African Kings and Black Slaves

THE EARLY MODERN AMERICAS

Peter C. Mancall, Series Editor

Volumes in the series explore neglected aspects of early modern history in the
Western Hemisphere. Interdisciplinary in character, and with a special emphasis
on the Atlantic World from 1450 to 1850, the series is published in partnership
with the USC-Huntington Early Modern Studies Institute.

African Kings
and Black Slaves

Sovereignty and Dispossession
in the Early Modern Atlantic

Herman L. Bennett

PENN

UNIVERSITY OF PENNSYLVANIA PRESS

PHILADELPHIA

Published by
University of Pennsylvania Press
Philadelphia, Pennsylvania 19104-4112
www.upenn.edu/pennpress

Printed in the United States of America on acid-free paper
1 3 5 7 9 10 8 6 4 2

Library of Congress Cataloging-in-Publication Data

Names: Bennett, Herman L. (Herman Lee), author.
Title: African kings and black slaves: sovereignty and dispossession in the
    early modern Atlantic / Herman L. Bennett.
Other titles: Early modern Americas.
Description: 1st edition. | Philadelphia: University of Pennsylvania Press,
    [2019] | Series: The early modern Americas | Includes bibliographical
    references and index.
Identifiers: LCCN 2018015360| ISBN 9780812250633 (hardcover: alk. paper)
Subjects: LCSH: Slave trade—Political aspects—Atlantic Ocean
    Region—History—15th century. | Slave trade—Political aspects—Atlantic
    Ocean Region—History—16th century. | Africa, West—Relations—
    Portugal—History—15th century. | Africa, West—Relations—Portugal—
    History—16th century. | Portugal—Relations—Africa, West—History—
    15th century. | Portugal—Relations—Africa, West—History—16th century. |
    Power (Social sciences)—Africa, West—History—15th century. | Power
    (Social sciences)—Africa, West—History—16th century. | Power (Social
    sciences)—Portugal—History—15th century. | Power (Social sciences)—
    Portugal—History—16th century.
Classification: LCC HT1331.B46 2019 | DDC 306.3/62091821—dc23
LC record available at https://lccn.loc.gov/2018015360

For Jennifer L. Morgan

CONTENTS

African Kings and Black Slaves

Prologue

Years ago, on entering the Arquivo Nacional do Torre do Tombo, Portugal's national archive, an exhibition on early modern exploration caught my eye. It was 1998, six years after Spain had commemorated the anniversary of Christopher Columbus's 1492 voyage. Not wanting to be outdone by Spanish nationalism, the Portuguese staged an equally impressive celebration of Bartolomeu Dias's rounding of Cabo da Boa Esperança (Cape of Good Hope) and Vasco da Gama's actual voyage to India, which were accompanied by a world expo and numerous international cultural festivals acknowledging Portugal's former place in the world. In addition to reprinting many fifteenth- and sixteenth-century chronicles testifying to Portugal's global footprint, the national archive curated various exhibitions to display the cultural patrimony.

Perusing the contents of the exhibition, I could not but notice the scrolls, papyri, and embellished and laminated texts that, alongside the esoteric scripts, announced far more than the Portuguese exploration of North and East Africa, West Central Africa, the Middle East, and South and East Asia. The Portuguese court received the inhabitants of those regions as notables who, on delivering their respective sovereign's correspondence, enjoyed the protected status of emissaries. In this enactment of "renaissance diplomacy," the Portuguese, the emissaries, and the authors of the various texts steeped their rhetorical protocol in ornate forms of address. They stood and spoke as equals, which the lords, emirs, negús, emperors, pashas, manicongos, and princes conveyed through the detailed invocation of their royal titles. Pressed for time, I pushed on and into the archive, but not before taking a long look at the letters crafted in Amharic that Ethiopia's ruler addressed to his Christian brother and peer, the Portuguese sovereign.

* * *

Little did I understand then that this correspondence, embellished with royal titles and diplomatic in scope, troubled the conventional representations shared by contemporary Africans and their global descendants regarding the early modern European encounter with the larger world. In the popular narrative defined by conquests, colonial imposition, possession, and dispossession, what role—if any—did royal titles play? If titles did not matter, why were all the parties involved constantly invoking them? In the eyes of the Europeans, what function did they serve?[1] How might these titles reveal something different about a well-known past typified by the easy juxtapositions of conquerors and conquered, winners and victims, colonizers and colonized, masters and slaves? Stated differently, in the contemporary African and its related diasporic imaginary, but also among scholars of colonial slavery, the foundational premise resides in the abject and violated body of the enslaved, the object unmoored and alienated from all preexisting social ties. Dominance resulting in objectification, always already conceived as secular in form, did not engender an inquiry into a previous status. For this reason, the process of enslavement foreclosed an engagement with the past, thus constituting the slave as an epistemic object of the here, now, and future. Simply stated, a master was a master and a slave a slave.

But language matters, and as a historian of Africans, I was keen on knowing if the use of royal terminology in the texts before me was related to a grammar of politics that perhaps informed Europe's encounter with Africa and the subsequent histories that unfolded.[2] The answer to this query resides in what follows. At its core, this book asks what role, if any, did the acknowledged existence of politics in Africa play in shaping early modern European expansion—to which a final related question has been appended: how might this political grammar be illustrative of pasts that have been lost under the subsequent weight of successive colonial impositions and our restricted political imagination?

The terminology used in the letters allowed me to conceive of the pervasiveness with which European chroniclers and travel writers used Iberian royal tropes to describe the earliest encounters with Africans. Royalty saturated the landscape. With this awareness, I re-immersed myself in the familiar travelogues and chronicles describing the European encounter with Africa. It was immediately clear that the terminology formed a corpus, a "register" if you will, questioning the idea of European apotheosis that, in turn, telescoped the emergence and dominance of a slave trade mediated by commodification in which tenuous relations were market driven. In pondering the ubiquitous use of royal terminology, I asked if one could read this phenomenon as an acknowledgment of African sovereignty that was simultaneously constitutive of early modern Iberian imperial statecraft. Incessantly focused on the Europeans' pervasive deployment of royal terminology in reference to African sovereigns, I intentionally relied on the narrative literature, composed of chronicles and travelogues, that has been foundational to framing the earliest encounter between Africans and Europeans. In the extant documents, I glimpsed traces of a past that tacked between African and European history, which begged for a reconsideration of the New World's origin story of blackness, the early modern African diaspora, and Atlantic history.

The interpretive practice of rereading the early modern colonial library for evidence, understandings, and events complicating the inaugural moments of European expansion also offered the possibility to enrich knowledge production as it relates to the formation of the African diaspora. Rereading the familiar engenders an origin story still in need of being conceived that— irrespective of the demands of our postcolonial present—has implications for how the subsequent past unfolds. Obviously, the narrative of slavery and freedom stood on the horizon, but a strategic rereading of the early modern colonial library also questions truths bequeathed to us from a subsequent liberal era that to this day still colonizes our imaginary when it comes to framing the fifteenth-century European encounter with Africa.

Stated less abstractly, the European encounter with Africa is generally not seen as a site of theorization with regard to the political. But the political informs every text of this encounter.[3] At the level of generality, I am interested in rhetoric and performances of lordship alongside the legal regimes, ceremonies, and pomp constitutive of early modern politics both in the form of sovereign power and sovereignty. Scholars of the slave trade usually look at these "anecdotes"—at best as curiosities that figure in cultural history—as exceptional instances that are quickly relegated in favor of serial data or abstraction. I am intent on reading the rhetoric, incidents, ceremonies, and rituals embedded in the chronicles and travel accounts as political tropes.[4] These tropes and anecdotes, prominently manifest in the well-used tomes of the colonial library, engender an equally valid reading of the colonial past as it relates to Africa, Africans, and the formation of the African diaspora.

*   *   *

Let us turn from the texts on display in Portugal's national archive to one of the most iconic moments of the European encounter with Africans. In 1441, building on years of previous Portuguese trading, hunting, and fishing expeditions that scoured the Atlantic coastline south of Cape Bajador, a small fleet of caravels anchored at Lagos on the southern Portuguese coast. As the returning crew discharged their cargo in the presence of Infante Dom Henrique, popularly known as Henry the Navigator, the spectacle of the handful of "captives" drew the attention of the royal party. Though few in number, the captives sparked commentary but also expectations. Recalling this event and anticipating the future it foretold, the royal chronicler Gomes de Zurara speculated about royal sentiment. "May we not think thou didst feel joy," Zurara conjectured about the prince's reaction, "not so much for the number of the captives taken, as for the hope thou didst conceive of the others thou couldst take?" In projecting royal will, the chronicler envisioned how the prince's imaginary transformed "captives" into slaves while conjuring a robust slave trade into existence. Zurara was quick to add that the prince was not unduly focused on the wealth accruing from a future trade in slaves. "Thy joy," observed the chronicler, "was solely from that one holy purpose of thine to seek salvation for the lost souls of the heathen." Enslavement afforded the captives salvation and "true freedom." "And yet," wrote the chronicler, "the greater benefit was theirs for though their bodies were now brought into subjection, that was a small matter in comparison of their souls, which would now possess true freedom for evermore."[5]

One can easily dismiss Zurara's musings about the "soul," "salvation," and "true freedom" as ideology at work, which, in fact, it was. But an undue focus on ideology privileges secular skepticism at the expense of faith, reduces Christianity to an instrument of power, and, most germane to the narrative that follows, has caused scholars to lose sight of Catholicism's formidable yet layered political history with Africa and Africans. The scholarship on the Catholic encounter with Africans obviously has transcended the image of a solitary priest baptizing enslaved Africans as their captors compelled them on board. Catholic missions, though sparse, were an established reality in a number of sixteenth-century West and West Central African kingdoms. Catholicism had acquired considerable depth because African converts—notably the elites but also commoners—had transformed it into an indigenous phenomenon.[6] While the earliest missions, especially among the Kongo peoples, have attracted scholarly attention, we still have yet to fully consider Christianity's institutional and intellectual complexity, which sanctioned the presence of the imaginary priest and insinuated Catholicism into Africa. Even if we concede the limited role that the Church's conscience played in this process, one needs also to ponder the efficacy of scripture, theology, papal *anuncios*, the particulars of Church-state relations, and Christian relations with the *extra ecclesiam*—the Christian designation for all people who did not accept the Catholic faith. To acknowledge that the priest's gesture was superficial should not foreclose an examination of the institutional mechanisms and intellectual traditions that mediated the Catholic encounter with Africa and Africans. In the eyes of the Church, the priest's presence transcended the issue of a Christian conscience. Church-state relations—but also theology, papal authority, papal bulls, and the evolving Episcopal Church centered on a diocese, Church canons, and canon law—came to the fore when medieval Christians encountered not just infidels but also pagans.[7] Framed differently, in overlooking Catholicism's institutional history and its related intellectual currents, we have lost sight of a tradition of Christian politics that brought into relief the simultaneity of early modern African and European sovereignty, which perhaps explains why the priest stood at the quay.

African Kings and Black Slaves delineates how and under what circumstances Catholic dogma, institutions, and law mattered in the European encounter with Africans. This history magnifies a field of politics engendering early modern sovereignty that culminated in a taxonomy of African difference, which in turn rendered the inhabitants of some polities into slaves. Even before the systemization of the slave trade and slavery—which only two centuries later came to be exclusively linked with people of African descent—we see how Christianity mediated encounters with pagan polities resulting in different outcomes. To say as much calls into question the telos that has long served to absorb the African-European encounter and its immediate history into the story of New World slavery, thereby overlooking the part that Africa and Africans played in the evolution of Iberian sovereignty and imperial expansion before 1492. Though familiar with the Portuguese and Spanish encounters with Africans, scholars rarely reflect on the earliest sequence of events involving Iberians interacting with African polities and how that history might trouble the existing narrative of the West and its emergence.[8] Instead, the emphasis has been on the inauguration of the slave trade and slavery and assigning economic prominence to those institutions in the unfolding histories of the Americas.

As a site of metamorphosis (recall the opening scene of the mariners unloading the captives before the entourage of nobles)—sites where elites, buyers, and owners reduced Africans into slaves—the priest's location symbolically delineated the boundaries between an African polity and the beginnings of

Christian jurisdiction. As we shall see, trade signified the existence of sovereign authority—both African and European—which, in turn, highlighted an often overlooked Christian intellectual and institutional legacy. Scholars and popular lore are quick to stress ideological contortions rather than exploring the efficacy of African sovereignty and Christianity's institutional practices in Atlantic Africa. In reducing the earliest encounter with Africa to the slave trade and slavery to a New World commercial phenomenon, we have lost sight of a distinct narrative of power in Africa along with the fact that Africans stood for more than objects acted upon.

Rather than view what follows as an assertion of African agency, I am more interested in the implications that this past might have for narrating the history of Europe. The narrative of power that historians and theorists associate with the West has woefully underexamined and undertheorized the African presence. This presence, I argue, is a site yet to be examined for its role in Western formation—a history in which Africa and Africans figured as objects but occasionally also emerge as historical subjects. Despite the colonial turn in European history, Africa and Africans rarely feature in the earliest narratives of the Portuguese and Spanish past beyond the status of chattel already detached from what in modern terms might be described as the political. Consequently, the objects of the slave trade and slavery enter history—the European past—devoid of those claims, ties, and associations that had positioned them as subjects, clients, and vassals of African lords and elites whose own status fluctuated over time. From this perspective, it is easy to imagine and project natal alienation—social death—as a timeless phenomenon rather than as a dramatic act involving force and violence that sundered roots into rootlessness. What is more, we ascribe a hegemonic singularity to the early European past: Europe in its relationship to Africa is always already a secular and dominant fully forged entity with a singular political rationale. Europe, in this configuration of the past, is already the West rather than an entity or idea that emerges through time and through its encounters with Africa.[9] Through the complexities that framed the encounter with Africa—complexities that were brought to bear in the encounter but also were shaped by the variety of social formations manifest in Africa—Portugal and Spain constituted the early modern European social formation that subsequently shaped the histories of the Americas and Asia. To argue as much positions this study in the realm of both postcolonialism and black studies.[10]

"Black studies," writes the cultural theorist Alexander G. Weheliye, "represents a substantial critique of western modernity," which leads to an insistence that "although much of the critical, poetic, and quantitative work generated under the auspices of black studies has been concerned with the experiences, life worlds, struggles, and cultural productions of black populations around the world, the theoretical and methodological protocols of black studies have always been global in their reach, because they provide detailed explanations of how techniques of domination, dispossession, expropriation, exploitation, and violence are predicated upon the hierarchical ordering of racial, gender, sexual, economic, religious and national differences."[11] Though Weheliye is, of course, correct, this critique need not be interpreted as a disavowal of "western modernity." Instead, it might profitably be seen as an engagement with the very elements that were constitutive of blackness in the first instance—the formative cultural encounters between an emerging Europe with an equally emergent Africa, the slave trade and slavery, colonial trade and dispossession alongside the shifting regimes of differences. Black studies, precisely by attending to the formation of blackness, entails knowing and representing the history of the West, Europe's encounters with Africans, and the evolving narrative of racial becoming. For this reason, understanding the European past creates a condition of possibility for histories of Africans and racial formations. Such a perspective simultaneously underscores the need for a nuanced engagement with the European past and its shifting rationale in order to represent the histories of Africans and its diasporic permutations. The Europe of the Enlightenment cannot stand in for all previous and subsequent incarnations without limiting our understanding of various African pasts.

*   *   *

Through an evocative engagement with the writings of the cultural critic Hortense Spillers and philosopher Sylvia Winter, Weheliye demonstrates an awareness of the interdependence of Europe and the black past by offering a prescient critique of contemporary theorizations of power associated with Giorgio Agamben and Michel Foucault for their woeful neglect of racialized and colonized "assemblages." I understand Weheliye to be offering a more transcendent critique of Western theorists and theorizations of power, which in the instance of Foucault and Agamben invariably have subsumed racial and colonial experiences without engaging their historical specificities, complexities, and defining significance. This is not, however, true for the particularity of European experiences, which, as the foundational locus, always stands in for the timeless universal. Even in the wake of Paul Gilroy's brilliant exegesis,

The Black Atlantic: Modernity and Double Consciousness, in which the cultural critic reminded us that "the history and the legacy of the Enlightenment were worth understanding and arguing about" so as to demonstrate that "the experiences of black people were part of the abstract modernity," most theorists still implicitly question this claim through their very framing of modern history and the narrative of power.[12] *African Kings and Black Slaves* treads similar theoretical ground as Weheliye and Gilroy but focuses on an earlier, no less important historical moment that a considerable body of scholars and theorists have rendered as a transitional one, thereby overlooking how Catholicism, Africa, and the slave trade were instrumental in the formation of early Western modernity.

In *The Rise of African Slavery in the Americas*, the economic historian David Eltis routes the early modern history of liberty through the ascendant capitalist ethos in Northern Europe. As commercial capitalism gained sway over the landscape, nascent social forms, including liberty and individualism, appeared among the thicket of preexisting social relationships from which they only gradually became disentangled. According to Eltis, both concepts had secured considerable roots among Northern Europeans by the beginning of the eighteenth century, specifically in the Dutch Republic and England, ensuring that cargoes of slaves sold in public squares constituted a disconcerting spectacle. The specter of slavery in the urban metropolis, Amsterdam and London in contrast to Madrid and Lisbon, reified newly cherished notions of liberty and in some instances violated the sensibility of individuals who had only recently forged a tradition of freedom. But then, with ironic cadence, Eltis notes that in the Americas, the Dutch Republic and England were "associated with the harshest and most closed systems of exploiting enslaved non-Europeans."[13] For Eltis, tracking the divergence of European freedom and American slavery represents "the focus" of *The Rise of African Slavery in the Americas*. In doing so, Eltis builds on the venerable intellectual tradition linking slavery to the elemental formation of Western modernity. In addressing the ways that European freedom engendered American slavery, Eltis delineates how both were implicated in the formation of Western modernity. Instead of framing liberty's relationship to bondage as a paradox, Eltis views both social practices as constitutive of the modern. As Eltis sees it, the most advanced European economic sector, Northern Europe, liberated from the absolutism of church and state, displayed a marked propensity for highly regimented slave regimes, which, in turn, accentuated the accumulation of capital that enabled the maturation of existing social forms (liberty and individualism), all the while spawning new ones (popular sovereignty, secularization, and so forth) that collectively defined the modern. In suggesting as much, Eltis locates the origins and formation of modernity among Western Europeans. In the ascendance of the modern, causality, in short, resided with Europeans. As an economic historian, Eltis, of course, is writing against a tradition of thought that has long sought to root the rise of racial slavery in the realm of ideology, whereby slavery rendered as a metaphor and metonym of "white over black" arises from an idealist tradition.[14]

As historians of race and slavery—well before the publication of *The Rise of African Slavery in the Americas*—ventured into the archives and drilled down into sources, the field-defining, theoretically charged panoramic writings of W. E. B. Dubois, Fernando Ortiz, C. L. R. James, E. Franklin Frazier, Gilberto Freyre, Oliver Cox, Eric Williams, Frank Tannenbaum, Eugene Genovese, and Stanley Elkins occupied the sidelines as casualties of specialization predicated on empirical evidence and specific facts. This was, in one sense, reflective of a larger shift away from systemic approaches, in which race and slavery were situated in writings from the 1930s to the 1960s, that sought to explain the emergence and divergences in the modern world.[15] But on the American scene, the politics of race played a considerable role in both intellectual and scholarly circles. In the second half of the twentieth century, scholarly efforts to decenter race as the explanation for the slave trade and slavery were a significant influence in diminishing the currency of politics, especially configured around the state's role in modern development. "Race relations," argued the historian Eugene Genovese, "did not determine the patterns of slavery in the New World; the patterns of slavery, as conditioned by past and present, history and ecology, and manifested in particular forms of class rule, determined race relations."[16] For Genovese, the slave trade and slavery had economic or, more broadly, a material basis. Such claims, widely debated in the second half of the twentieth century, offered an explanation for how and why Africans were rendered into slaves and sought to shift the focus away from racism or some intrinsic European cultural characteristic. Similarly critical of the idea that slavery originated in ideologically driven motives, the historian Ira Berlin observed that "plantation slavery did not have its origins in a conspiracy to dishonor, shame, brutalize, or otherwise reduce black people's standing on some perverse scale of humanity—although it did all of those at one time or another." Pointing to the institution's rationality, Berlin goes on to say: "Slavery's moral stench cannot mask the design of American captivity: to commandeer the labor of many to make a few rich and powerful. Slavery thus

made class as it made race, and in entwining the two processes it mystified
both."[17] Genovese's observations anticipated Berlin's, but together they emphasized the centrality of capitalism, class, and labor, which stressed how "objective" material forces prevailed over ideology. Genovese framed the relationship
between slavery and colonialism in the following manner: "The general character of modern slaveholding classes arose from two separate sources: from
a common origin in the expansion of Europe, which historically meant the
expansion of the world market and, accordingly, established a pronounced
tendency toward commercial exploitation and profit maximization."[18] This line
of reasoning minimized the earliest instantiation of the slave trade and slavery that still witnessed discernible distinctions between colonial and capitalist
expansion, especially during the early modern period when the latter was still
at a rudimentary stage of development and engaged in a protracted struggle
from which it would only subsequently emerge triumphant.

The relegation of race to an ideological formation engendered the subordination of earlier explanations that acknowledged the slave trade's impact on
both African and European societies, notably framed around the alleged symbiosis between development and underdevelopment. The ascendant consensus contributed to further rendering of the slave trade and colonial slavery into
(liberal) economic phenomena as opposed to relations embedded in the social
formation. From this analytical perspective, scholars depicted the slave trade
as an economic process (trade, transactions, and commodities)—elements
of early modern capitalism from which politics and political traditions had
been exorcized. This very modern framing of the economic and, specifically,
the early modern slave trade circumvented the lexicon of early modern Christian polities—including concept terms such as sovereigns and subjects. In
the resulting parlance, slaves and New World slavery acquired a modern
(economic) valence long before the ascendancy of numeracy and the realization
of distinctive economic and political spheres in which the separation of the
political from the economic enabled the market to assume hegemony over
social life.[19] In describing the long marginalized Iberian and African pasts, including their respective commerce in slaves, scholars used modern concepts
and cultural logics, even though they represented radically distinct histories.
To recuperate this relegated past—one of the intents of this book—we need
not completely dispense with the logic of capitalism, but rather excavate and
historicize earlier forms that prevailed in characterizing the political that for
centuries would still govern the early modern order of things.[20] Karl Marx, as
I argue, exhibited an awareness of this distinction in delineating primitive

capital accumulation, in which the political played a crucial role in the formation of early modern capitalism whereby the market and commodity fetish engendered discipline. Interestingly enough, theorists of the capitalist transitions in Europe steadfastly took up, challenged, and revised the evolutionary paradigms that allegedly explained the makings of the modern world. Feudalism, capitalism, and bourgeois revolutions—but not colonialism and slavery—occupied pride of place.[21] Even as slavery in Greece and Rome commanded attention as political forms delineating mastery, absolutism, the public and private alongside freedom—especially as they related to the genesis of capitalism—writers conceived the transatlantic slave trade and New World slavery in fundamentally different ways. For theorists of the capitalist transition, enslavement and bonded labor fueled the emergence of capitalism, but the slave trade and colonial slavery were conceived in economic terms. Theorization of the transition not only relegated colonial slavery to the economic domain; it also privileged an implicit secular world in which Christianity was represented in instrumental ways that neglected how the Church for centuries governed existing political traditions, including encounters and the transformations of Africans into slaves. In neglecting this phenomenon, scholars of the fifteenth and sixteenth centuries have condensed the distinctive early modern era into a uniform modern period, thereby losing sight of how the complexities characterizing the European encounters with Africa relegated a history of politics that played a crucial role in modern Europe's emergence. For scholars of the slave trade and Atlantic slavery, equating "Europe" and "modern" remains a standard practice.

The political scientist and scholar of black studies Cedric Robinson questioned this allegedly "objective" formulation, arguing that "the historical development of world capitalism was influenced in a most fundamental way by the particularistic forces of racism and nationalism. This could only be true if the social, psychological and cultural origins of racism and nationalism both anticipated capitalism in time and formed a piece with those events which contributed directly to its organization of production and exchange."[22] For Robinson, "the particularistic forces of racism and nationalism," which preceded the emergence of capitalism, had engendered a unique social formation—"racial capitalism." In the study that follows and in line with Robinson, colonialism represents more than an economic system or simply a regime of class exploitation. It constitutes an assemblage in which competing domains (political, institutional, and legal traditions) vie for primacy as they compete for economic, social, cultural, and political preeminence. The state is more than the instrument of the ruling class; the objectives of power are never singular, sequential, or contiguous. Yet, at the same time, I depart from Robinson's formulation in that I see institutional and intellectual life as being shaped by far more than "the particularistic forces of racism and nationalism." To begin with, early modern institutions and intellectual legacies had yet to experience thorough secularization, which would allow for the existence of a modern state, capitalism, race, and class. States, in the form of kingdoms, existed, as did markets and private property, but the fifteenth century was not yet the era of secularized entities such as citizens, classes, and laborers. Instead, lords, masters, and sovereigns competed with one another, and with the Church, in defining the experiences of subjects and slaves.

Church-state relations, though rarely attended to in standard histories of black studies, figure prominently in Europe's history with Africa and Africans. At best, theorists, along with imperial historians, point to the state's role in regulating the slave trade through the *casa de escravo, asiento,* and *pieza de india,* thereby sustaining absolutism fiscally. Imperial historians noted as much. But in their hands the slave trade and slavery represented a facet of the commercial nexus defining the imperial framework. Here empire was not a constitutive element of absolute sovereignty, nor was slavery foundational to the formation of absolutism. In that respect neither the slave nor slavery configured in the emergence of absolutism or the framing of state sovereignty. The slave trade was not constitutive of European political formation. In turn, there was little recognition of how sovereignty, political traditions, or politics on the African side shaped how Europeans interacted with Africans in order to lubricate the trading mechanism of the slave trade. When the focus turned to wars, diplomacy, or political economy (wealth in people), the scholarly perspective merely rendered them as facets of trade thereby overlooking the existence and importance of African sovereignty. Consequently, trade—the slave trade—appears in our histories as an entity or epiphenomenon divorced from the world of politics.

From these aforementioned observations flows an assertion: until Europe is understood in its historical specificity, its early modern encounter with Africa cannot be fully realized. At its starkest, Europe and its encroachment on Africa unleashed unrelenting violence, highlighting the Janus face at the core of modern life, but this representation also flattens and condenses a complex past that grants Europeans far too much power. For Africa, Africans, and the African diaspora, the stakes are considerable. Concepts like tradition, authenticity, autonomy, cultural memory, agency, and resistance—which always

acquired valence through analogy and negation in the wake of encounters—
cannot be conceived, in their complexity, until the historical specificity of the
European past is clarified. As a postcolonial history but also a history that acknowledges the complex entanglement with Africa and Africans in the making of European social formation, *African Kings and Black Slaves* gestures
toward an earlier European past which constitutes a necessary representation
for writing histories of both the early modern and contemporary African
diaspora.[23]

Let us employ the purported relationship between the African diaspora,
slavery, and the modern to assert that contemporary representations of the
Atlantic slave trade and New World slavery privilege a decidedly modern
conception of political economy. Through this modern-inflected prism,
both slavery and the slave trade appear as phenomena configured in relation
to the *oikos*, economic life, and commodification. In our thinking and writings, the economy and its constitutive elements—property and private life,
the market and commodities, trade and trading relations—embody discrete
entities that, in turn, define the social logic of the early modern slave trade
and slavery. The assumption of an autonomous economic life belies the historical process whereby "the economic" emerged distinct from and eventually
triumphed over other realms of social life.[24] In directing attention to this historical process, we discern how newly emergent "economic" practices associated
with the early modern European-African encounter inaugurated a transition
against the dominant practices of the day.[25] *African Kings and Black Slaves*
delineates the historical process through which economic life assumed sovereignty. Rather than track and trace the emergence of this economic dynamic,
the project at hand has a different aim. Composed of six chapters tackling
distinctive themes, it routes us through both late medieval and early modern
political thought alongside contemporary forms of the political so as to outline a neglected history of the European encounter with Africa. In doing so,
African Kings and Black Slaves argues for the primacy of politics—intellectual,
juridical, and customary—in mediating the earliest contact between Africans
and Europeans. Here then is a story of medieval and early modern power that
preceded the ascendance of political economy, one in which laws, political
thought, and ceremonial practices configured Africans as subjects, sovereigns,
and occasionally even as gods.[26]

Gods, sovereigns, and subjects trouble the narrative of power that presently
frames the histories of the slave trade and slavery, the process of enslavement
and the Middle Passage, whereby Africans were rendered into chattel slaves.

Aside from being prompted by the initial sighting of the correspondence between sovereigns in the Portuguese national archives, *African Kings and Black
Slaves* was also motivated by an alleged encounter with the divine—a constitutive myth in the making of the New World. Decades after it occurred, the
surviving but defeated native peoples of Tenochitlán, the Mexica, recalled an
encounter in tales about their defeat which they conveyed to Franciscan missionaries. Here myth encountered history. Gods, of course, played a decisive
role in orchestrating the drama involving emperors, lords, and fearless warriors.
The strangers, when they arrived, were identified as gods, and came in various hues. In the discerning eyes of the Mexica, such distinctions among the
coterie of stranger-gods were carefully observed. For in a universe of capricious
divines, the lives of mere mortals often rested on their ability to anticipate the
will of gods, and attentiveness to their form, tastes, and proclivities, the Mexica
believed, could incur a god's favor or at least forestall sudden wrath. Among
the pantheon of strangers, some stood out, and the Mexica anointed them
as "soiled gods."[27] But for the Spaniards, the Spanish-speaking Africans and
blacks that accompanied the *entrada* (the juridical term the Spaniards
employed for the conquest) were simply servants and slaves. Attending to
these divergent fictions alongside the letters in the Portuguese archive prompted
this inquiry into the genealogy of a transformation—an exploration into how
the earliest Africans became slaves. *African Kings and Black Slaves* offers a
glimpse of a lost past—a past buried beneath layers of contemporary historiographical sediment.

By recasting the initial century of African-European interaction—beginning
in 1441 and culminating around 1560—the history that follows takes on a
myriad of theoretical concerns underscoring the temporality that shapes this
historical moment, best described as "after postcoloniality," whose intellectual and political horizon necessitates distinctive representations of the past.
What are the implications for such a history of African-European interaction? Previous histories largely focused on the economics of enslavement and
slavery that, in turn, served to counter the dynamics of cultural difference in
the guise of race, which allegedly shaped how Europeans initially perceived
and then interacted with the Africans they encountered. In the long history
of the African-European encounter preceding colonial rule in the nineteenth
century, the slave trade and New World slavery occupied a dominant role that
was exclusively depicted as the instrumental history of racial formation or the
story of class differences. By questioning this narrative of difference and
capital—again a scrutiny animated by the temporality associated with after

postcoloniality—*African Kings and Black Slaves* delineates new analytics for framing the earliest history of the African-European encounter.

The foundational encounters between Africans and Europeans embodied more than an aberrant yet overlooked moment in the long history of the slave trade and New World slavery. In analyzing the earliest phase of the slave trade, we discern long-standing *traditions*—specific institutional practices, established customs, and intellectual norms—whose social logic preceded but also survived the immediate African and European encounters. Various reasons explain how successive new social forms supplanted these traditions, eventually even eliminating their traces. In the process of epistemological erasure, pride of place belongs to the triumphal liberal narrative that framed the history of the slave trade and its decline at the hands of an enlightened West in a manner that disavowed the veracity, complexity, and intrinsic value to preceding histories and traditions involving the African-European encounter.[28] It is to this tradition that we now turn before routing the story of the slave trade and slavery through the earliest phase of the early modern period, whose meaning, significance, and form often get suppressed by subsequent eras.[29]

CHAPTER I

Liberalism

In 1852, eight years before assuming the coveted position as clerk of the Privy Council, the Englishman Sir Arthur Helps published a two-volume history, *The Conquerors of the New World and Their Bondsmen: Being a Narrative of the Principal Events Which Led to Negro Slavery in the West Indies and America.* These books, the product of research in the Royal Academy of History in Madrid, constituted Helps's inaugural tome on Spanish America. Nineteen years later, he had published five additional books, totaling nine volumes, on the early history of Spanish America and its Spanish protagonists, including *The Spanish Conquest in America, and Its Relation to the History of Slavery and the Government of Colonies* (4 vols., 1855, 1857–1861); *The Life of Las Casas, the Apostle of the Indians* (1868); *The Life of Columbus* (1869); *The Life of Pizarro* (1869); and *The Life of Hernando Cortés* (1871). In the nineteenth century, only the American William H. Prescott, among non-Iberian and non-Spanish American writers, rivaled Helps in producing Iberian and Spanish American historiography, the latest installment of the Anglo-imperial library.[1] Though both authors addressed the same subject—New World conquests—their focus differed. Prescott explored how the Renaissance monarchy affected Spanish expansion, culminating in the conquest of the Americas. Spaniards and Indians—at the exclusion of Africans—inhabited Prescott's histories. Helps employed a broader canvas and insisted that the earlier Iberian encounter with Africa, including the history of slavery, figured in the formation and governance of the New World. Acknowledging that slavery "lacks a dramatic interest," Helps observed how "it has no thread to run upon like the account of any man's life, or the history of a nation. The story of slavery is fragmentary, confused; in a different state of progress in different parts of the world at the same time, and deficient in distinct epochs to be illustrated by great adventures. Moreover, people think that they have already heard about it; which is not so."[2]

To observe that "the story of slavery" exists "in a different state of progress in different parts of the world at the same time" reads at once as a self-congratulatory nod to British liberalism and as a critique of existing slaving empires and nations. By 1852, Britain had suppressed its own slave trade (1807), emancipated the enslaved throughout most of its empire (1833), and for much of the nineteenth-century led a crusade against human trafficking. By the mid-nineteenth century, most European nations had capitulated to British diplomatic demands, allowing triumphant English liberals to lament slavery's existence, if not expansion, in the hands of African and Arab despots. Helps's musings, along with the countless expeditionary reports, travel accounts, and histories written by other European authors, fueled the English appetite for encroachment on African and Arab sovereignty—the reign of illiberal tyrants, as they saw it—so as to suppress slave trading and slavery, which, by the mid-nineteenth century, Western writers had defined exclusively as the black man's burden. From liberalism's triumphant perch, one could discern in Helps's writings the conflation of historiography with ideology. His was a history of slavery that inveighed against human bondage and in doing so called for the benevolence of imperial intervention.

In a sense, Helps strikes a familiar chord: the critique of the "chattel principle" bequeathed by the liberal world order.[3] He offers an outline of European expansion, but one in which slavery figures as "a much more momentous question" necessitating "a history of its own." Writing at British liberalism's apogee, Helps did not explicitly acknowledge colonial slavery's elemental role in imperial Britain's formation. He transposed that relationship to the Iberian past, thus exonerating both English liberalism and imperial Britain. By doing so, he invoked an earlier imperial formation with unquestionable ties to slavery. Helps did, however, underscore how the slave trade's ascendancy and, more important, its demise resided in English hands. Conceived in this manner, the slave trade and slavery represented an English story before descending into the domain of despots and tyrants. Subscribing to this fiction, Western scholars and theorists have overlooked slavery's earlier relationship to early modern imperial governance.

Helps alludes to this connection in his initial exploration of Spanish history, *The Conquerors of the New World and Their Bondsmen*; but in the subsequent and expanded version that draws on the same material, *The Spanish Conquest in America and Its Relation to the History of Slavery and the*

Government of Colonies, Helps explicitly demonstrates how Iberian expansion and encounters with Africans united slavery and colonial governance—the process of subjecting and ruling peoples. While the title *The Spanish Conquest in America* ostensibly situates the history in the New World, Helps devotes considerable attention to the African past, notably to the iconic events that framed the Iberian-African encounters during the "age of discovery." To view these descriptions of the initial century of contact as a representation of European hegemony presaging liberalism's ascendancy misses the point. The expeditions under Prince Henry's patronage, the inaugural encounter with black Africans, the acts of enslavement, Cadamosto's voyage, the foundation of El Mina, and the assassination of Prince Bemoin—once well-known imperial dramas that fueled the imagination of Western schoolchildren and with which today's imperial historians still remain familiar (and which figure in this project)—illuminate the relationship between slavery and governance in a distinct historical moment in which African sovereignty and the European recognition thereof was unquestioned.

Helps clearly offers a more nuanced narrative of the African-European encounter, which in the liberal imaginary typically conflated historical agency with Europe's inhabitants. Reflecting the tenor and ambiguity of the Iberian sources, Helps conveys some of the complexity that shaped African polities and the dynamism of their rulers. Though framed in the genre of romance, Helps narrates how heroic African kings and tragic black princes, courtly pageantry, royal processions, and valiant foes played leading roles in the encounter with Europeans. By doing so, he draws on well-worn sources and canonical events of the early modern period, familiar episodes and historical figures around which this book also takes shape. In Helps's narration of the past, the iconic and the familiar convey a history that yielded insight into a previous era that his and now our present leave largely unacknowledged. Equating this past in relation to the earliest moments of the African-European encounter with "old slavery," Helps declares,

> The peculiar phase of slavery that will be brought forward in this history is not the first and most natural one, in which the slave was merely the captive in war, "the fruit of the spear," as he has figuratively been called who lived in the house of his conqueror, and laboured at this hands. This system culminated amongst the Romans; partook of the fortunes of the Empire; was gradually modified by Christianity and advancing civilization; declined by slow and almost impercep-

tible degrees into serfage and vassalage; and was extinct, or nearly so
when the second period was marked by a commercial character. The
slave was no longer an accident of war. He had become the object of
war. He was no longer a mere accidental subject of barter. He was to be
sought for, to be hunted out, to be produced; and this change accordingly gave rise to a new branch of commerce. Slavery became at once a
much more momentous question than it ever had been and thenceforth, indeed, claims for itself a history of its own.[4]

Building on the histories of a previous generation of liberal thinkers, including
the Scottish political economist Adam Smith, Helps conveys how commercial imperatives—not chivalry, honor, or Christianization—drove European expansion and determined the nature of colonial rule. In this telling of
the New World epic, European motivation resided in acquisition, commerce,
and profit. The same held true for the latest incarnation of slavery. But then
Helps cautions the reader from viewing "the history of slavery" as "merely
an account of commercial greediness and reckless cruelty carried to the
uttermost."[5]

Even as he configures the link between African slavery and New World
conquests through a politics of "dramatic interest"—as opposed to a stark
focus on market phenomena, trade, and the making of chattel—Helps still
narrates a liberal story that simultaneously delineates the transitory compo-
nents of the early African-European encounter distinguishing between "old"
and "modern" slavery. By acknowledging the "history of slavery," Helps offers
us a sighting of a lost moment—events, experiences, histories, and texts—that
feature in what follows. Here the focus does not reside in some ancient tradition or what Helps variously labeled the "first," "natural," or "old" slavery. Instead, Helps gestures to an interstitial moment situated precariously between
that "peculiar phase of slavery." Ill defined, "this system" emerges in the vortex of a shifting chronology that at once "culminated," "was gradually modified," "declined," and finally "was extinct, or nearly so." Indeed, we may want
to read his tentative, if not halting, attempts to describe the antecedents of
his present—a past that is not synonymous with antiquity—as already privileging a secular liberal worldview that disavowed an earlier Christian discursive formation. Though the liberal imagination is not the central plot of the
succeeding story, as the silhouette through which we narrate the history of
the slave trade and slavery, it casts a formidable shadow over historical memory and must be engaged critically if we are to develop a new interpretation.[6]

Indeed, it is important to ask why this emphasis on representation might matter. Simply put, histories of the African past and its diaspora refract how we narrate the European past. From this perspective, the history of the West is cast as foundational in the formation of the African diaspora, and, in turn, the emergent African past is inextricably linked to a nascent Europe. The European story that liberal writers like Helps crafted still enjoys a dominant role in how subsequent scholars configure the history of slavery and, by implication, Europe's relationship to Africa and Africans. The resulting idea of Europe frames the history of slavery so thoroughly that any engagement with the African past exists in a dialectic relationship with prevailing representation of Europe. Obviously, the specificity of the European past matters. To acknowledge as much requires scholars of the African past or the African diaspora to wield an equally discerning historical sensibility in their rendering of Europe as we now expect from our engagements with Africa.[7] Stated differently, might we suspect a misaligned representation of the fifteenth-century past if scholars configured Europe as a secular entity in which the logic of capitalism stands ascendant in its initial encounter with Africa? What such a static configuration of Europe implies for histories of the European encounter with Africans cannot be overstated.

Though the African past and even the African diaspora, as a formation engendered by European expansion, have always manifested a degree of autonomy, much that we know about Africa and Africans relies on the configuration of the European past. In recent years, no field of study has done more to acknowledge this dynamic of interpolation than postcolonial scholarship.[8] As critique, epistemological intervention, and history writing, postcolonial scholarship has questioned the assumptions that naturalize Europe as the universal subject of history. Here the critique has largely focused on the eighteenth century and beyond, a period when Britain and France played leading roles invariably encapsulating the European experience. For this reason, postcolonial criticism offers a challenge to the world that liberalism invented. This critique, as scholars of Latin America have noted, focuses principally on English and French experiences with the larger world, thereby coming at the expense of earlier colonial histories that precede the eighteenth-century inventions of Europe and the European past.[9] Helps and his contemporaries crafted this liberal order that sublimates for a singular European past. An unquestionably liberal Europe, therefore, frames the history of Europe and its expansion. Traditions, experiences, and histories that precede the advent of liberalism are often rendered merely as earlier versions of the same.

What this has meant for a framing of earlier histories has preoccupied some scholars, but this critique has not made significant inroads into the earliest histories of European expansion or, for that matter, into representations of the slave trade. The Europe that frames the history of these encounters is the ascendant, if not hegemonic, Europe of the late eighteenth century simply projected on an earlier setting. To acknowledge as much underscores the symbiosis shaping the formation of both Africa and Europe and positions this study of the African diaspora in the contested terrain of historical representation. By implication, the African diaspora—the momentous human dispersal of African peoples inaugurated during the fifteenth century and the subsequent Atlantic encounters that engendered both the destruction of social formations and the creation of profound social transformations—emerges as a constitutive element in the early formation of Europe, thus composing a defining feature of the modern world. In saying as much, it is also critical to discern a distinction between being a "feature" of the modern world and how contemporary scholarship interpolates the relationship between the African diaspora, the slave trade, and the modern.

*   *   *

It should be said that this project did not begin exclusively in the merchant ledgers, ship manifests, or royal tax records featured prominently in the slave trade archive. After the sighting of those initial letters, this project emerged through a steady engagement with the library of the "Black radical tradition," most notably the writings of C. L. R. James, Eric Williams, and Walter Rodney.[10] As intellectuals—colonial, nationalist, and postcolonial—they touched on the slave trade to comment on the related histories of colonial expansion and slavery, bringing to light distinctive dynamics in the overlapping African, European, and New World past.[11] They wrote compelling histories that also served as commentaries on the state and situation of the black world. In these narratives, I first witnessed history writing as critical engagement with the present. Even though I read these seminal works decades after they had been crafted, the urgency, political significance, and theoretical relevance still seemed vibrant. In these histories, the colonial experience took on meaning for the formation of various black and African worlds that to this day remains germane. Colonialism and its very elements—the slave trade, slavery, the structuring of difference and capitalism—mattered then and now. These narratives offered up histories of the modern world in which power played a

dynamic role without obliterating the potential for change.[12] As classical materialists but also colonial subjects, these iconic figures of the "Black radical
tradition" expressed an intimate familiarity with the history of late modern
Europe that could be nuanced through an engagement with the early modern instantiation of imperial expansion in which the history of Spain and
Portugal represented more than a long preface to the "real" colonial past. Perhaps we should approach this by asking a different question: how might we
reconcile these disparate histories of Europe without simply viewing the three
centuries before the advent of English and French capitalism merely as a long
prehistory, extended detour, or ill-defined route ultimately not taken?[13] As a
scholar of Africa and Africans working on the Latin American past, it seemed
natural that I found an opening through Walter Rodney's *A History of the
Upper Guinea Coast.*

A deeply nuanced study grounded in Portuguese archival sources dating
back to the sixteenth century, Rodney's book addressed many of the salient
historiographical themes of the African past, including the issue of migrations
and the spread of human civilization in West Africa, cultural diffusion, the
basis of social differentiation, slavery and the slave trade, the formation of states
and empires, the spread of Islam, and the arrival of the Europeans to include
the advent of colonial rule. On the basis of its impeccable research, *A History
of the Upper Guinea Coast* became a field-defining study in the fledgling historiography on Africa.[14] Yet for Rodney, the stakes involved far more than
scholarly debate. The history of the Upper Guinea coast presented an opening
to comment on the postcolonial condition, particularly the role of African
elites whose avarice fueled the slave trade, which in due course paved the way
for European colonial domination. In drawing this conclusion about the
past, Rodney simultaneously commented on the postcolonial present in both
Africa and the Caribbean. Rodney wrote,

> It is an obvious and well-recognized fact that the African chiefs and
> kings were actively engaged in partnership with the European sla-
> vers all along the coast, but the impression given of inter-tribal con-
> flicts has usually seemed to outweigh that of internal struggles. . . .
> Tribal divisions were not, then, the most important. When the line
> of demarcation is clearly drawn between the agents and the victims
> of slaving as it was carried on among the littoral peoples, that line
> coincides with the distinction between the privileged and the un-
> privileged in the society as a whole. The Atlantic slave trade was

deliberately selective in its impact on the society of the Upper Guinea Coast, with the ruling classes protecting itself, while helping the Europeans to exploit the common people. This is of course the widespread pattern of modern neo-colonialism; and by the same token the period of slave trading in West Africa should be regarded as protocolonial.[15]

Clearly, Rodney's engagement with the past enabled a critique of the present. In the present, the manner in which the African and black elite mobilized political sovereignty to advance particular agendas needed to be questioned if not politically challenged. As Rodney saw matters, the African elite engaged in practices only too reminiscent of an earlier historical moment. Such behavior highlighted class interest rather than a lack of agency. "It must be borne in mind that when the Europeans arrived they dealt with the Africans through the ruling class," observed Rodney, noting how "the responsibility for the slave trade, as far as Africans themselves bear part of this responsibility, lies squarely upon the shoulders of the tribal rulers and élites. They were in alliance with the European slave merchants, and it was upon the mass of the people that they jointly preyed."[16] Since governance resided among Africa rulers, Rodney did not view the matter as evidence of failed sovereignty. Rodney repeatedly reiterated, "There was no semblance of European political control over the African rulers."[17] Critical of elite politics in the present and the past but also intent on highlighting the existence of the political in precolonial Africa, Rodney drew on political sociology for terminology that allowed him to traverse the premodern and modern divide. In doing so, he promiscuously employed terms like *regime, social formation, state, stateless, empire, emperor, king, kingship, class, war, rule*, and *sovereignty*.

Rodney's account of the African-European encounter, despite its secular framings, acknowledged the historicity of the engagement between the Portuguese and the peoples of the Upper Guinea Coast. In situating that narrative in the fifteenth century, Rodney elided the historical dynamic of a subsequent colonial moment, one in which the relations of power skewed in favor of the Europeans. The imbalance in power, a product of the future, reflected a history in which Europeans but also Africans contributed. In assuming the existence of human agency, Rodney illuminated a dynamic ancient African past alongside the more recent fifteenth century that welcomed the Portuguese presence (on African terms) but to which the new arrivals had to accommodate. In this context, the Portuguese encounter with peoples of the

Upper Guinea Coast mediated existing political practices and traditions that
the various sides brought to bear. For the Portuguese, this meant engaging
with Africans through the conceptual optic of their time. As Rodney noted,
the Portuguese employed feudal terminology in their representations of and
interactions with Africans. Social distinctions among Africans, meanwhile,
conveyed an indigenous cultural logic rather than a recent imposition, yet
through time hardened the competition for resources and stratification between sectors in society. Engendered by existing forms of differentiation, slavery and the slave trade eventually came to monopolize the trade between the
Portuguese and Africans, but through the eighteenth century, as Rodney
stressed, Africans wielded authority in their relations with Europeans. The result was a history but also a critique building on an exploration of the past so
as to engage the postcolonial present without resorting to simple ideological
contortions. Along with acknowledging complexity in the African-European
encounter, Rodney questioned the idea of European dominance in the earliest engagement with Africans. Ironically, the Africanist John K. Thornton has
taken Rodney to task for precisely the opposite view.

For more than a generation, Thornton's *Africa and Africans in the Making of the Atlantic World*—based on a fundamental mischaracterization of
Rodney's *A History of the Upper Guinea* along with a questionable deployment
of Rodney's polemic *How Europe Underdeveloped Africa*—has been a standard
of Atlantic historiography. No other book rivals *Africa and Africans* in both
framing and representing Atlantic African history. Its canonical status derives,
in part, from the absence of an empirically grounded and accessible African
past reconcilable with the thematic concerns informing the study of American slavery—the African-European encounter, the evolution of race and
American democracy, the political economy of slavery, and the politics of resistance and cultural survival. The text's alignment with the empiricism that
informed the earlier historiography of European imperial studies enhanced
its canonical status while securing its prominence in Atlantic studies.

Intent on vindicating the African past—an impulse prompted by liberal
historiography—Thornton ascribed Africans agency while illustrating little
awareness as to why Rodney, as a critic of liberalism, assumed as much. *Africa
and Africans* positions all Africans—not solely the elites, rulers, despots, and
tyrants—as agents of the slave trade. In bestowing agency onto Africans
rather than assuming its existence, Thornton crafted a simplified African past
for American consumption: a history that circumvented the thematic structure of American historiography but embraced the conceptual space assigned

to Africans. By insinuating liberal causality and an ill-defined African agency, Thornton flattened a layered political history, which Rodney had built around elites, power, political authority, and sovereignty. In the process, Thornton not only distorted Rodney's findings but also pointedly dismissed him for being a "nationalist" and "radical historian" associated with the "neo-Marxist focus" that allegedly reduced Africans to passivity.[18]

Notwithstanding its canonical status, *Africa and Africans* begs such questions as the following: What are the implications of assigning Africans agency when Western humanism assumes as much with regard to philosophical Man? Does not the very act of bestowing agency foreclose its unquestionable universalism? Asked differently, does the gesture of granting agency not risk giving legitimacy to the very political-conceptual practice that exercised its existence among Africans in the first place? For the better part of a generation, as the canonical status of *Africa and Africans* has remained unquestioned, scholars of Atlantic history have avoided addressing such vexing questions. For this reason, the moral cost for incorporating Africans into Western and in particular U.S. historiography remains unquestionably disturbing, conceptually troubling, and fundamentally problematic.

Thornton's aim, of course, resided in having African history acknowledged as an analytic of the American intellectual scene. In the face of slave regimentation directed toward production at the expense of an autonomous formation of culture, African cultural persistence represented both a defiant act and an elemental aspect of American culture. Indeed, it should be noted that Thornton's focus resided with the African and not the slave past. Thornton took issue with "historians of American slavery in the era of the civil rights struggle and black power movements in the United States" intent on overturning the image of the compliant slave, but in doing so, they solely configured cultural vitality through the matrix of slavery. Arguments for "slave culture" reduced "the African identity of the slave," thereby disavowing the African past.[19] In staking claims around the terrain of African culture, Thornton argued for its vibrancy in early America. In a universe that from its inception exhibited relentless hostility and at best indifference to Africans, stressing African cultural vitality represented far more than an antiquarian endeavor. For Thornton, the existence of African culture countered the racist ideologies intent on denying the humanity of blacks. As the anthropologist David Scott has observed in relation to Thornton, "The basic questioned to be answered, . . . was Atlantic slave plantation power so limiting or stultifying as to prevent or preclude the persistence of African languages, religion, kinship patterns, and so on? . . . For Thornton, slave plantation power is pictured principally as a negative or limiting force, and the central preoccupation is whether or to what extent the regime of plantation slavery restricted, blocked, paralyzed, or deformed the transformative agency of the slave."[20] Scott's nuanced reading of *Africa and Africans* underscores how Thornton, like Rodney, though from a different vantage point, addressed the issue of power. Postcolonial critics like Rodney obviously engaged the terrain of power and cultural contestation but focused far more on the consciousness that impeded African elites from navigating the shoals of the postindependence period on behalf of the common good. "Animated by a fundamental and sympathetic humanism," Scott observes, "this concern obliges . . . Thornton . . . to look for the agency that transgresses it, survives it, overcomes it, and to look in turn for the sources (cultural or otherwise) that enabled or fed that transgression, survival, or overcoming."[21]

By mobilizing culture, Thornton circumvented the indifference to and exclusion of the African past. Ironically, in advancing a conceptual approach styled "Africanist," Thornton strongly critiqued anthropologists, notably those of the mid-twentieth century whose principal focus was the African present. At its core, Thornton was critical of the historical stasis characterizing mid-century African anthropology that found its way into the writing of the African past. "The interest in the African background of American culture," observed Thornton, "led many historians of the Americas back to Africa." In then making a now familiar critique, Thornton noted how historians "studied Africans' culture through the medium of modern anthropology rather than the careful study of contemporary documents. Because anthropologists' knowledge is based on fieldwork in contemporary (usually mid-twentieth century) Africa, until quite recently their statements about earlier times were based on theoretical supposition or an assumption that African society and culture did not change."[22] Here the issue rightly focused on the lack of historicity in certain, if not most, mid-twentieth-century anthropological studies. These studies, as anthropologists themselves have pointed out, embraced the prevailing evolutionary thinking of the times. Thornton's critique obviously carried considerable validity. In emphasizing Africa's salience in the formation of early black societies in the Americas, scholars should not have simply relied uncritically on the studies of British social anthropologists. Interestingly enough, in method and form, *Africa and Africans* resembled anthropological studies of the African past while Thornton's critique of that discipline overlooks an important dynamic.[23]

Until the mid-twentieth century, American historians, with a few notable exceptions, manifested a profound indifference to African history and the history of blacks beyond the narrative of slavery. During the same period and on the basis of a restricted thematic focus that included racial pathology, crime, and poverty, scholars confined the story of blacks to the field of sociology. When historians invoked the black experience, the focus was invariably on slavery and the postbellum dilemma of race. Indeed, the first to take up the subject of race and therefore the experience of blacks were white Southerners—who often employed history to fight a war that had been lost on the battlefield. The outcome resulted in negative portrayals of black freedom, insinuating that slavery had been a beneficial and modernizing institutional experience for Africans and subsequently blacks. Though this aspect of history writing no longer holds sway in the American narrative nor is representative of thinking in the historical profession, we are only now fully realizing how naturalized this ideology had become as a manifestation of U.S. history.[24] Thornton, by focusing on the question of African culture as opposed to the incorporation of Africans into the American historical narrative, circumvented the thematic structure of the American past. For this reason, though adamant in his critique of mid-century anthropologists, Thornton shares with them—notably Melville J. Herskovits—a similar engagement with culture and the American historical narrative. For Herskovits, a focus on culture averted the negation of the African past that sanctioned racists in barring blacks from citizenship. Clearly, the terrain of culture occasioned but also channeled racial advocacy, engendering appeals for inclusion.

In the middle of the twentieth century, Herskovits reconfigured the study of the African past in the New World. By questioning the "myth of the Negro past," Herskovits staked out the conceptual terrain from which successive scholars staged new studies of the African diaspora. Viewing Africans and consequently blacks as cultural beings, Herskovits aligned with a small but influential group of critics who questioned normative racist thinking. In doing so, he built on the work of his adviser at Columbia University, the German anthropologist Franz Boas, who earlier had challenged the dominant evolutionary paradigms that viewed Africans as inferior racialized beings. For Herskovits, culture superseded race as the register through which an authentic understanding of the New World black experience could be discerned.

In privileging a cultural perspective over the discourse of race, Herskovits was at the helm of a small community of social scientists who were forging new approaches for studying the long-neglected "New World Negro." Even though they disavowed the explicitly racist views that had framed the study of Africans and their New World descendants, their modernist ahistorical treatment of culture reinscribed the "myth of the Negro past." Herskovits insisted that an African cultural legacy prevailed throughout the Americas, but he too employed a decidedly modern framing of culture. Arguing for a cultural baseline, Herskovits minimized the specificity of the African past while severing the ideal type from history and the political. In contextualizing the New World's African past but not, as we shall see, its relationship to the dominant forms of American history and the historical formation of Africa, Herskovits bypassed political traditions and political histories characterized by social differentiation, the politics of kingship, ethnic conflict, and state formation. By disavowing preexisting political histories and statecraft, Herskovits conceptualized the very break that defines deracination—the sundering of roots. Culture, in this formulation, did not assume expression through institutional forms, institutionalized rituals, cultures with rules, or customary practices rooted in space and dominion. Stated differently, Herskovits replaced one myth of the African past with another: one of cultural forms that hovered above and beyond historical reality. As a testament to Herskovits's legacy, scholars largely configured the African diaspora as a cultural phenomenon ranging from the nostalgia of return to an embodied African consciousness as opposed to an engagement with specific histories in which state formation and its destruction played a decisive role. Rarely have studies of the African diaspora attended to diaspora as an act of state destruction—whereby an imperial assault violates the sovereignty, if not destroys the polity, of another people, thus rendering them stateless beings.[25] Instead, the prevailing focus has been on culture disruption, collective trauma, and individual resilience. In the process, we have lost sight of the travails of war alongside the drama of state destruction that represented the historical consequences of the empires at the core of Herskovits's Africa. But in representing the cultural memory of the enslaved, we eschew specifics in favor of a collective communal African past.

For the most part, Herskovits focused on the West African imperial polities of Oyo, Dahomey, and Asante. This imperial perspective came at the expense of subaltern politics but also regions and peoples beyond empires, especially northern West Africa.[26] What prompted this indifference to nonimperial formations? Asked differently, why focus on Asante, Dahomey and Oyo as opposed to other imperial formations? Though a few scholars have taken issue with Herskovits's regional focus, the African imperial perspective alongside the West African emphasis comes as a surprise. One might, for instance, ask why the African baseline is configured around a West African locus. Why neglect West Central Africa? Herskovits clearly constructed an image of Africa that reified his indifference to the prevailing scientific tradition on the "Dark Continent." Interestingly enough, he does not, for example, reference the German explorer Georg Schweinfurth's *The Heart of Africa* (1874)—which, according to the art historian Suzanne Blier, had a profound impact on the cultural and scientific patrons connected to New York's Museum of Natural History and therefore the American public interested in Africa—but he does acknowledge Sir Richard F. Burton's popular travel narrative *A Mission to Gelele, King of Dahome with Notices of the So-Called "Amazons", the Grand Customs, the Yearly Customs, the Human Sacrifices, the Present State of the Slave Trade and the Negro's Place in Nature.* Though acknowledging familiarity with Burton's text, Herskovits avoids the imperial traveler's cultural conceptions in favor of a more abstracted notion of culture. But well into the nineteenth century, royal subject status in Dahomey involved far more than abstracted cultural forms. Power and force configured the subject. Subject status in Dahomey acquired valence through the culture of militarism, tribute, and discipline alongside submission, fear, awe, and personal obedience to the sovereign. For this reason, the culture of royal subjects entailed more than abstracted customs. Dahomey's victims, those most likely transformed into New World slaves, forged cultural abstractions out of necessity, underscoring how the African diaspora entailed deracination but also the loss of sovereignty—the destruction of state forms that previously had been the habitus for cultural practices.[27] So here in the New World was a people who had to engage in abstracted cultural survival, precisely because the customary beliefs, norms, and practices were severed from state forms and institutional mechanisms. Culture or customs, in other words, assumed relevance in relation to the institutional function in the larger web of signification through which the collective constituted society and the individual emerged. In the wake of Herskovits, most scholars of Atlantic history and New World slavery have configured the African diaspora through modern formulations of culture or a cultural engagement abstracted from the polis. In contrast to empires and statelessness, culture and shared consciousness stand in for the histories of the African diaspora. Such representations privilege, above all, the realm of ideas, memory, and cultural practices. As a cultural formation, we might ask whose culture stood at the center of the African diaspora, but also why we position culture at the heart of our histories of the African diaspora in the first place.

Questioning the claim that culture is the central feature of the African diaspora challenges the framing at the heart of black studies. The stakes do not simply involve some greater truth claim that now takes precedence over earlier positions and claims. There is also an acknowledgment that the "problem space" of earlier moments—liberal historiography but also those associated with anticolonial nationalism and its immediate postcolonial sequence—demand that new questions be posed so as to repurpose the political-intellectual project associated with the earliest history of the African-European encounter. Much that we thought to be true—framing our positions and claims—simply cannot be sustained. In many respects, the time has come for us to jettison the Herskovitzian cultural paradigm that both explicitly and implicitly continues to configure thinking about the earliest histories of the African-European encounter and on which both the genealogy and the epistemological endeavor of black studies still rest. In asking for a fundamental reconsideration of the African American intellectual enterprise, we stake new claims around the formulation of the African diaspora and by implication the very framing of power ascribed to the European past.

*   *   *

A strain of thought among an emerging community of scholars in the first half of the twentieth century steadily emphasized the shift from race to culture. Though they did not overturn the dominance of the racist paradigm, the emphasis on viewing culture as unhinged from institutional moorings called into question previous normative assumptions. This cultural framing came with a cost. A decidedly modern concept of culture overlooked the existence of sovereign power inextricably tied to African lordship, which fifteenth-century Iberians had posited as a distinct African reality securing Christian protection and trade. Simply put, the earliest extant sources acknowledged the royal manifestation of power in Africa.

Since their lives but also diplomacy and trade depended on a keen understanding of relations of power, fifteenth-century Iberians offered detailed descriptions of the hierarchies they encountered ceremonially (in ritual), institutionally (in court), or transactionally (in tribute). While the emphasis, in initial encounters, usually swirled around the medieval marvel and the exotic—the ontology for that very modern concept of otherness—even a casual reading of the period's travel accounts, chronicles, and histories details the routine nature in first sightings and their immediate aftermath, which might be best described as the absence of wonder. As the travelers stumbled ashore, they along with indigenous Africans enacted established protocols that mediated their encounters. Even as curiosity prevailed, the extant sources highlight how hierarchy and order shaped the pace, form, and nature of first interaction. To interpret these acts through a modern register invokes by definition the concept of culture. *African Kings and Black Slaves*, by revisiting these familiar narratives, accounts, chronicles, and histories of inaugural sightings, affords a glimpse of clear yet overlooked references to relations of power in Africa. References to power did not disappear overnight as the dust of arrival settled, but they have been lost in our imposition of the liberal future onto the past. In the early European encounter with Africa, as we shall see, the earliest explorers, merchants, court historians, chroniclers, and theologians experienced the political, a trope that subsequent writers and theorists have lost sight of by projecting their contemporary perspectives on a previous period.

Stating that the prevailing scholarly perspective configures the slave trade and slavery primarily as an English story is not an exaggeration. Empire and liberalism stand triumphant, underscoring their continuing legacy in framing the past. In this past, the African-European encounter has lost a significant dimension of its complexity; imperial rule prevails, the English stand in ascendancy in their relations with Africans, and the slave trade represents a mere economic appendage of capital fueled by the perception that all Africans embody savage difference. But the slave trade and slavery always represented far more than an English story or for that matter a symptom of Europe's economic and political supremacy. To acknowledge as much in narrating Africa's Atlantic past entails more than ascribing Africans agency. It requires— to invoke the historian Dipesh Chakrabarty—the provincializing of the European past: that very act of delineating a history in all of its specifics that preceded the emergence of ascendant "Europe." Stated differently, the specifics of the past that predated Europe—not some generic eighteenth-century Europe—need to be excavated in order to discern the very making of Africa and Africans. This endeavor of historical excavation, akin to what the French political philosopher Michel Foucault categorized as historical archaeology, animates what follows.

CHAPTER 2

Mythologies

In present-day Ghana, Elmina to be exact, long before Asante ascendancy or the earlier Anlo-Ewe arrival, an African lord approached a group of strangers who had recently landed. At that moment—which the Portuguese date to 1481 but whose reckoning for local Africans remains obscured in their distinct cultural configurations of the past—the lord encountered the largest contingent of Europeans to set foot in the "land of Guinea." As he greeted the strangers, the *Caramança* made clear that he held their lives in his hands. Hours earlier the Portuguese commander, Diogo de Azambuja, instructed his factor to secure landing rights and an audience with the reigning lord, whose title was Caramança, though the Portuguese initially mistook this as his name. Now, the Portuguese arrivals stood in formation awaiting the Caramança. Even if Azambuja extended the request as a routine formality, his gesture—especially in view of the larger contingent of Christians present—acknowledged the Caramança's dominion. After decades of fleeting contact, Guinea's sovereigns, whose dominion extended to the West African and West Central African coast, still exacted respect for their position as lords and landlords—respect that the Portuguese accorded in ceremonial form. Ceremonies along with diplomacy enacted through discernible gestures and motions facilitated trade while implicating the Portuguese in local kingship rituals directed at them and local subjects. As one contemporary noted, the Portuguese "carried on their business in peace and friendliness, without those warlike incursions, assaults and robberies which happened at the beginning."[1]

As the Portuguese awaited the Caramança's arrival, the cacophony "of bugles, bells and horns, which are their instruments" announced the lord's procession. Surrounded by an armed escort and accompanied by nobles, each trailed by two naked pages carrying their ruler's stools and weapons, the

Caramança approached with measured poise, naked yet bedecked in gold. He enacted his omnipotence over all the locals, including the inhabitants of Elmina (literally, "the mine")—the name the Portuguese gave to the land jutting into the Atlantic where they hoped to erect a fort so as to secure access to the inland gold trade. Soon after the event, the Portuguese chronicler Rui de Pina (1440–1521) recounted how "the king came naked, and his arms and legs were covered with chains and trinkets of gold in many shapes, and countless bells and large beads of gold were hanging from the hair of his beard and his head."[2] Another Portuguese chronicler, João de Barros (1496–1570), who was personally acquainted with many of the Portuguese nobles present at the scene, described the procession in even greater detail:

> [Caramança] came with many people in war-like manner, with a great hub-bub of kettle-drums, trumpets, bells, and other instruments, more deafening than pleasing to the ear. Their dress was their own flesh, anointed and very shining, which made their skins still blacker, a custom which they affected as elegancy. Their privy parts only were covered with the skins of monkeys or woven palm leaves—the chiefs with patterned cloth, which they had from our ships. All, in general, were armed after their manner, some with spears and bucklers, others with bows and quivers of arrows; and many, in place of helmets, wore monkey skins studded with the teeth of animals. . . . Those who were considered noblemen were followed by two pages; one of whom carried a round wooded stool so that they might sit down and rest when they wished; the other a war buckler. These noblemen wore rings and golden jewels on their heads and beards. Their king, Caramança, came in their midst, his legs and arms covered with golden bracelets and rings, a collar round his neck, from which hung some small bells, and in his plaited beard golden bars, which weighed down its untrimmed hairs, so that instead of being twisted it was smooth. To impress his dignity, he walked with very slow and light steps, never turning his face to either side.[3]

As the king reached the center of the Portuguese formation, Azambuja descended from a makeshift platform. He reverently approached the Caramança, who took his hand only to release it so as to "touch his fingers and then snap the one with the other, saying in his language 'Bere, bere,' which in ours means 'Peace, peace.'" After Azambuja responded with a gesture of his own, the nobles who accompanied the king repeated the hand-finger ritual. "But," Pina recalled, "the manner in which they snapped their fingers differed from that of the king: wetting their fingers in their mouths and wiping them on their chests, they cracked them from the little finger to the index finger, a kind of salute here given to princes; for they say that fingers can carry poison, if they are not cleaned in this manner."[4] Following this series of gestures, principals on both sides extolled rhetoric of goodwill and friendship but also warnings. If the Portuguese acted contrary to his will, the king proclaimed, "they would cause more harm to themselves than him." With this stern admonition, the Caramança conveyed what the rituals and his presence dramatized: as the sovereign authority, he wielded power over life and death.

*   *   *

In a magical landscape inhabited by gods, royalty, the living, and the dead, the majesty of form engendered through coronations, processions, and sacred rituals constituted far more than a minor affair.[5] As sources of authority, spectacles conveyed the mystery of power embedded in lordship.[6] Trivializing symbolic enactments, if not overlooking them altogether, results in a distorted geography of power.[7] In neither Atlantic studies nor the history of the African diaspora do symbolic enactments in Africa figure as sites for theorizing the evolving history of sovereign power.[8] The spectacles enacted along Africa's Atlantic coast during the fifteenth century and beyond suggest that the region constituted a crucial site of lordship and sovereignty and an evolving history of power. But the same should be said for the encounter between Africans and Europeans. Spectacles and ceremonies—ceremonies of encounter as well as ceremonies of possession—repeatedly dramatized sovereignty while displaying authority over sacred knowledge, territory, and people.[9] In the fifteenth century, an African lord's loci of power invariably centered on his ability to marshal vassals and retainers whose fortune, status, debts, and ties (or lack thereof) triggered a political calculus that transformed subjects into slaves— the charter beings of the early modern African diaspora. Focusing on the earliest spectacles and ceremonies recalibrates the locus of Atlantic encounters while bringing forth new domains for examining the history of sovereignty.[10]

At one level then, this book highlights the staging of lordship, the ceremonies and pomp expressive of early modern practices of sovereignty, in which Africans figured. Here the mystery of power, authority, and rule resided in rituals and rites. Generally overlooked in secular conceptions of power (state as opposed to sovereign power) that since the eighteenth century, have framed representations of the African-European encounter, the scholars that do focus on these rituals and rites generally reduce them to cultural traditions.[11] Flourishing at the moment of contact, these spectacles, even in the fifteenth century, drew on hybrid forms composed of novel terminology, pidgin languages, currencies, sacred knowledge, and rituals that have long invited scholarly attention but largely as cultural affects rather than as instruments of power.[12] It is fitting to view these forms and practices simultaneously as novel cultural effects and trappings of power intent on harnessing the presence of strangers.[13] The spectacles were, in fact, staged for European consumption. But they were also directed at the subjects of an African lord intent on asserting autonomy in the periphery that he inhabited in relation to the lords of the interior. In this respect, the opening performance constituted a multidimensional ceremony. First, the Portuguese directed it at themselves and other Christians at a distance. The African lord, in turn, focused the Europeans' gaze on his authority. By these actions, the lord marshaled the attention of his subjects through the assertion of dominion over foreigners, thereby charting a new locus of sovereignty from that wielded by established lords situated inland.[14] We, therefore, need to see the encounter as engendering a spatial reconfiguration of power that eventually led to the emergence of new (breakaway) social formations whose very origins and cultural logic resided principally in the expanding Atlantic complex.[15] For this reason, the earliest encounters between Africans and Europeans embodied more than an aberrant yet overlooked moment in the long history of contact and trade. Diplomacy—a term rarely invoked in African-European interaction—may best characterize such encounters.[16]

In an age marked by discoveries, encounters, and conquests, the performative, discursive, and material foundations of power—the collective locus of sovereign power—structured the ways that lords and subjects, Africans and Europeans, interacted. Expansion in the form of discoveries, encounters, and conquests brought distinct manifestations of power and, by implication, competing forms of sovereign power into relief. These diverse traditions of sovereignty surfaced during encounters when those who embodied sovereign power (in their relationship to the occult, in their regulation of legitimate violence, in their dominion over people, or in their control over territory) insisted on being understood on their own terms. The resulting dynamic—acts of translation—configured the way in which power both composed and suffused the social landscape.

The anatomy of power has occupied a vast array of thinkers, but philo-sophically and historically, its form and formation have been almost exclu-sively framed in a manner privileging the Western experience. Even the language for discerning power in non-Western and culturally hybrid contexts draws narrowly on the decidedly modern Western experience.[17] Here we might note that the modern classical expression of power, which the German social theorist Max Weber identified as the state embodying a monopoly on legiti-mate violence, continues to wield hegemonic influence over our theoretical imaginary. Although Weber's analytics of power were admittedly formulated as a general definition of the state and its role in framing the modern experi-ence, subsequent writers have had few philosophical qualms about projecting his analytics into the past.[18] Rather than take issue here with the anachro-nism of utilizing a modern entity as the universal embodiment of the state form, I wish to direct our attention to the claims concerning the state's pur-ported monopoly over power. Weber's definition, though mindful of a con-tested terrain, contends that the viability of a state rests on its ability to exercise hegemony over competing forms of power.[19] The state, we are told, exerts force exclusively in its domain. That being the case, one must still ask what the analytical implications are for sites of encounters where distinct authorities and lords stood face to face. Are we to assume that contestation foreclosed a monopoly over violence, thereby rendering the site stateless? Posed differently, how should we configure power at moments and sites of encounters? By insist-ing on the mutually constitutive nature of sovereign authority in early modern Africa and Iberian imperial absolutism—one of the book's principal claims—I argue for a wider, Atlantic African theorization of power that brings into relief the way writers have naturalized histories of political practice in Africa and Europe as mutually exclusive phenomena.[20] My insistence on the mutu-ally constitutive nature of power and statecraft in the early African-European encounter does not deny either African or European forms a primordial exis-tence; rather it questions theorization that excludes Africa as a formative site in sovereignty's early modern history while emphasizing that the still defini-tive expression of power—the monopoly over violence—constitutes only one modality for discerning sovereign might. The histories of power in Africa and Europe have steadily evolved, but during the earliest phase of the African-European encounter, they played a crucial role in shaping the nature of sovereign authority in the emerging Atlantic complex. As a constituent ele-ment of a cataclysmic era, early African-European diplomacy engendered novel social forms throughout the Atlantic littoral. To ignore these diplomatic enactments, as we have, results in static, ahistorical, and overdetermined understandings of European power, on which scholars of African studies, the African diaspora, and Atlantic history still rely to represent the story of Europe and the legacy of the encounter. For this reason, we see new political orientations and politics arising, which would also require the deployment of new ideologies and practices of legitimacy.

Political theater, an embodiment of politics, clearly played an important role in the early history of the Atlantic but so did the prevailing registers of political thought, which, along with the complex European legal regimes (Roman civil and canon law) in tandem with the will and authority of African lords, brought into relief the practices and discourses of *dominium* that acknowledged African sovereignty. *Dominium*, by shaping the earliest interaction between Europeans and Africans, engendered a far more complicated history than is gestured toward by the still prevailing trope of African alterity, whereby perceptions of savage difference resulted in African enslavement and colonial domination. To be sure, the occasional Christian prince heralded conquest, forced conversion, and enslavement for pagan foes, but a more complicated social reality, as we shall see in Chapter 3, tempered the rhetoric mediated through Roman law. Intent on bringing this fifteenth-century social reality into relief in the European encounter with Africa, this book delineates a far more layered intellectual and cultural landscape than we are accustomed to imagining for early African-European encounters.

As expressions of the political, the principal forms of the early modern African-European encounter—the slave trade and slavery—remain remarkably underexamined.[21] In view of how contemporary political theorists frame the early modern African presence, this lacuna should not surprise. In his pioneering discussion of New World encounters, the historian of political thought Anthony Pagden devotes considerable energy to discussing Aristotle's theory of natural slavery. But in stark contrast to the ways in which he conveys the layered Spanish perception of Indians, Pagden simply notes that African enslavement did not represent a matter of concern—theological or otherwise.[22] For the political theorist Istvan Hont, the matter is simple: before the philosopher David Hume joined the economic to the political, sovereigns manifested a marked indifference to commercialization.[23] In contrast to the omissions of modern scholars, as a commentary on nascent imperial governance and *policia* (order), the slave trade and slavery invited considerable theological scrutiny in the sixteenth century; this scrutiny was explicitly configured around slavery in Spain, a widespread institution that only in the late fifteenth century became an increasingly Africanized social phenome-non.[24] By constricting the African presence in Spanish thought to the sixteenth-century New World, Pagden and others problematically equate Af-ricans with slaves, but in doing so, they foreclose a more ample perspective—rooted in the fifteenth-century Atlantic encounters among Africans and Europeans—that brought the issue of dominion to the fore along with long-standing debates about the legitimacy of conquest, territorial dispossession, and enslavement.[25] As the medievalist Steven A. Epstein notes, "The European background to New World slavery matters."[26] By situating slavery and the slave trade on a wider and earlier intellectual canvas, we are afforded a dis-tinct perspective on the African-European encounter—a perspective that complicates the teleology that still frames the history of slavery. Doing so would enable us, along with the medievalist James Muldoon, to observe how "medieval ideas and institutions continued to shape the way in which Europeans operated long after the supposed end of the Middle Ages some-where in the fifteenth century."[27]

Among the various terms that defined the lexicon of early modern Euro-pean political thought, slavery figures prominently. Western writers and in-tellectuals have long addressed themselves to the issue of slavery. Long before Scottish political economists and French physiocrats linked bondage to des-potism and economic malaise, scholastics and humanists invoked slavery to meditate on the human condition, status, and the nature of an existing social order. Greek philosophers, Roman jurists, Christian theologians, and Renais-sance humanists, drawing on their respective authorities, their legal statures, and the Old Testament, defined slavery as the modality of subjection. Slavery framed lordship; in so doing, it configured mastery and liberty alongside tyranny and despotism but also brought into relief the relative status of others. For this reason, it is surprising to see that scholars deemphasize the historical, philosophical, and etymological relation between privatization and depriva-tion. In this history that preceded the master-slave dialectic configured by the German philosopher Georg Wilhelm Hegel, the master's power originated in the commutation of actual for social death and by confining the slave along with wife and children to the household, thereby depriving them collectively of a public existence. In terms of a customary status, slavery steadily ceded ground to serfdom in many parts of Christendom during the High Middle Ages, but its institutional legacy was still manifest in treatises concerning the social order.[28] As the subjects of Christian polities encountered diverse *gens* (people) and a plethora of nations, slavery figured prominently in the ethnographic imagination as a trope for expounding on such social phenomena as honor, virtue, shame, violence, hierarchy, authority, dominion, sovereignty, life, and death. Indeed it was the rare discussion of power that did not reference slavery as its antithesis and the analogue of liberty. But as New World slavery came to be framed in opposition to liberty—personal liberty—the term's more expansive meaning contracted. Though slavery represented the antithesis of personal liberty, the association of bondage with American Indians and particularly Africans resulted in an embodied difference whereby slavery became synonymous with blackness and freedom with whiteness. In this transformation, slavery exemplified personal status—the status of the individual—thereby diminishing the term's more complicated relationship to power. Here then we can delineate the ways slavery was semantically transformed into a racially charged form of dominion severed from the political formation.[29] Though still associated with terms that carry political valence—despotism and tyranny—writers employ this nomenclature to reference the masters' authority or to comment on the coercion required to ensure the institution's productivity. Slavery, in effect, became synonymous with individual dominance or its productive capacity. This transformation engendered a now neglected history. For this reason, slavery remains remarkably underexamined at the experiential level as a social relation and as a thematic in the history of political thought.[30]

Such claims are even more pronounced in relation to the slave trade. In the Western imaginary, the slave trade—both the act of enslavement and the Middle Passage—has not occupied an analogous role to slavery. As an exemplar of extreme horror, writers generally have let the phenomenon speak for itself.[31] Perceiving enslavement as the spoils of war and conquest, they implicitly distinguished the slave trade from slavery. In the formative years of the Atlantic slave trade, several popes and the occasional theologian questioned the morality of enslavement, but their concerns, as we shall see in Chapter 6, were largely driven by apprehension toward the new commercial ethos to which human trafficking was linked. The Atlantic slave trade thus avoided scrutiny until the late eighteenth century, when British abolitionists, prompted by their cause, conducted empirical research on mortality rates among the traffickers and their human cargo. To this day, the abolitionists' thematic concerns, temporal delimitations, and moral critique configured the intellectual approach to the slave trade. This is because, as the intellectual historian Christopher Brown has noted, "we have inherited the world that the abolitionists and their allies helped to make."[32] In short, the fact-finding of British abolitionists still provides the foundational perspective on the slave trade and, by implication, the history of African-European diplomacy. For this reason, the abolitionist imaginary—moral reform forged in the crucible of liberalism and empire—also delineated the epistemological terrain that supplanted an earlier Iberian history of that diplomacy.[33]

Here it is fitting to note that I come to this project as a historian of the African experience in Latin America who has long been intrigued by the anomalous location of both the African and blackness in Latin American history. I am convinced that this is related to how scholars of Spain, Spanish America, and now the Spanish Atlantic have been able to conceive of a Spanish imperial formation that eschews Spain's initial involvement in Africa, as if these practices had no bearing on the history of the Indies beyond the story of chattel slavery.[34] Historians of colonial Latin America, if they acknowledge Spain's conflict with Portugal in the early Atlantic, largely treat that experience as an aside and confine it to the conflict over the Canary Islands, Portugal's detaining of Columbus following his initial landfall in the Indies, and the events leading up to the Treaty of Tordesillas (1494), the papal-administered accord that parceled trade routes into Portuguese and Spanish spheres of influence. With the notable exception of the conflict of the Canaries, scholars limit this narrative to the period of 1492 to 1494, thereby obscuring nearly a century of Iberian imperial practices in which both the Castilian and Portuguese monarchy, along with theologians, gave considerable thought to Africa and their subjects' encounter with Africans. In rendering this history—beginning with the Conquest of Ceuta—as an aside in the formation of the West, the fabrication of imperial Spain, and the history of the Indies, scholars have configured Spanish interaction with Africa as the history of slavery in which "just war" legitimized the process of enslavement and Roman law governed master-slave relations.[35] But, as we shall see, much is lost by this circumscribed perspective. Over the course of the fifteenth century, Europeans—both the Portuguese and Spaniards—manifested a shifting political rationale in relation to Africans and the African Atlantic that belies the conventional representation that culminates in the slave trade. In their conflict with each other—in which the competing legal regimes and political (social) thought played a significant role—alongside the diverse practices that African rulers extracted from Iberians on the ground, a far more complicated historical experience and story of power emerges than the claim that perceived or embodied differences—racial alterity—configured the experience leading to enslavement. If, however, our *telos* configures Africans as slaves who solely represented property, we, in turn, lose sight of how competing legal regimes and an acknowledged sovereignty shaped Iberian imperial expansion.

Scholars of Spanish America and the Spanish Atlantic rarely relate slavery to empire. The study of slavery, largely limited to a category of possession and labor but by implication also dominance, stands in stark contrast to imperial histories. Empire defined slavery but also the Iberian Atlantic slave trades. Both also conspired in the formation of imperial absolutism. New World slavery materialized in the wake of European expansion, which corresponded with Western absolutism's emergence. While scholars of nineteenth-century Latin America have begun to explore the relationship between slavery and empire, this has not been the case for early modernists or social theorists.[36] Indeed, the centrality accorded to early modern capitalism in studies of slavery has overshadowed absolutism's formative relationship with human bondage in both Guinea and the Indies. Even as the extant pockets of merchant capitalism sustained Christian expansion and colonization, it also required sanction from absolutist rulers, in the form of charters. In return for real and symbolic obeisance, royal subjects requested and received approval to contract trade, discover new territories, and even extend the Christian presence. Such endeavors, in the absolutist era, almost always necessitated royal authorization. In the Iberian Atlantic—where absolutism initially took hold—the sovereign's authority reigned ascendant over all domains until the end of the Baroque era.[37] As an early embodiment of absolutism, the Castilian monarchy assumed prominence in ruling—a marked contrast to the subsequent English experience, in which the Crown assumed a more limited role and an individual's authority over private property gradually reigned supreme. In this respect, the Spanish colonies represented an anomaly—or a route not taken. Out of a desire to regulate, a feature of absolutism's rationale, Castile's sovereigns subjected trade, discovery, and settlement to their authority in hopes of extending royal dominion and benefiting materially.[38] Their governance also assumed knowledge about places, commodities, and populations. The institutional structures that sustained absolutism, which included the Christian Church, thus served as instruments of ethnographic production—instruments designed to gather information about the populace and thereby control the king's various vassals, including slaves. For these reasons, the absolutist monarchs manifested intense interest in regulating the slave trade and slavery ostensibly since those institutional formations touched on more than property.[39]

Slaves represented both property and people. Scholars have long been sensitive to the ambiguity that the enslaved embodied. But modern studies of slavery, by projecting liberal historicism onto an earlier era, conflated the ascendancy of property with sovereign power. From this perspective, power in the form of ownership, dominance, and work shaped the slave experience. But in early modern Spanish America, masters were not the only ones defining the nature of slavery or even the most powerful authorities manifesting dominion over the enslaved. Masters competed with royal and ecclesiastical officials as they attempted to extend their dominion over persons simultaneously defined as chattel, vassals, and Christians.[40]

In early modern Spanish America, absolute authority did not accompany slave ownership. As Spain's rulers extended their dominion throughout the unfolding Atlantic world, they consistently encroached on the domain of private property, which occupied a privileged place in the mercantile economy throughout Europe. While Roman law, in theory, accorded masters' complete authority over slaves, Spain's monarchs frequently violated the owner's dominion while expecting their slave vassals to adhere to existing laws. Intent on upholding imperial rule, Castile's sovereigns often transgressed the masters' domain. Yet in intervening on the sanctity of the master-slave relationship, the Catholic monarchs eschewed doing so in an arbitrary manner. Instead they relied on existing laws—natural law, canon law, civil law, and customary law—that constituted slaves as vassals and Christian subjects. Jurisdictional conflicts surfaced, of course, with consequences for empire and slavery. These conflicts and their consequences insinuated an added layer of politics into the African-European encounter.

In conceding that "politics" were present in the early modern African-European encounter, the formative century of the slave trade and its resulting diasporas are restored to an imperial past that historians generally do not configure as the domain of Africans or slaves. As a discursive entity, early modern Africa initially emerged through the Portuguese and Spanish imperial encounters that simultaneously engendered the African diaspora. In the making of early modern Africa and the African diaspora, empire played a foundational role. As the imperial encounter bestowed the foundational grammar that brought these abstractions into existence, they transformed the imperial formation. Indeed, in the fifty years before Christopher Columbus's monumental voyage, sailors, merchants, and the occasional missionary in the service of Iberian royal households brought novel representations of Africa and Africans into relief. As referents of early modern Africa and some of the earliest contributions to the Africanist archive, these accounts, chronicles, and hagiographies were simultaneously constitutive of Europe and the European encounter with Africa and Africans.

Restoring the African experience to its imperial origins represents far more than a historiographical intervention. This act requires both an acknowledgment that African history occupies an underdeveloped status in Iberian and Latin American studies beyond the instrumentality of chattel slavery and a recognition that historical reconstruction needs to be configured in tension with the temporal specificity of an evolving imperial formation.[41] At first glance, it may seem counterintuitive to formulate the problem of the African past by situating it in relation to Iberian or Latin American colonial studies. But if we begin with the supposition that each analytical field (i.e., Latin American history, American history, and black studies) engenders specific demands and pasts, then this focus seems appropriate.[42] Interestingly enough, Latin American postcolonial scholars have been particularly attuned to this dynamic.

In *Genealogical Fictions: Limpieza de Sangre, Religion, and Gender in Colonial Mexico,* the historian María Elena Martínez states that her priorities are "to highlight some of the specifications of Spanish colonialism." Martínez writes, "Although there are continuities and similarities between different colonial projects, colonialism cannot be reduced to a single model; it has multiple historicities. The Spanish colonial project, the earliest in the Americas was driven by historically and culturally specific forces, and its course was determined by early modern dynamics on both sides of the Atlantic. It differed most from modern imperial projects."[43] In making this claim, Martínez adds her voice to an illustrious group of Latin Americanists, including Fernando Coronil, Jorge Klor de Alva, Walter Mignolo, and José Rabasa, all of whom are intent on reformulating the dominant conceptions of colonialism. In an exchange that has been stylized as the "postcolonial debate," these scholars of Latin America display a rigorous historicist sensibility. While we are now constantly reminded of the need to historicize our understanding of the colonial experience, an examination of what this might mean for the slave, black, or African experiences, which were constitutive of the Iberian colonial experience, has yet to emerge as a subject of inquiry.

My insistence that we historicize the African-European encounter, notably the slave trade and by implication slavery in the Americas, is analogous to Latin American postcolonialists' efforts to configure the history of Latin America in relation to Iberian temporalities, thereby disavowing the English and French experience as the normative incarnation of the colonial.[44] In fact, the

Latin American postcolonial critique of Anglo- and Francophone postcolonial studies anticipates my concerns directed at late eighteenth- and early
nineteenth-century representations of the slave trade—rooted in Anglophone
moral judgments that have rendered the slave trade into a transcendent historical phenomenon. The slave trade in the fifteenth and sixteenth centuries
embodied distinct forms from subsequent incarnations of the trade; still scholars generally project backward without engaging the distinct temporality and
its implication for the very categories and meanings that have become constitutive of the slave trade. What this calls for, among other things, is the reconstruction of African history (for Latin America) that does not circumscribe
the story to the history of numbers and abstracted cultures that privilege a
formulation of the slave trade and slavery anchored in a triumphant narrative
of capitalism.[45]

By conveying both the routine and the exotic, travelers produced representations of Africa that built on but eventually broke from classical depictions of the African continent. Early modern images of Africa were also distinct
from subsequent perceptions of Africa that legitimized the European partition
of the African continent in the nineteenth century. To perceive the image of
Africa as singular—invariably configured as the embodiment of alterity, radical
difference, or the "other"—both trivializes and exorcizes a distinct historical
moment in which rituals, spectacles, and symbols but also laws, courts, and
African lordship were instrumental in configuring sovereignty and power.
Consequently, our histories along with contemporary criticism, as Chapter 3 illustrates, have lost sight of the complex calculus of power that shaped
the early interaction among Africans and Europeans, engendering an early
modern Africa and producing the African diaspora. Clearly, fifteenth- and
sixteenth-century accounts, chronicles, and hagiographies reflected the ways
in which early modern European travelers perceived the encounter with
Africa and Africans, but these same sources also convey much about the enactment of power, lordship, and sovereignty in Atlantic Africa. In essence, the
Africanist archive offers far more than a glimpse of its discursive content.
Rather, it displays the very effects shaping the European-African diplomacy.

A century before priests, theologians, civilians, and canonists debated the
relative merits of Spanish dominion in the Indies, an array of individuals voiced
analogous concerns about Spanish and Portuguese expansion into the Atlantic littoral. The novelty of the Indies and their inhabitants overshadowed the
earlier, fifteenth-century discoveries but not before theologians, civilians, and
canonists concluded, on the basis of both natural and canon law, that the newly

encountered peoples, though viewed as barbarians, wielded sovereignty and legitimate property rights. As lords, in their own right and on the basis of natural law, African sovereigns manifested an acknowledged *dominium* that precluded Christian invaders from encroaching on their lands and making off with their possessions. Even a cursory glance at the language and terminology of the extant chronicles and travel literature conveys the pervasiveness of *dominium* in the earliest history of the African-European encounter. Novel discoveries along with dramatic conquests in the Americas have cast a shadow over this idiom in relationship to the African past while relegating fifteenth-century texts and commentaries to obscurity. Africanists have complicated this process by rendering, at best, a gloss of the extant sources. They thereby offer an anachronistic and decontextualized reading of papal bulls, the fifteenth-century treaties, and the extant travelogues while historians of slavery and scholars of racial formation largely neglect this vibrant intellectual history in favor of a perspective privileging trade and the social implications of the chattel principle. As a result, far more than just a vibrant intellectual tradition has been lost; the *episteme* through which a discourse of *dominium* and the ritualized practices associated with the landlord-stranger reciprocity mediated the earliest encounter among Africans and Europeans has been uprooted from the past. In its stead, a history predicated on difference, rupture, and apotheosis defines Europe's encounter with Africans.

In the long history of the African-European encounter that preceded nineteenth-century colonial rule, writers have confined the slave trade and slavery to the history of racial formation or the story of capital. Variations of this theme have resulted in narratives of difference constituted around culture, ethnicity, and now the subtlety of commodification. Still, the salience of difference—variously rendered as culture, race, and civilization—and capital stand steadfastly at the expense of alternate forms of historical emplotment. Viewed from the perspective of Europe's history with Muslims and Jews in and beyond Christendom, alongside first contact with diverse peoples and polities throughout the age of exploration, the monolithic depiction of European interaction with Africans stands out as an anomaly. At the precise moment that Christians wielded various strategies for engaging the diverse peoples they fought, lived, and contracted trade with, the portrayal of the African-European encounter still retains a uniformly flattened form. Stated succinctly, a "savage to slave" trajectory frames the narrative of the early modern African experience. By questioning this narrative convention, initially formulated around the principle of difference or capitalism, this study stresses the need for more

robust engagement with the prevailing fifteenth-century traditions and practices so as to undo the stasis informing our perspective on the earliest phase
of the European-African encounter.

*   *   *

Attention to a more layered historical process, in this case diplomacy between
Africans and Europeans, underscores the manner through which cultural effects linked to "economic" practices inaugurated a transition in and against
the very cultural order that composed social life. In questioning the imposition of this modern logic of historical representation onto the inaugural century
of African-European interaction, I insist on circumventing the practice of
modern scholarship and the collective memories of various publics that configure the histories of the encounter leading to the slave trade as a timeless
and self-evident social phenomenon. As a challenge to the existing historical
practice, I call for a consideration of the "political" in the narration of African-
European interaction in the form of political thought, the evolution of the
early modern Atlantic legal regimes, and the prevailing contests over dominion. Attention to these early modern manifestations of the "political" underscores much more than the naturalized state of economic or racial hegemony
in historical perceptions of African-European interaction. In the formation
of the New World, these enactments of politics position the African Atlantic
as a constituent element in the narrative of modernity.

   Building on the discursive tradition of Renaissance humanists, theologians, and imperial polemicists, contemporary philosophers and theorists now
readily acknowledge the centrality of 1492 in the formation of the modern.
As the moment that inaugurated a new epoch, thereby severing the present and
its futures from the preceding "traditional" era, as a structurally constituted
process associated with novel institutional forms, or as a collective sensibility,
modernity defines the analytical contours of a contemporaneity that dates
from 1492. As the French philosopher Tzvetan Todorov noted, "None is more
suitable, in order to mark the beginning of the modern era, than the year 1492,
the year Columbus crosses the Atlantic Ocean. We are all the direct descendants
of Columbus, it is with him that our genealogy begins, insofar as the word
beginning has a meaning."[46] To frame modernity in relation to 1492 is also to
recognize the importance that discoveries, encounters, and conquests played
in its formation. Occasionally acknowledged in the past but now more frequently asserted, documenting how imperial expansion engendered Europe's

modernity still remains an elusive endeavor.[47] Elusive, in part, because archives and their sources rarely—in a single record—identify decisive breaks,
momentous ruptures, or cataclysmic transformations, discoveries, encounters, and conquests call for reflection while privileging philosophical intuition
over empirically rendered proof. Philosophical intuition, however, offers little
by way of a corrective to the ideological dominance that 1492 wields over our
collective imaginary as modernity's inaugural moment.[48] What if we took
issue with the idea that 1492 constituted a defining moment, offering in its
stead the entire fifteenth century or the fifty years preceding 1492? In other
words, what historical process comes into relief when our inquiry into the
relationship between Iberian imperial expansion and Europe's modernity
begins circa 1450?

In conventional Atlantic historiography, the sixteenth century constitutes
a transitional epoch, a period characterized by a series of condensed antecedents
in which the hallmarks of our political modernity (the absolutist state, capitalism, and embodied difference) staged inaugural yet shallow appearances.
Constitutive of modernity, though rarely theorized as such, the slave trade
conjoined capital, statecraft, and race. Unlike their interest in modernity's other
institutional expressions, scholars manifest an indifference to historicizing the
slave trade, thus permitting it to acquire the status of an epiphenomenon—
a universal tragedy oblivious, with the exception of its volume, to historical
specificity. But can we legitimately assume that the cultural logic informing
the early modern slave trade remained intact over the course of four centuries?
Obviously, the answer is no. What then would it mean to configure the early
modern Atlantic slave trade historically? At first glance, this question seems
oxymoronic given that the early modern slave trade belongs to a distant era,
having been conceived, transpired, and brought to conclusion during a finite
span of time. To speak of the Atlantic slave trade is to reference the past. Yet
its vast temporal span—inaugurated in the fifteenth century and concluded
in the late nineteenth century—underscores that the slave trade traversed
multiple eras embodying distinct contingencies of time and being. Philosophers, intellectual historians, and anthropologists have long perceived how
temporality imbues reality, including history, with specific meaning.[49] In
view of the shifting dialectic between temporality and meaning, it seems
reasonable to ponder how one might configure the slave trade historically. To
insist that the nineteenth-century Portuguese slavers conceived of the time-being
nexus in a manner that distinguished them and their activities from the Portuguese who inaugurated the trade in the fifteenth century seems anything

but far-fetched. Surely the chattel principle of nineteenth-century capitalism carried a different, if not radically distinct, valence from the trading ethos
of the fifteenth century. In suggesting as much, my intent resides in discerning how one might engender a more nuanced history of the early modern
Atlantic slave trade, a history that transcends the liberal triumphalism of the
nineteenth century, which to this day frames the African-European encounter as a singular event—the slave trade—and defines the African diaspora
both as an economic effect—capitalism and the quantification of reality—
and a cultural tragedy—modern slavery and the apotheosis of race.[50]

*   *   *

In April 1569, months after a Spanish armada commanded by New Spain's
(Mexico's) newly appointed viceroy, Martín Enríquez, destroyed a small English squadron anchored in the harbor of Veracruz, the English captain John
Hawkins filed a civil claim in Her Majesty's High Court of Admiralty against
Spain's Philip II. Barely escaping with his life, Captain Hawkins, accompanied by a handful of English survivors, registered a complaint against Spain's
sovereign for the forfeit of life and liberty "eyther slayne in the fight of Vera
Crux or taken by the spaniardes." Having lost the bulk of his fleet and hundreds of lives to Spanish forces and the sea, John Hawkins sought restitution.
Yet this court favorite did not express concern about the loss of English lives
or the plight of his surviving countrymen, who as Lutheran heretics now stood
accused before the Holy Office of the Inquisition.[51] Instead, Hawkins confined his claim to the lost cargo; in the process, he implicitly distinguished
between English bodies and those "negros of goodlie stature, shape and per-
sonage, and yonge of yeres beinge the choise and principall of all the negros
w'ch wer gotten and purchased in this last voyage at Guiney."[52] As a claimant
before the Admiralty Court, Hawkins knew that the loss of the Africans
represented a civil proceeding in which human life, transformed into a commodity, acquired a specific value.

    In framing the claim against Christendom's mightiest sovereign, Hawkins
and his associates did not evoke nationalist rhetoric or manifest a Protestant
lament. He simply tallied the losses by conveying value through a convertible
currency and a near universal commodity—gold. "The said lvii (57) negroes,"
Hawkins told the High Court, "might have ben soulde at Vera Crux for iiii[e]
Pesos of Goulde everie negro."[53] By acknowledging the conditionality of
value—"negroes . . . might have ben soulde"—Hawkins displayed his strate-

gic awareness of the Spanish imperial landscape, including the geographic distribution of buyers who, in turn, influenced market conditions. Far from being restricted to him or other English traders, Hawkins declared that "Englishmen, frenchemen and portugalls doe bringe meny Negros to the . . . West Indias . . . but none . . . to the haven of Vera Crux, being aboute vi^e leages sailing beyond these hether places." For this reason, concluded Hawkins, "the Negroes and all other wares must be derer bought and soulde there."[54] The factor William Clarke, a Hawkins associate, concurred, speculating that "as towchinge ther value . . . they might be worthe a pece at the haven of Vera Cruz . . . cccL pesos of goulde."[55] As Hawkins and the other litigants ascribed value to the African cargo, they quantified distance traveled and the risk that a specific port posed, thereby enhancing the value of their loss. In the alchemy of calculation, the Atlantic passage entailed numerous quantifiable factors that added value to the cost of procurement—value that furthered the transformation of Africans into slaves. At this historic moment when the English represented interlopers in the New World, the African cargo's worth resided in its exchange value as opposed to its use value, a form of valuation that would increase once the English began to settle permanently in the Americas.[56] For this reason, Hawkins and the other European traders demanded "rialls of plate spanishe money" and, of course, gold in exchange for their cargo. As commodities, Africans enabled the English to trade for convertible of currencies—specie and bullion.

Claims, value, commodities, risk, market price, and currency constituted the sinews of merchant capitalism, which in the sixteenth century still was in its formative phase. In the wake of European expansion, distinct practices of mercantile activity converged, resulting in new social forms but also in the replacement of existing ones. Defined as momentous, this dynamic has, since the sixteenth century, attracted the attention of contemporaries and historians who discern in this era the origins of the modern. By means of this logic, Hawkins's voyage, ostensibly configured around transporting African slaves to the Americas, characterized a more modern zeitgeist. Far from fantastical, a scholarly consensus surrounds this claim. Still, it could be argued that scholars do not sufficiently stress the novelty of the voyage, which, from the moment he set sail to filing his claim, symbolized the emergence of a new era—also a new era in the history of the slave trade that played a significant role in mediating European interaction with Africans. The novelty does not reside in the trade of sub-Saharan Africans, which, in fact, preceded Columbus's voyage by a half century, but rather in the commercial ascendance in defining

African-European interaction. As a social practice, commercialization has a history still in need of a narrative, yet the century of African-European interaction that preceded Hawkins's voyage also requires a representational form that engages a complex past too often condensed and flattened by the monolithic depiction of a thoroughly commercialized slave trade alongside the histories of race.

Within the moment and register that we now inhabit, economic life constitutes a distinct realm from other forms of social life. In short, the economy and its constituent elements—the market and commodities, trade and trading relations, property and private life—appear as historical givens. But the representation of a discrete entity identified as "the economic" belies the historical dynamic whereby this phenomenon was distinguished from and eventually triumphed over other realms of social life. The German philosopher Karl Marx drew attention to this historical process often overlooked in discussions of the earliest encounter between Africans and Europeans. Toward the end of the first volume of *Das Kapital*, Marx sought to explicate the origins of capitalism. Having detailed and analyzed the workings of modern capitalism, Marx confined himself to documenting its historical genealogy. By discerning capitalism's historical trajectory, Marx delimited the process as "so-called primitive accumulation," noting that it "is nothing else than the historical process of divorcing the producer from the means of production."[57] In contrast to "bourgeois historians" who identified the process as a form of freedom, Marx was less than sanguine about the stakes involved. "Hence the historical movement which changes the producers into wage-labourers appears," observed Marx, "on the one hand, as their emancipation from serfdom and from the fetters of the guilds. . . . But, on the other hand, these newly freed men became sellers of themselves only after they had been robbed of all their own means of production and all the guarantees of existence afforded by the old feudal arrangements. And this history, the history of their expropriation, is written in the annals of mankind in letters of blood and fire."[58] In grounding the genesis of capitalism in primitive capital accumulation, Marx identified a relentless process of expropriation. By describing the mechanism—legal and extralegal—whereby producers were detached from their land, thereby transforming peasants and serfs into a rural workforce, Marx illustrated how capitalist farmers and the landed gentry engendered the capitalist transition in the countryside and the social landscape in general. Though scrupulously attentive to the economic process informing primitive capital accumulation, Marx insisted that expropriation was above all else a political event. The po-

litical nature of this process—embodied in statecraft—underscores a phenomenon that remains underanalyzed in the history of the slave trade.[59] Though
the history of violence and existing social structures are acknowledged, political theater, including rites and rituals, diplomacy, and laws, which collectively embodied statecraft, have been studiously ignored. But manifestations
of sovereignty, as Marx illustrated in the case of Europe, accompanied the economic effects of primitive capital accumulation. In responding to popular
sentiments that ideological factors—racism—fostered the origins and early
history of the slave trade, scholars have relegated political developments and
social relations among sovereigns and merchants and individual actors to the
analytical margins. Consequently, cultural representations of the initial contacts between Europeans and Africans in the fifteenth century, along with the
origins and early history of the slave trade, tend to privilege trade and trading
mechanics, type and volume of goods, and the transformation of humans into
commodities. By means of this economic perspective, designed as a corrective
to the popular perception that racism engendered the slave trade and slavery,
we have lost sight of a significant political dimension of first contact.[60]

CHAPTER 3

Law

Circa 1441, on the return to Sagres, a Portuguese caravel carrying pelts and oil set anchor off the northwestern coast of Africa. During the hiatus in present-day Mauritania, the commander of the "little ship" implored the nineteen-man crew to strive for more than the "small service" that they had performed in gathering their merchandise. Antáo Gonçalves waxed poetic: "O How fair a thing it would be if we, who have come to this land for a cargo of such petty merchandise, were to meet with the good luck to bring the first captives before the face of our Prince." Persuaded by Gonçalves's exhortation, the crew strove for valor and through successive skirmishes at nightfall acquired a man and a woman.[1]

The Portuguese raid, scholars of early modern colonialism tell us, marks a critical moment in Europe's overseas expansion resulting in a series of Atlantic encounters and ultimately the commodification of labor—a process initiated by the Portuguese as the architects of the transatlantic slave trade.[2] Commercialization, a signpost of an emergent modernity, united these phenomena. For some scholars of Atlantic slavery, the commercialization of Europe's material life was at the heart of the enslavement process, the institution of slavery, and the experiences of the enslaved.[3] Others insist that the crew's enslavement of Africans represented more than the appropriation of property since the process engendered modern race making. Here alterity, an embodied radical difference, inaugurates a break and introduces a new era.

These various claims underscore the significance of the Portuguese raid but also point to its consequences. Still, the transformations associated with the raid were not immediately apparent or ascendant. The Atlantic complex had to be established and then was constantly being remade; the commodification of labor took centuries before being fully realized, thereby underlining the fiction of absolute property; race making, like the Atlantic complex, experienced numerous incarnations invariably tempering Manichaean assertions. In stressing the raid's historic distinctiveness, even careful scholars compress time in favor of phenomena and ideas associated with later temporal moments. As this and the following two chapters illustrate, forward-focused writing—concerned with consequences—has in the case of the early African-European encounter foreclosed an engagement with the specific corpus of legal, theological, and institutional practices that wielded currency in the fifteenth century.

Roman law is a case in point. It was authoritative on civil matters, and scholars insist on its ascendancy in property-related issues. Notwithstanding its authoritative position, Roman law never secured hegemony over civil affairs in the fifteenth century and beyond or even over the social life that preceded the African's transformation into a slave. In always already conflating *African* with *slave* and then condensing the slave's relationship to the Western legal corpus down to the domain of property, slavery scholars—by projecting the cultural logic of an eighteenth-century market society onto earlier manifestations of bondage—ascribe an unwarranted hegemony to Roman law.[4] Roman law, in fact, flourished in a wider legal and social arena that even in the face of the violence accompanying Christian expansion, afforded non-Christians rights. The fifteenth-century European legal corpus, by conceding *dominium* to infidels and pagans, implicitly recognized a sovereign African existence that preceded the human calculus transforming subjects into captives and slaves.[5] Based on an established corpus of thought, law, and theology configuring Christian institutional relations with non-Christians, African polities wielded legal tender in the Christian imaginary.

Even as the nascent commercial sensibility gained ascendancy over the chivalrous creed that flourished during the Reconquista, ecclesiastical authority still tempered the prince's dominion when it involved infidels and pagans. Even as *extra ecclesiam*, Guinea's inhabitants, both infidels and pagans, had natural rights. In asserting its authority over the *extra ecclesiam* who, in turn, acquired additional obligations and rights, the Church complicated matters. Ironically, ecclesiastical authorities appropriated this imperial posture long before a single clergyman set foot in the "land of the blacks" and before the Portuguese encounter with Guinea's inhabitants. As mediator, the Church did not embrace a neutral stance. Ecclesiastical authorities, on the basis of theological grounds, inserted the Church's corporate interests into the institutional and intellectual arenas engendered by European expansion. In the wake of

Portuguese and Spanish expansion, the resulting jurisdictional conflict had considerable implications for native experiences. At the most elemental level, natural law acknowledged native (African) sovereignty even as Christian thought, theology, and law sanctioned the enslavement of Africans.

Attention to these laws and discourses widens the intellectual horizon beyond the materialist (slave, property, capital) and ideological (alterity, savage, race) parameters through which scholars of colonialism and racial slavery still narrate the early African-European encounter. By bringing these long-obscured intellectual genealogies into relief, we do far more than trouble the familiar narrative of the African-European encounter: we glean how the slave trade and the African diaspora emerged from a rights discourse—a discourse that acknowledged native sovereignty by restricting Christians from conquering and dispossessing alien subjects. In the juridical breach that Christian thought, along with the conflict that the coexistence of Roman, canon, and "feudal" law, engendered, African sovereignty came into relief, eventually pressing Christians to distinguish between sovereign and enslaved Africans. By rendering the early African-European encounter visible through the prism of a subsequent cultural logic—a logic that privileges (alterity in the form of the African slave) the racial slave—Africanists, colonial historians, and slavery scholars neglect the foundational genealogy of Atlantic history.

*　　*　　*

In contending with Portugal's encounter with Guinea's inhabitants and subsequently adjudicating over Portuguese and Castilian territorial claims in the Atlantic, successive fifteenth-century popes drew on a canonical tradition dating from Innocent IV's thirteenth-century commentary. Before his election as Pope Innocent IV in 1243, Sinibaldo Fieschi was an influential canonist. As pope (1243–1254), the erstwhile canonist took an active interest in Christian-Moslem relations since the Christian Crusades, the Reconquista, and Christian territorial expansion lacked a firm legal basis in canon law. In his influential commentary, Innocent IV raised the question, "Is it licit to invade the lands that infidels possess, and if it is licit, why is it licit?" According to one leading scholar, "Innocent was not . . . interested in justifying the crusades; the general theory of the just war did that. What interested him was the problem of whether or not Christians could legitimately seize land, other than the Holy Land, that the Moslems occupied. Did . . . Christians have a general right to dispossess infidels everywhere?"[6] Innocent acknowledged that the law of nations had supplanted natural law in regulating human interaction, such as trade, conflict, and social hierarchies. Similarly, the prince replaced the father as the "lawful authority in society" through God's provenance, manifesting his *dominium* in the monopoly over justice and sanctioned violence.

All "rational creatures," for example, the ancient Israelites in selecting Saul as king, were entitled to elect their rulers—a right that in the Old Testament was not predicated on living in a state of grace. Viewing infidels as "rational creatures," Innocent deemed that they also could decide on their rulers. The pope, however, bore responsibility for the infidels' souls. In outlining his opinion, Innocent delineated a temporal domain that was simultaneously autonomous yet subordinate to the Church. Laws of nations pertained to secular matters, a domain in which a significant tendency in the Church, known as "dualism," showed increasingly less interest. But in spiritual matters, the pope's authority prevailed, since all humans were of Christ though not with the Church. "As a result," the medievalist James Muldoon notes, "the pope's pastoral responsibilities consisted of jurisdiction over two distinct flocks, one consisting of Christians and one comprising everyone else." Since the pope's jurisdiction extended *de jure* over infidels, he alone could call for a Christian invasion of an infidel's domain. Even then, however, Innocent maintained that only a violation of natural law could precipitate such an attack. By adhering to the beliefs of their gods, infidels and pagans did not violate natural law. Thus, such beliefs did not provide justification for Christians to simply invade non-Christian polities, dispossess its inhabitants of their territory and freedom, or force them to convert. Innocent IV's theological contribution resided in the fact that he accorded pagans and infidels *dominium* and therefore the right to live beyond the state of grace. Although some canon lawyers questioned the assertion that infidels and pagans possessed rights— including Henry of Segusio, a former student of Sinibaldo Fieschi known widely as Hostiensis—"by the end of the fourteenth century Innocent IV's commentary . . . had become the *communis opinio* of the canonists."[7]

A half-century later, the imperial activities of Christian rulers again raised the issue about the infidels' *dominium*. While Innocent IV's commentary prevailed and continued to mediate European imperial expansion and Christian interaction with non-Christians, the Christian princes' strength and growing autonomy vis-à-vis the papacy along with their desire for legitimacy brought renewed interest in Hostiensis's commentary. Despite the shifting alliance characterizing Church-state relations in the late Middle Ages, temporal authorities in Christian Europe legitimized their rule and defined their actions on scriptural and spiritual grounds. Christianity represented their ontological myth, the source of their traditions, and the banner under which they marched against infidels. Initially, the Christian princes manifested some reluctance to distance themselves from this founding ideology, since to discard Christianity would mean that their *dominium* merely rested on the might of one particular lineage over another. Moreover by abandoning the pretense to just war against the infidels, Christian sovereigns risked revealing that profit motivated their desire for expansion. In the context of the late Middle Ages and the beginning of the early modern period, commercial considerations stood in opposition to a Christian sovereign's purported interests in honor and justice. In the early modern period, Christianity still served multiple purposes: it legitimized the ascendancy of a particular noble house while sanctioning elite *dominium* over the nonelite. In the face of powerful noble lineage, the position of the nascent absolutist rulers remained tenuous at best, and the prince was reluctant to dispense with the protective veneer that even diminished papal authority accorded. Still, the ambitious Iberian sovereigns manifested a willingness to interpret canon law in a manner that furthered their claims over infidels and Christians.[8] As a result, secular authorities relied increasingly on Hostiensis's commentaries and those theologians who displayed less conformity than canon lawyers on the rights of the *extra ecclesiam*.

Developments in Christendom also brought the *dominium* of the *extra ecclesiam* under renewed scrutiny. Since the Church defined all nonbelievers, including Saracens (a widely used term for infidels or those who willfully rejected the faith) and pagans (individuals who existed in ignorance of the faith) as the *extra ecclesiam*, it used the same laws and traditions in their treatment. In effect, the Church did not distinguish between the non-Christian minority in Europe and the *extra ecclesiam* residing beyond its de facto jurisdiction. Therefore, laws and practices shaping Church-state relations with nonbelievers in Europe set the precedent for Christian interaction with non-Christians in the wider Atlantic world. Beginning in the thirteenth century and in the context of the Reconquista, some Christian lords on the Iberian Peninsula started undermining the corporate bodies of Jews and Saracens by ordering those populations to adhere to Christian legal precepts and Iberian customary laws. While indicative of the Christians' victory over the Moors, such practices represented a departure from Reconquista ethics. Throughout much of the Reconquista, victorious Christians and Moors often allowed their adversaries who remained under their territorial jurisdiction to adhere to their own beliefs and traditions. By the thirteenth century, when the tide favored Christians, the victorious rulers displayed less willingness to respect Moorish and Jewish corporate institutions and practices.[9] This intransigence flourished at the very moment that Castilian scholars rediscovered Roman civil law, which they codified along with their customary practices in the *Siete Partidas*. Following this legal transformation, the Christian monarchs continued restricting the judicial autonomy of their Jewish and Moorish subjects. In 1412, this culminated in the most draconian legislation to date when it "forbade Jews and Moslems alike to have their own judges. Thenceforth, their cases, civil and criminal, were to be tried before ordinary judges of the districts where they lived. Criminal cases were to be decided according to Christian custom."[10] Though the temporal authorities relaxed the 1412 legislation with a decree in 1479, the systematic assault against customary courts of non-Christians continued unabated.

Though inimical to Innocent IV's commentary granting the *extra ecclesiam dominium*, the practice of curtailing Jewish and Moorish traditions reflected the ascendant hegemony of Hispania's Christian rulers. These sovereigns, though zealous Christians, saw all corporate privileges as a threat to their centralizing aspirations.[11] In their opinion, the inhabitants of their territory represented their subjects. Jews and Moors were not an exception. By their actions, Hispania's Christian rulers contrived new forms of personhood.[12] In a world defined by corporations with their accompanying rights and obligations, Jews and Moors embodied corporate-less beings that Christian authorities compelled to adhere to Christian laws and customary norms thereby forsaking their own legal traditions and customs.[13] By undermining Jewish and Moorish courts, the Christian rulers redefined more than their relations to Jews and Moors. As they dismantled the courts that had once enabled Jews and Moors to reproduce their distinctive juridical status, the Catholic sovereigns actually reconstituted the meaning of being a Jew or a Moor.[14] Standing before Christian courts and officials whose rulings owed much to Christian ethics, the various diasporic populations—Jews, Moors, and Africans—lacked the protective shield of a culturally sanctioned corporate status. As such, they embodied one of the distinguishing features of the early modern period—individualism.

Understanding Portugal's initial encounter with Guinea's inhabitants requires juxtaposing the Church's historical provenance over the *extra ecclesiam* against the secular state's ascendancy. Despite the precedent established by Innocent IV's commentary, temporal authorities drastically transformed their institutional interaction with the non-Christian minority, which carried over into their relationship with the peoples of Guinea. As the Church's hegemony receded, the monarch's power expanded, but dogma continued to affect the secular authorities' practices and nascent traditions. Much of the imperial activity in the fifteenth century represented secular expansion that the papacy approved after the fact. Despite the secular nature of the Infante's imperial activity, Henrique (Prince Henry) continued to rely on the Reconquista rhetoric of just war and Christian conversion. But the motives informing Gomes Eanes de Zurara's text and the language through which the Portuguese represented the "conquest of Guinea" also underscores a discursive shift symbolized by the gradual ascendancy of Hostiensis's commentary. Like transitions in general, the formally reigning discourses remain part and parcel of the newly ascendant view. Consequently, the issue of whether the infidels manifested *dominium* remained a persistent question for early modern jurists, theologians, canonists, and Christian princes. Irrespective of the transformations in Europe, which signaled a shift in the relationship between Christians and the *extra ecclesiam*, secular expansion, for reasons of legitimacy, had to contend with a tradition that acknowledged the infidels' and pagans' *dominium* and right to live as sinners. Grace, in other words, did not form the basis on which the rule of law rested. Non-Christian princes did, therefore, wield legitimate authority and constitute sovereign temporal authorities. As the Portuguese and subsequently the Castilians ventured farther south into the "land of the blacks," they constantly had to contend with theoretical and practical recognition that Guinea did not represent *terra nullius*.

*   *   *

"Here beginneth the Chronicle in which are set down all the notable deeds that were achieved in the Conquest of Guinea." With this auspicious inauguration, Gomes Eanes de Zurara, the House of Avis's royal chronicler and archivist, introduced one of Portugal's foundational texts: *The Chronicle of the Discovery and Conquest of Guinea*.[15] Commissioned by the House of Avis, Zurara knew only too well that historical writing represented a construction—a process whereby patrons determined the primacy of certain narratives over others. "Our Lord the King," Zurara remarked, "ordered me to work at the writing and ordering of the history in this volume so that those who read might have the more perfect knowledge."[16] Zurara's candor underscores his sovereign's desire to link the House of Avis's imperial activities, especially in "the land of Guinea" and the Canary Islands, with kingship in Portugal. "The notable deeds . . . achieved in the Conquest" therefore constitute the founding acts around which Zurara narrated a hagiography of Infante Henrique (Prince Henry) seamlessly uniting the House of Avis's *dominium*, Portugal's nascent *imperium*, the ascendancy of a Christian-Portuguese nation, and an unwavering Christian presence on the Iberian Peninsula.[17] In this narrative's production, the trope of Reconquista—the ideological myth of unwavering Christian opposition to Muslim domination of the Iberian Peninsula—was so pervasive that it conflated Islamic Moors and pagan Africans, a representational gesture that precluded first the Portuguese and subsequently the Castilians from marveling at their novel encounter with Guinea's inhabitants.[18] This lack of marvel—a product of Reconquista historiography—coupled with canon law distinguished those Africans who were enslaved from the natives of the Indies, the early modern period's invented "other"; it constituted the former, on the basis of their conceptual familiarity, as distinct subjects.[19] The contrast with "Indians" or even with Europeans did not, however, elicit images of a homogenous "black" subject. The discourse of Reconquista, but especially canon law, wrought juridical differences among "Africa's" inhabitants—differences manifested in the language of sovereignty or the lack thereof.

According to Zurara, the "notable deeds" of his compatriots rested on a series of conquests. Yet a cursory examination of these "deeds" brings into relief the new meanings ascribed to the term *conquista* (conquest) during Portugal's incipient phase of overseas expansion. In the context of the Reconquista—the Christian-Moorish conflict over the possession of the Iberian Peninsula that began in the eighth century—*conquista* represented a Christian sovereign's *dominium* extending from a permanently settled village, town, or city to the immediate hinterland and its inhabitants.[20] But as *The Chronicle* unfolds, the Portuguese do not act in accordance to existing definitions of conquest. During their initial voyages along Guinea's coast, the Portuguese not only eschew establishing a settlement, either peacefully or by force; they also make no effort to contract a treaty so as to acquire a territorial claim to "the land of blacks."[21] With several noteworthy exceptions, the initial Portuguese encounter with Guinea constituted chattel raids. Such raids underscore the commercial imperatives of those "notable deeds" and of Portugal's conquests. With Christian ascendancy over the Moors largely ensured, the Portuguese and subsequently the Castilian temporal authorities attached new meanings to the term *conquista*. In the Reconquista's waning decades, commerce and the possession of bodies, not territory, signified the "notable deeds . . . achieved in the Conquest of Guinea."[22] Despite their increasing temporal preoccupations, the princes and their chroniclers employed the conquest rhetoric so as to invoke images of Christian Crusades, just wars, and the conversion of infidels. For Portugal's princes, Christian zeal played a connected yet secondary role to profit and strategic knowledge about commercial opportunities.

This nascent commercial sensibility and the manner in which the Portuguese represented these secular concerns had profound implications for Guinea's inhabitants. Prompted southward by profit, the Portuguese charted Guinea's physical and human landscape in accordance with their commercial sensibility. While the quest for profits propelled the Portuguese encounter with Guinea's inhabitants, long-standing practices scripted the interaction between Christians and non-Christians and led Zurara to depict the Portuguese expeditions as a *reconquista*. During the Reconquista, Christians enslaved infidels under the pretext of a just war, yet irrespective of these religious imperatives, ransom still represented a viable option. But when blackamoors, as opposed to Moors, became the victims of the Portuguese raids, the practice of accepting ransom for religious captives ended—since they quickly became slaves for life. This transformation underscores developments in the emergent Atlantic economy and the concomitant evolution of an early modern commercial sensibility that gradually untangled itself from its Christian foundations. Though its hegemony over the meanings of conquest had diminished, Christianity retained its ascendant position over the princes' affairs and for the time being kept the sovereigns' ambitions and nascent commercial sensibility in check. Consequently, the Church continued to accord infidels and pagans the right to have an existence beyond the state of grace, while consenting that those who had been legitimately enslaved could be reduced to chattel. Yet even among chattel, the Church maintained some dominion—especially over their souls—and in an effort to affect the Christian *república*'s spiritual well-being, imposed itself between masters and their property.[23]

In the aftermath of Portugal's conquest of Ceuta (1415), the Moorish stronghold in Morocco and "key of all the Mediterranean," Zurara crowed that Christendom prospered "from this achievement." Though the Portuguese deprived the Moors of "the great city of Ceuta," a city symbolic of Islam's military prowess, Zurara described the victory solely in commercial terms. According to the royal chronicler, the "East and West alike . . . can now exchange their goods, without any great peril of merchandise."[24] For Zurara, Infante Henrique's valor and military prowess, honed repeatedly in "Africa," united the "East with the West, in order that the nations might learn to exchange their riches." As the Portuguese shifted their gaze southward under Henrique's influence, their motive was commerce not conversion. Henrique wanted "to know the land" so that "many kinds of merchandise might be brought to this realm, which would find a ready market."[25] At this historic moment, however, commerce could not enter posterity as the sole motive behind a noble's behavior. Thus, in listing five reasons why the Infante manifested an interest in "the land beyond," Zurara wrote that Henrique's final reason represented a "great desire to make increase in the faith of our Lord Jesus Christ."[26]

In 1434, under the Infante's encouragement "to gain . . . honour and profit," the squire Gil Eanes finally reached "the land beyond" when he rounded the Cape of Bojador. On his return, Gil Eanes informed his sovereign that the mariners had been right, noting "there is no race of men nor place of inhabitants in this place."[27] Successive voyages did, however, produce signs of habitation, and the Portuguese gradually distinguished "Africa" from "Guinea." In contrast to the "land of the Moors," Guinea, the "land of the blacks," represented the more fertile region. According to Zurara, they "saw a country very different from that former one—for that was sandy and untilled, and quite treeless, like a country where there was no water—while this other land they saw to be covered with palms and other green and beautiful trees."[28] Eventually the Portuguese rendered geographical dissimilarities into customary and ultimately juridical distinctions, separating Moors from blackamoors. The quest "to know" and the concomitant desire for "profit" encouraged the Portuguese penchant for specificity. In his quest to offer the "more perfect knowledge," Zurara revised his earlier observations that Guinea included the "land of the Moors." He declared that "although we have already several times in the course of this history, called *Guinea* that other land to which the first [Portuguese] went, we give not this common name to both because the country is all one; for some the lands are very different from others, and very far apart."[29] This difference, in the first instance, resided in a geographic fertility that the Portuguese equated with commercial opportunities. The relationship between fertility, commerce, and imagined profit underscores the discriminating nature of the early modern Portuguese explorers and their motives. Through this discerning prism, the Portuguese made ever more subtle distinctions among Guinea's various inhabitants.

*   *   *

In 1441, twenty-six years after the conquest of Ceuta, the Portuguese expedition under Antão Gonçalves landed near Cabo Blanco in present-day Mauritania. Following a brief skirmish "in the land of Guinea" with a "naked man
following a camel," the Portuguese enslaved their first Moor. Near nightfall,
the Portuguese encountered and seized a "black Mooress" who, according to
Zurara, "was [the] slave of those on the hill."[30] By their actions, the Portuguese launched the transatlantic slave trade in whose wake the early modern
African diaspora emerged and in which the "slave" constituted the charter subject. Through the capture of the "Mooress," but in particular by marking her
as distinct from the Moors on the basis of juridical status and phenotype, the
Portuguese introduced a taxonomy that distinguished Moors from blackamoors, infidels from pagans, and Africans from blacks, sovereign from sovereignless subjects, and free persons from slaves. Shortly thereafter, the Portuguese
employed this human measure, formulated via a black woman's body, so as to
delineate who could be "legitimately" enslaved.

Though the Portuguese discerned a difference between the Moors and the
blackamoors, this initially did not preclude the enslavement of the former.
Arriving in Gonçalves's wake, Nuno Tristão "brought with him an armed
caravel" intent on capturing "some of the people of the country." On learning
of his compatriots' deeds, the zealous Nuno Tristão insisted that "what is still
better . . . [is] for us to carry many more; for . . . profit." According to Zurara,
Tristão led a nocturnal raid against the Moors who Gonçalves had previously sighted. In the ensuing raid, the Portuguese took an additional ten
"prisoners," including a noble named Adahu. The raiding party, keen on discerning "the state and conditions of the people of that land," lingered on the
coast for several days. To that effect, the Portuguese brought an "Arab" interpreter who questioned the captives. "But the noble in that he was of better
breeding than the other captives . . . understood that Arab and answered to
whatever matter was asked of him by the same." Afterward, the Portuguese
captains sent the "Arab" and the blackamooress ashore so as to instruct the
Moors of their terms for ransom. Soon thereafter, the raiders departed for
Portugal.[31]

In Sagres, Zurara's concerns shifted from the profit obtained through
raiding to the captives' spiritual salvation. Zurara insisted that "the greater
benefit was theirs, for though their bodies were now brought into some subjection, that was a small matter in comparison of their souls, which would now
possess true freedom for evermore."[32] After recounting the intricacies of the
captives' partition, Zurara directed his attention to the noble Adahu. "As

you know," Zurara stated, "every prisoner desireth to be free, which desire is all the stronger in a man of higher reason or nobility." "Seeing himself held in captivity," Adahu offered Gonçalves "five or six Black Moors" in return for his freedom and promised a similar ransom for two youths that were also held captive. Tempted by his desire to "serve the Infante his lord" who was intent on "know[ing] part of that land," Gonçalves immediately committed himself to another expedition that included Adahu and the two youths. "For as the Moor told" him, "the least they would give for them would be ten Moors." According to Zurara, "It was better to save ten souls than three—for though they were black, yet had they souls like the others, and all the more as these blacks were not of the lineage of the Moors but were Gentiles, and so the better to bring into the path of salvation."[33] In addition to the quantity of souls, Adahu promised "the blacks could give . . . news of the land further distant."

Prompted by profit, souls, and strategic curiosity, the Portuguese expedition under Gonçalves landed near the Rio d'Ouro (River of Gold) where they met two Moors who instructed them to wait. The Moors returned with an entourage numbering a hundred "male and female," thus revealing "that those youth were in great honour among them." Gonçalves exchanged his two captives for "ten blacks, male and females, from various countries." Adahu, who had been released earlier with the pledge that he personally would bring his ransom, "never returned to fulfill his promise." Zurara, in turn, chided "the Moorish noble" for not remembering "the benefits he had received" and informed his readers that "his deceit thenceforth warned our men not to trust one of that race except under the most certain security."[34]

Despite Zurara's protestations about Adahu's treachery, for which the Portuguese would hold "that race" forever accountable, the episode underscores Portuguese awareness of differences among Africans. Accordingly, it was the Moor who, because of his superior status, valued freedom more than blacks. The Portuguese quickly equated status with sovereignty and the lack thereof with the legitimate enslavement of certain individuals. Though the Portuguese captured both Moors and the "black Mooress," they had already started distinguishing between sovereign "Moorish" subjects and those "Moors," "Negros," and "blacks" that they could legitimately enslave. Zurara observed that the "black Mooress," unlike the valiant yet vanquished "Moor," represented the "chattel" of a larger Moorish contingent. Here already "blacks" represented the "legitimately" unfree. In narrating this initial encounter between the Portuguese and Guinea's inhabitants, Zurara employed an unstable definition of who constituted a "Moor"—but he sought to resolve this ambiguity by using "Moor" to signify a sovereign subject. As the Portuguese encountered more of Guinea's inhabitants, the terms "Black Moors" "blacks," "Ethiops," "Guineas," and "Negros," or the descriptive terms to which a religious signifier was appended, such as "Moors . . . [who] were Gentiles" and "pagans" gradually constituted the rootless and sovereignless—and in many cases, simply "slaves."

As the Portuguese perceived distinctions among the peoples they encountered and began acting in accordance with these perceptions, Infante Henrique sought to cultivate papal approval for his subjects' deeds. By linking Portugal's activities in Guinea with the conquest of Ceuta, the Infante stressed how spiritual imperatives motivated exploration along the Atlantic littoral. In his diplomatic entreaty, Infante Henrique minimized the commercial incentive and fashioned the "toils of that conquest" into a "just war" under the banner of a Christian Crusade.[35] In his response—a papal bull—Eugenius IV unwittingly underscored the extent of the Infante's misrepresentation and the Church's willingness to perpetuate this fiction. *Romanus pontifex* (1433), the first in a series of papal bulls issued during the fifteenth century that regulated Christian expansion, sanctioned the Infante's request and Portugal's alleged mission in Guinea since "we strive for those things that may destroy the errors and wickedness of the infidels and . . . our beloved son and noble baron Henry . . . purposeth to go in person, with his men at arms, to those lands, that are held by them and guide his army against them."[36] For Pope Eugenius, the Infante's alleged "war" constituted a Christian counteroffensive, which if successful would undermine the "Turks'" military presence in the Mediterranean—a presence that was increasingly felt on Western Christendom's eastern rim. Though Pope Eugenius claimed that his "beloved son" and "Governor of the Order of Christ" intended to "make war under the banner of the said order against . . . Moors and other enemies of the faith," Henrique's and his subjects' motives did not resonate in the "aforesaid war." The territorial charter granted by Portugal's regent prince, Infante Pedro, to his brother, Henrique, included exclusive jurisdiction over Guinea and thus underscores the Infante's true interests and commercial acumen.[37] Desiring legitimacy for his commercial imperatives and wanting to prevent other princes from encroaching on Portugal's "conquests," Infante Henrique invoked the rhetoric of a just war so as to solicit papal patronage.[38] In order to receive the charter from Portugal's regent and his brother, Infante Pedro, Henrique did not need to mask his intentions in the trope of the Reconquista. Through tactical representation, Henrique acquired an exclusive charter to mediate between Christians and Guinea's inhabitants.

In soliciting papal approval, Henrique manifested the ways in which the early modern prince—a temporal authority with decidedly secular interests—continued to rely on Christian legitimization. Henrique, by his actions, acknowledged the Church's imagined jurisdiction beyond Christendom's borders and over the *extra ecclesiam*. In the fifteenth and sixteenth centuries, the Church still maintained a hold over the Christian princes' expansionism and their interactions with the *extra ecclesiam* both in and beyond Christendom.[39] In regulating this interaction, the Church drew on a rich corpus of texts but relied on canon law and especially the ecclesiastical consensus that formed around Innocent IV's commentary.[40] On the basis of canonical precedent, the Church increasingly intervened in the domain of laws of nations (*ius gentium*) as it adjudicated over the affairs among Christians, infidels, and pagans. While the secular domain gradually ascended, temporal authorities still needed to contend with Christian dogma's lengthy history, even though some postulated that their activities were subject to *ius gentium*. Well into the early modern period, the Church presided over the temporal authorities' imperial activities; even after the Protestant Reformation, the pope still meddled in the "Catholic sovereigns'" nascent but not entirely secularized domain: the affairs of state. While such affairs increasingly defined treaties and trade between nations as secular matters and property relations as the sole provenance of individuals, on the grounds of spiritual considerations and concerns about orthodoxy, the Church continued to assert its dominion over the incipient temporal realm.[41] For the infidels and pagans who as the sovereignless and as chattel fell into Christian hands, the Church and to a lesser extent the Crown expressed a keen interest in their spiritual well-being.[42] In the Church's eyes, infidels and pagans, both sovereign and sovereignless, constituted the *extra ecclesiam* who wielded a juridical position in and beyond Christendom. In constituting the *extra ecclesiam*, the Church relied on rediscovered teachings of the ancients, the Bible, natural law (*ius naturae*), customary law (*ius gentium*), commentaries, canon law precedents, theological treaties, and papal bulls. Collectively, these texts and institutional practices outlined the obligations but also the rights of non-Christians both within and beyond an imagined Europe.

* * *

Following their initial chattel raid in 1441, the Portuguese launched numerous expeditions against the inhabitants of Guinea's northwestern coast and
the adjacent islands.[43] These expeditions simply amounted to slave raiding,
and the Portuguese displayed no interest in Christian conversion nor did they
seek to assess the "power of the Moor." The Portuguese did, however, discern
differences among the various peoples they captured. In noting phenotypic
distinctions, the Portuguese reproduced their own cultural predilections but
fashioned somatic divisions into cultural divides among Guinea's inhabitants.
Zurara observed how "amongst them were some white enough, fair to look
upon, and well proportioned; others were less white like mulattoes; others
again were as black as Ethiops, and so ugly, both in features and in body,
as almost to appear the images of a lower hemisphere."[44] Zurara's descriptions
underscore how the Portuguese associated aesthetic distinctions with corporeal differences. The dark and unsightly captives who verged on being bestial
actually embodied their difference. As the Portuguese entered the "land of the
Negroes," these distinctions continued to suffuse the slave raiders' imagined
taxonomy, which linked phenotype, the corporeal, and geography.[45]

As the first caravels entered the "land of the Negroes," the Portuguese
manifested great interest in the southern region's fertility for they believed it
offered them more "opportunities." Guinea presented such bountiful "opportunities" that the whole "country" exuded fecundity. Zurara related how "some
of those who were present said . . . that it was clear from the smell that came
off the land how good must be the fruits of that country, for it was so deli-
cious that from the point they reached, though they were on the sea, it seemed
to them that they stood in some gracious fruit garden ordained for the sole
end of their delight."[46] By rendering Guinea into Eden waiting to be harvested
"for the sole end of their delight," Zurara's text underscores a distinct sensory
reaction to the "land of the Negroes." The Portuguese had finally left behind
the Moors' barren desert and arrived in a land so ripe that they could actually
smell it from a distance. Guided by their senses, the Portuguese distinguished
"Negros" from "Moors" on the basis of the fecundity of the former's territorial
domain. Throughout this period, the Portuguese repeated this process and, in
fact, chartered Guinea's landscape in accordance with perceived natural resources and the commercial possibilities that each area afforded. Consequently,
the Portuguese bestowed commercialized toponyms on Guinea, including
Cabo d'Ouro (River of Gold), Cabo Verde (Green Cape), Madeira (the Wooded
Isle), and el Mina (literally, the Mine, though in English it was referred to as
the Gold Coast). As this landscape entered Portugal's cosmographic archive,

the Portuguese used it to ascribe cultural specificity to Guinea's diverse peoples usually in relations to provenance, territory, and purported political jurisdiction. But ethnic labels often simply reflected the commercialization of the landscape.

The relationship between topographical fecundity and commerce reinforced perceived distinctions between Moors and "Negros." Zurara observed that "the people of this green land are wholly black, and hence this is called Land of the Negroes, or Land of Guinea. Wherefore also the men and women thereof are called "Guineas," as if one were to say 'Black Men.'"[47] As the Portuguese awareness of the landscape increased, Zurara corrected his earlier claims, noting that "although we have already several times in this history, called Guinea that other land to which the first went, we give not this common name to both because the country is all one, for some of the lands are very different from others."[48] In Guinea, the "land of the Negroes," the Portuguese finally "found many things there different from this land of ours." Despite the importance Zurara placed on Guinea's unfolding novelty, Dinis Diaz's success in finally capturing *negros* "in their own land" interested him more. For Zurara, this represented a notable feat since the Portuguese could now both act on their nascent taxonomy but, more important, disregard the Moors as middlemen and slaves.

As they harvested Guinea's diverse fruits, the Portuguese confronted tenacious opposition from the region's inhabitants. After mounting numerous raids against the Azenagays, the Portuguese finally faced an opponent who successfully challenged their presence and wanton acts. Cape Verde's inhabitants even displayed an unwillingness to allow the Portuguese to anchor. When the Portuguese captain Gomez Pirez did land, he placed "a cake and a mirror and a sheet of paper on which he drew a cross" on the shore before returning hastily to the safety of his vessel. The coastal inhabitants, however, destroyed the signs and symbolically obliterated the Portuguese presence. Zurara recorded how "the natives when they came there and found those things, broke up the cake and threw it far away, and with their assegais they cast at the mirror, till they had broken it in many pieces, and the paper they tore, showing that they cared not for any of these things."[49] In retaliation, Pirez ordered his bowmen to fire a salvo at the Cape Verdians who replied in kind. As a result the Portuguese retreated, eventually tacking northward to the now more familiar "land of the Moors." After acquiring water on Arguim Island, Pirez navigated his ship up the Rio d'Ouro, where he encountered Moors who sold him "a black for the price of five doubloons."[50] During this encounter, the

Portuguese captain expressed his desire for more extensive trade, indicating that he would return the following July for additional blacks and gold. In 1446, a year later, Pirez did return and by his actions commercialized the enslavement process. Encountering Moors on an estuary of the Rio d'Ouro, Gomez Pirez "began to speak with them by means of his interpreters, asking them to have some Guineas brought there, in exchange for whom he would give them cloth." The Moors, however, responded, "We are not merchants. . . . They are all engaged in trafficking in the Upland; yet, if they knew it, they would make great endeavor to come here, for they are men well supplied both with Guineas and gold, as well as some other things with which you might be well content."[51]

Although the Portuguese periodically still preyed on the coastal and island inhabitants, the momentum for raids waned in favor of "traffic of merchandise." As this shift occurred, the Portuguese focused their attention on "knights," "lords," "governors," and "kings," those that could enforce or hinder trading relations. In an initial encounter signifying this shift toward diplomacy, Fernandaffonso, the second in command on a Portuguese expedition in the Cape Verde archipelago led by the Dane Vallarte, instructed the messenger—through his *negro* interpreter—to "tell your lord . . . we are subjects of a great and powerful Prince . . . who is at the limits of the west, and by whose command we have come here to converse on his behalf with the great and good King of this land."[52] After this salutation, the Portuguese handed the messenger a letter from Infante Henrique, the content of which the interpreter revealed orally. At the conclusion of this ritualized interaction, the Portuguese sent the messenger to Guitanye, his lord, who was to convey the contents of this interaction to the "great King" Boor. In dispatching the messenger, the Portuguese sent more than a message. The letter symbolized a new—diplomatic—phase of Portuguese interaction with Guinea's purported lords.

Despite some notable exceptions, diplomacy enacted through protocol—the ritualized performance of hierarchy—began to characterize Portugal's relationship with Guinea's diverse nations. While both sides constantly struggled to impose their traditions on the commercial formalities, the African elite usually dictated the terms of trade and interaction. Portuguese subjects who violated African laws quickly risked stiff fines or found their lives in danger. Recourse resided with African "lords," not the king of Portugal. In Guinea, subjects of Portugal's king had entered the jurisdictions of non-Christian princes who, like sovereigns everywhere, dispensed justice as they saw fit. Though the Portuguese initiated the transition from raids to diplomacy, their lack of military successes against Africans affected this shift in imperial policy. African successes revealed Portugal's conquest of Guinea as a fiction designed to stave off other Christian "princes" from staking claims in the newly "discovered" territories. As they extolled their Reconquista rhetoric, the Portuguese's intended audience remained strictly Christian and European. Though the Portuguese referred to Africans as objects, in practice they could not render Guinea's inhabitants into this prescribed role and desperately sought an effective strategy with which to obtain "profit" from the "land of the Blacks." Diplomacy, with its focus on institutional formalities and mutual, if grudging, respect for difference, generally offered personal securities and tenuous recognition of private property that effectively facilitated trade. Through diplomacy and its formalities, Portugal's temporal authorities acknowledged that Guinea's diverse lords manifested *dominium* and ceased to "conquer" Guinea. "The affairs of these parts," Zurara lamented "were henceforth treated more by trafficking and bargaining of merchants than by bravery and toil in arms."[53]

*   *   *

As a prelude to conquest, "discovery" occupied a prominent role in Zurara's history. But disclosing, unveiling, and subjecting Guinea to the Portuguese gaze elicited little wonder and even fewer marvels.[54] In Guinea, the Portuguese found unfamiliar beliefs and practices but nothing so unusual that it remained indiscernible and, therefore, could not be assimilated. According to one scholar of early modern European colonial encounters, "Anything . . . which fell right through [the European] conceptual 'grid' could only ever be relegated to the 'marvellous' or the 'wonderous.'"[55] Despite their imperial pretense of having "discovered" Guinea, the Portuguese, according to Zurara, found little that baffled them in the "land of the blacks." They explained the extant manifestations of marvel through the teachings of the ancients or simply allowed it to disappear in the Reconquista's historiographical wake since much that seemed incomprehensible became a Moorish trope in need of exorcism.

Steeped in the uncompromising rhetoric of a militant Christianity, the historiography associated with the Reconquista aimed at restoring a broken link between Hispania and imperial Christian Rome.[56] As a romance, this discourse represented Hispania's Christian princes' legitimating ideology both in war and peace. Predicated on Christian victories against the Moors—beginning with the mythical victory at the caves of Covadonga (722) and leading to the more tangible victory at Las Navas de Tolosa (1212)—the Reconquista historiography denied Islam's century-long dominion over the peninsula and its Christian subjects. In an effort to occlude five centuries of Islamic hegemony and an eight-century-long Islamic presence, the Christian princes relied on more than the cross and the sword. The chronicles and histories, defined as war by means of the pen, represented the nascent Catholic sovereigns' most effective offensive against Islam.[57]

In drafting Christian charters, chronicles, and histories, the scribes, archivists, and historians drew on the heroic genre of uncompromising valor and chivalry. As legitimizing ideologies, these tracts harked back to an imaginary Europe symbolized by imperial Rome and ancient Greece. As Christian Europe's foundational metropolis, the ancient Greek polis and Rome represented a cultural provenance untainted by an expansive and cosmopolitan Islam. In reclaiming a lost heritage, Christian archivists and historians sought to order the past and simultaneously invented a functional Greco-Roman-Christian cultural tradition whose direct heirs they claimed to be. The imposition of this classical-Christian ontology onto the world of Hispanic letters signaled the end to the Christian-Jewish-Islamic cross-fertilization that characterized the period of Islamic domination. Allegedly restoring the traditions of "their" ancients, Christian Europeans merely invented an interpretive framework through which they filtered experience and ascribed meanings. In this context, the discoveries and encounters of Portugal's mariners—though at odds with the teachings of the ancients—assumed meanings through cultural conceptions that accorded with classical-Christian texts. Since the authors of these texts had imaginary, if not actual, familiarity with "Africa," "Egypt," "Ethiopia," and "Libya," which was then transposed onto Guinea, the Portuguese found little among the blackamoors that could not be processed through their conceptual grid. This phenomenon, a product of Reconquista historiography, positioned Guinea's inhabitants as knowable objects whose customs, habits, and practices could be apprehended.

From their initial encounter, the Portuguese positioned Guinea's inhabitants in relation to Adam, Christianity's paterfamilias. As Zurara defended his moral sentiments for the enslaved, he insisted, "I pray Thee that my tears may not wrong my conscience; for it is not their religion but their humanity that maketh mine to weep in pity for their sufferings. And if the brute animals, with their bestial feelings, by a natural instinct understand the sufferings of their own kind, what wouldst Thou have my human to do on seeing before my eyes that miserable company, and remembering that they too are of the generation of the sons of Adam?"[58] Although Reconquista and Renaissance historiography ascribed everyone and everything a position in the Christ-centric universe, the former tradition eschewed comparative ethnology, occluded alterity, and initially denied the limitations of Western Europe's canonical texts in light of observations and experiences to the contrary.

As ideologues of a fragile and contested narrative tradition, the architects of Reconquista historiography resisted experiences and novel ideas that threatened their sovereigns' newly ascendant position. Hispania's narratives of discovery and conquest of Guinea and subsequently the Indies tended, therefore, to render those encounters meaningful in terms postulated by ancient and canonical authors. For instance, after the Portuguese landed the initial slaves in Sagres, Zurara observed, "Here you must note that these blacks were Moors like the others, though their slaves in accordance with ancient custom, which I believe to have been because of the curse which, after the Deluge, Noah laid upon his son Cain, cursing him in this way: that his race should be subject to all the other races of the world."[59] Although Zurara clearly sought to validate his compatriots' actions, his reliance on a Judaic trope that entered Christian theology at its very founding underscores the ways late medieval contemporaries still relied on ancient sources to process their encounter with Guinea's inhabitants.

Guinea's discovery and conquest stood in marked contrast to those of the Indies. The Indies gradually emerged as the "New World" owing to the influence of Italian humanists who manifested a marked interest in Columbus's discovery and who were the first to assimilate the meaning implied by *Orbe Novo* or *Mundus Novus*.[60] Unlike the Indies, Guinea constituted a part of the Old World. Discernible in the region's inability to become the subject of intellectual obsession, Guinea largely avoided scrutiny. An unproblematic conceptual assimilation into medieval Europe's gnosis accompanied Guinea's lack of scrutiny.

Although Renaissance humanists barely took note of Guinea's emergence in the fifteenth century, novelty did not altogether elude the region. But the context in which marvel surfaced underscored how Europeans in the fifteenth century still adhered to an ontology based on ancient authors.

Though profoundly hierarchical, this explanatory system obviated a relationship between novelty and Guinea. In his account on João Fernandes, the mariner who spent seven months living among Guinea's inhabitants, Zurara highlighted the conceptual ambiguity that precluded him from actually believing that "blacks" constituted "images of a lower hemisphere." "I marvel," Zurara confessed, "at the affection which those who dwelt there came to feel for him. And albeit that his affability was very great towards all other people, I was astonished it could exist towards these, or how it could be so felt and returned by such savages, for I am assured that when he parted from the men among whom he had lived those seven months, many of them wept with regretful thought." [61] Though he abhorred the physiognomy of Guinea's inhabitants and their purported cultural practices, Zurara acknowledged that they, like all humans, shared the same psychic disposition. "But why do I say so, when I know that we are all sons of Adam, composed of the same elements, and that we all receive a soul as reasonable beings?"

Even as he denied that meaningful differences distinguished Christian Europeans from pagan Guineans, Zurara invoked a status differential that Aristotle had postulated and that verged on the corporeal. "True it is that, in some bodies, the instruments are not so good for producing virtues as they are in others, to who God by his grace hath granted such power; and when men lack the first principles on which the higher ones depend, they lead a life little less than bestial. For into three modes is the life of men divided, as saith the Philosopher."[62] Describing the "three modes," Zurara reproduced the social taxonomy that Aristotle sketched in *The Politics*. "The first are those who live in contemplation, leaving on the one side all other worldly matters and only occupying themselves in praying and contemplation. . . . The second are those who live in cities, improving their estates and trading one with another. And the third are those who live in the deserts, removed from all conversation, who, because they have not perfectly the use of reason, live as the beast live." Despite social gradations that anticipated Europe's racial discourse, Zurara acknowledged that "passions" produced a common humanity and explained why Guinea inhabitants wept at João Fernandes's departure. "But these last have their passions like other reasonable creatures, as love, hate, hope, fear, and the other twelve which all of us naturally have. . . . And by these primal passions I hold that these men were moved to the love of John Fernandez. . . . And it would be very fitting to speak a little upon these passion, and in what way they are universal in all men."[63]

Though this rhetoric shaped the earliest phase of the early modern encounter between Old World regions, the discovery of the Indies questioned
its continued valence. By the middle of the seventeenth century, many ancient
texts had lost currency as practical guides but in the preceding two centuries
continued translating some experiences into meaning.[64] For reasons of tim-
ing and familiarity—more imagined then real—Guinea entered the European
consciousness when ancient texts still wielded considerable influence and the
Reconquista historiography reigned ascendant. This confluence explains, in
part, the terms and conditions under which Guinea entered European historiography and the subject position the region's inhabitants acquired.

As a historiographical tradition, the Reconquista perspective constituted
an ideology that had serious implications for Guinea's inhabitants. Initially
representing Guinea's inhabitants as Moors, Portuguese historians, including
Zurara, gradually distinguished "Black Moors," "Ethiops," "Negros," and
blacks from "Moors." But even as blacks, Guinea's inhabitants symbolized the
familiar and knowable that could be incorporated into Portugal's and, therefore, Europe's cosmos. That which the Portuguese could not explain, they simply
designated as the sign of the Moor, thus shrouding the blackamoor in cultural ambiguity. But in general, the Portuguese manifested little marvel in
their encounter with Guinea and loosely ascribed the continents "black"
inhabitants a corporate place as the sovereignless that distinguished them
from the sovereign Moors—a gesture that eventually confined some "Ethiops,"
"Negros," "blacks," and "Black Moors" to the condition of slaves. Stressing
these purported distinctions, Zurara drew on classical and medieval psychology that implied that the enslaved found solace in their servile condition.
"These captives," Zurara intoned, "were very different from the condition of
the other Moors who were taken prisoners from this part." Zurara then
noted, "After they had come to this land of Portugal, they never more tried to
fly, but rather in time forgot all about their own country, as soon as they
began to taste the good things of this one." Identifying "Guineas" as "very
loyal and obedient servants, without malice," the royal chronicler proclaimed,
"that they were not so inclined to lechery as the others."[65] While identifying
the "Guineas" in relative terms, Zurara's observation reveals that the ubiquitous
Moor constituted the cultural standard with which the Portuguese measured
Guinea's inhabitants, thus underscoring that the Reconquista historiography forged
alterity around Islam, its adherents, and the most recent conquerors of Hispania.
At the time of Guinea's "discovery," Islam, despite the caliphate of Cordoba's
destruction, continued to pose a viable threat to western Christendom. In this

context, the Portuguese as crusading Christians could ill afford to marvel at the enemy because such behavior, in the Reconquista milieu, was tantamount to heresy.

*   *   *

In due course, a new taxonomy of difference reigned ascendant. At the time of its sixteenth-century emergence, the Portuguese had already assimilated Guinea into their conceptual order. Despite the competing discourses flourishing at the time of Guinea's "discovery," canon law continued wielding a hegemonic influence over Christian intercourse with the *extra ecclesiam*. By defining Guinea's inhabitants, both infidels and pagans, as the *extra ecclesiam*, the Church granted those outside its fold the right to exist unmolested until such time that they violated natural law. Binding Christian princes and their subjects to this protocol, the Church in tandem with African agency and Portuguese commercial motives curtailed wanton slave raids and established an institutional context through which some of Guinea's inhabitants assumed the status of sovereign subjects. Others, however, represented the sovereignless—both in the eyes of Africans and Europeans—and were "legitimately" enslaved. In this phase of the early modern African diaspora, canon law precluded, in theory, unprovoked aggression against the *extra ecclesiam* and competed in shaping the slaves' subject status.

By ignoring the diverse laws and discourses shaping the early modern Atlantic encounters, scholars of slavery have projected a subsequent teleology featuring a continuum from "savage to slave" onto an earlier period. Simply put, European labor needs and perceptions of Africans facilitated the transatlantic slave trade. As the reigning origin myth, the savage-to-slave trajectory still explains the African presence in the New World, while confining the genesis of the transatlantic slave trade to a racial or materialist interpretation of early modern politics. But by opting between the cultural, the economic, or some combination thereof, it obscures the confluence of other discursive traditions that defined Africans and then constituted some as slaves. Such simplicity comes at a cost; it saddles social theory with the flawed epistemological assumption about a homogenous "black" subject.

CHAPTER 4

Authority

In the few historical narratives of fifteenth-century African-Iberian encounters, "sovereignty" (*maiestas*) makes an infrequent appearance.[1] For scholars
of colonial studies and postcolonial critics, the explanation is simple. "No European power," observed the Congolese cultural critic V. Y. Mudimbe, "considered the natives to have any sovereignty or any accepted rights over their
land."[2] Sovereignty, from this perspective, represented a European affair.
To employ sovereignty without qualification in relation to fifteenth-century
encounters is indeed problematic but not simply for the reasons that Mudimbe, a leading theorist of coloniality, outlined. As late medieval Christians
confronted "nations" during their discoveries and conquests, they relied on the
concept of *dominium* as the referent for sovereign power well into the sixteenth
century, when the French jurist Jean Bodin theorized sovereignty into existence among the republic of letters.[3] The anachronistic use of sovereignty aside,
to suggest as contemporary theorists have that the *extra ecclesiam* did not wield
political dominion represents a far more problematic claim. Christian authorities commonly acknowledged the existence of pagan rights, particularly in
the guise of sovereign power but also of sovereignty. As we saw in the previous chapter, the state of grace did not represent a requirement for Christian
recognition of sovereignty. For this reason, we may assume that late medieval
Christians employed the wide-ranging concept of *dominium* in their interaction with distinct peoples. A perspective configured around the multiple
meanings of *dominium* calls into question the exclusively secular orientation
that frames Europe's early modern expansion in Africa and the privileged
status accorded to cultural forms of difference in that history.[4] By privileging
difference in our representation of fifteenth-century human encounters,
we have already lost sight of the two guiding principles—*dominium* and

authority—through which Christians mediated their interaction with distinct peoples. Indeed, an elephant named Hanno and a nameless rhinoceros
stirred the Renaissance imagination in such a spectacular manner that by
comparison, diminished wonderment, if not normativity, accompanied the
arrival of both North and black Africans as courtiers, servants, and slaves.[5] In
saying as much, my intent is not to suggest that Christians failed to perceive
difference—of course they did—but to direct our attention to the specific
registers whereby Christians processed expansion and the resulting human
encounters. Expansion, in a universe composed of jurisdictions and subjects
but also where the use of force and violence were ubiquitous, invoked the
prince's authority and simultaneously the anatomy and limits of his power.[6]
In this vibrant terrain, subjectivities were bestowed but also crafted, distinguishing between sovereign Africans and those lacking a recognized sovereign
status. By ignoring this terrain, histories of the Atlantic and the African diaspora circumvent the early modern history of power along with the discourses
on sovereignty and sovereign power that played a considerable role in making
Africans into slaves.

*   *   *

Fifteenth-century Christendom manifested a vibrant, overlapping, and ultimately contradictory discourse on sovereignty. Rooted in a discernible corpus of
Western thought, allegedly a continuous tradition dating to the ancient Greeks,
classical Rome, and early Christianity, sovereignty embodied multiple and
competing histories whose hegemonic status varied according to the currency of
particular authorities and contextual circumstances.[7] In an age when increasing
numbers of Christian subjects traversed established boundaries to trade,
conquer, convert, and settle, theologians and jurists pondered which rights
accompanied Christians while debating the existence of *dominium* among the
encountered pagans, infidels, and heretics.[8] A corpus of medieval thought—
though Africans rarely figured as agents and only occasionally as the referenced
objects—guided Christian interaction with the wider world, serving as the discursive register for acknowledged sovereignty among the *extra ecclesiam*.

   Secular conceptions of European expansion overshadow earlier and
equally complicated histories featuring competing interests among theologians, canonists, lords, princes, and court factions.[9] In addition, the formation of imperial polities tempers ideas about a monolithic state, the ceaseless
flow of capital, and the singular and fully formed European. The alleged

dominance of Roman law, as we saw in the previous chapter, alongside imperial expansion and the conceit of the chroniclers, has resulted in a history that simplifies the competing and conflicting interests that composed the idea of Europe. Stated differently, there was no singular rationality of power.[10] Since fifteenth-century encounters brought diverse forces to the fore and continued to engender the asymmetrical formation of subjects, reframing the static concept of the European past still represents an unfulfilled aspect of the earliest histories of the African-European encounter.[11] At an elemental level, imperial, Christian, or European lordship shaped subject formation, particularly the manner in which subjected peoples engaged laws, interacted with authority, and subsequently entered the colonial archive as diverse subjects. The gloss configured as a kingdom, an empire, the Church, or Christianity reveals little if any subtlety engendered by the elaborate corpus of Western thought nor for that matter acknowledges the complex political history enacted during the reconquest.[12] Even in the contours of violence and Christian conquest, a rights discourse prevailed that illustrates the entanglement of sovereignty, slavery, and liberty.[13]

In the surrender treaties that framed a Christian lord's ascendance over Al-Andalus, the Arab designation for Iberia, and its inhabitants—the story of the reconquest—sovereignty's complexity was brought into relief by victories that featured both territorial expansion and the acquisition of new subjects. By affording the defeated populace a series of rights, foremost the right to live, the victorious lords manifested their sovereign power. This power was, it should be noted, not associated with the orthodoxy and uniformity among subjects. As the historian Andrew Hess observed, "The social content of the various agreements with the conquered maintained an official respect for the laws and customs of Islam."[14] Beyond the acquisition of property, sovereignty resulted from the merciful gesture of the triumphant sovereign who in one act commuted two deaths—physical and social. In determining that the defeated could live, the sovereign also engendered freedom—an existence beyond enslavement. The merciful act, the site where sovereign power met justice, became a crucible of freedom—life in the first instance but also rights in and to property. Sovereigns availed themselves of this property through periodic and forced loans from subjects euphemistically identified as the "royal treasure," but the larger issue that individuals had a right to private property held true.[15]

Subtlety, if acknowledged, in relation to the fifteenth-century African-European encounters derives from the belated recognition of the former's resistance to the latter's encroachments that only momentarily staved off an inevitable colonial imposition. In hopes of eliciting a different perspective, we might ask this question: in view of the conflicted discursive tradition that accompanied the numerous fifteenth-century encounters between Africans and Europeans but also between Christians, Jews, and Muslims alongside a plethora of heretics and pagans, how might we recalibrate the conventional narrative still largely configured around tropes of alterity, the quest for gold, and simplified conquest?[16]

Representing the encounters of fifteenth-century Europeans and the ensuing yet conflicting discourses on sovereign rights requires an understanding of both the structural and institutional dynamics in operation as well as an immersion in the corpus of medieval thought as the Christian lexicon of power, which twelfth-century Roman and canon lawyers ("the most important political theorists of the time") crafted.[17] Beginning in the twelfth century, when jurists pondered "whether the prince was bound by any laws,"[18] they simultaneously examined the nature of authority. As jurists deliberated over princely authority—cloaked in terms like *plenitudo potestas*, *auctoritas*, and *plena potestas*—they drew on a diverse body of thought derived from nature, the Bible, and customs that had been codified into natural law (*ius naturae*), customary law (*ius gentium*), divine law, positive law, canon law, and Roman law. The result was a vast compendium characterized by its plurality, which along with the loosely configured legal archive was anchored in the *decretum*, *decretals*, commentaries, *consilia*, *reflectio*, and lectures of diverse authorities. As jurists in the twelfth century delineated the prince's authority, they also identified the rights of subjects by defining the limits of princely power. Even as theologians, canonists, and civilians deferred to the prince's will, they scripted ideas about justice with the intent of curtailing the abuse of power characterized as tyrannical authority. Over the course of the High and Late Middle Ages, Christendom's evolving practices of *dominium*—royal and papal—and the related yet conflicting discourses of authority structured Christian expansion. In its most spectacular, violent, and brutal form, power animated expansion and first contact but then, often, ceded ground to the enactment of political authority.[19] Since authority and its related concepts (justice, rights, and due process) composed the fifteenth-century grammar of Christian expansion, we might consider how this modality of power fostered a perception of *dominium* among the subjects of centralizing polities in a vanguard role while simultaneously according African "barbarians" sovereign rights.[20]

On grounds that simple ideological and material realities—unbridled bru-
tality or the threat thereof—configured how Europeans interacted with Africans, specialists in African studies and students of the African diaspora have
neglected late medieval intellectual history. The gloss of medieval stereotypes,
based on a mythology of the monstrous, the barbarous, and the savage, nurtured the Africanists' indifference to the medieval past while bolstering the
claims of theorists who insist that alterity had been the foundational and
enduring European image of Africans.[21] The Africanist David Northrup observed how Robert July's field-defining *The Origins of Modern African Thought*
"dismissed the importance of earlier encounters because, he [July] believed,
the Atlantic slave trade precluded meaningful cultural interaction." From
July's perspective, "West African society gained 'nothing of consequence from
Europe's vast store of scientific and humanistic knowledge . . . but some ac-
quaintance with guns and other war-making implements and an appetite for
European products.'" This characterization of the European encountered with
Africa prompted Northrup to write,

> July was right to fault the slave trade, but later scholarly investiga-
> tions suggest that contacts with Europe during these centuries were
> more important than he thought. Despite its prominence and horrors,
> the Atlantic slave trade was not the sum total of Africa's expanding
> Atlantic exchanges, nor did it affect all parts of the continent. Other
> commercial exchanges preceded the massive sale of slaves, continued
> throughout its existence, and rose to new levels of intensity as the
> slave trade declined. It is the nature of history that early stages of
> an encounter contain great meaning in explaining later outcomes.
> Those who seek to tie modern Africa's problems to the Atlantic slave
> trade are applying this maxim, even if they greatly oversimplify the
> historical dynamics of these centuries. The slave trade had lasting
> effects, but the patterns of cultural and commercial relations detailed
> in this work were equally significant and arguably of greater long-term
> impact.[22]

The subtlety that Northrup finds in history and the historiography of the slave
trade has nonetheless been overshadowed by discourses of race. As the postcolonial theorist Guarav Desai observed, Christopher Fyfe wrote "in an
intentionally provocative piece" that "'in colonial Africa, authority was
manifested very simply. Whites gave orders, blacks obeyed. A white skin

(or more properly, a skin imputed white) conferred authority. It was an easy rule to understand and enforce, and it upheld colonial authority in Africa for about half a century. Yet some historians seem unwilling to remember it.'"[23] In view that the European presence allegedly assumed two forms—the slave trade followed by colonialism—the general consensus among Africanists is to insist that the narrative of European power wielded a disproportionate influence over the continent and its inhabitants. This perception rooted in the eighteenth-century ascendance of the slave trade and the nineteenth-century colonial partition still composes the reigning (popular) image of Europe. Obviously, a considerable number of Africanists question the narrative of Europe's dominance by focusing on African agency. Taking up the idea that a distinct cultural logic, specific experiences, and particular institutional formations characterized the continent and its peoples, they have crafted a radically distinct understanding of the African past. In centering Africa and Africans, the resulting scholarship has engendered a shift in our thinking about the African-European encounter. This modification in thinking about Africans is not, however, synonymous with a reconfigured or transformed European past. To this day, an ominous Europe that for a brief moment commandeered African history lurks in the shadows of a jointly shared past. For this reason, deconstructing Europe's epistemological hegemony still represents a precondition for inscribing the story of Africa and Africans. Among the handful of Africanists expressing interest in medieval thought and its influence on the European encounter with Africa, the focus resides with the fifteenth-century papal donations and the subsequent Christian textual legacy that were allegedly foundational in "establishing Western sovereignty."[24]

Papal bulls figure prominently in the social imaginary related to colonial encounters. Preceding Columbus's momentous voyage, papal bulls symbolize Christian authority, while in the wake of 1492, writers have associated the bulls with the legitimacy bestowed on Christian colonial expansion. In the hands of early modern Protestant propagandists, however, the bulls conferred by the pope to Iberian monarchs symbolized Catholic tyranny and overreach.[25] Depicted as the charters of European colonial expansion and racial slavery, the fifteenth-century bulls—as opposed to the actual political history—loom ominously as the ideological foundation of modern power. The perceived dominance of imperial expansion, Roman law, and the rhetoric associated with papal bulls have resulted in a history that simplifies the competing and conflicting interests that composed the idea of Europe. Few scholars, aside from medievalists and early modernists, have questioned the papal bulls' actual authority in the unfolding drama of European expansion. Papal bulls were not, however, laws. They did not supersede the authority of natural, divine, or canon law. By the fifteenth century, they lacked even the ideological cachet to infringe on positive law and the law of nations. Bulls, in fact, carried little authoritative weight beyond conveying the papal will—a will bound by an elaborate corpus of Christian thought and rulings. In this respect, papal will, like royal authority, confronted discursively defined limits. Assertions about the bulls' authoritative presence—akin to the rhetoric of Roman law and sovereign power—illustrate how the critical purchase of myth and discourse reside in the work that they perform rather than in actual relation to reality.[26]

To be sure, popes and monarchs often spoke in absolute terms, but jurists, theologians, and royal officials on the spot alongside the Saracens and pagans invariably tempered sweeping proclamations. Stated differently, crusading knights bent on wholesale conversion, territorial dispossession, and the enslavement of "barbarous" Africans capture an aspect of reality but not its entirety. Recourse to papal charters, grounded in the extant legal discourse, typically sanctioned expeditions and voyages, but how might we more effectively "read" these bulls? A strategic rereading of the bulls not only questions the idea that the European presence resulted in an immediate imperial imposition, which at its most extreme can only be described as a colonial apotheosis; it challenges the phenomenological claims of a fully defined West fashioning African alterity wholesale. The Cameroonian political scientist Achille Mbembe seamlessly reproduced this phenomenological maxim in his acclaimed *On the Postcolony*, observing how "it is in relation to Africa that the notion of 'absolute otherness' has been taken farthest."[27] Such rhetoric, stark and seductive, may be fruitful to think with but, in ascribing vast power to the West at the moment of the encounter—a time when Iberian polities were still in formation—projects a calcified narrative of power that simultaneously also condenses African history. We lose sight of the mutually constitutive nature of fifteenth-century African and European history, especially in regard to a politics configured in relationship to dominion. One of the intellectual endeavors of this project has been to press us into thinking about the earliest histories of the African-European encounter in relational terms, whereby Africa figured in the formation of Iberian colonialism and thus the emergence of early modern Portugal and Castile. Stated differently, a perspective

that accounts for the complexity in medieval thought and thus the papal bull
elicits a different history of the African-European encounter. Such a perspective
assumes (along with the theologians) the existence of sovereignty beyond a
state of grace. The acknowledgment of pagan sovereignty demonstrates that
dominium—configured around authority, obligations, and rights—positioned
Africans, sovereigns and slaves, in a complex relationship to Iberian imperial
formations well before the discovery of the Americas.

In *The Invention of Africa: Gnosis, Philosophy, and the Order of Knowledge*,
Mudimbe launched a searing assault against Western knowledge production.
Building on the structural critiques of anticolonial nationalists and the initial
generation of postcolonial critics—prompted by the persistent dilemma of African underdevelopment—Mudimbe sought to discern how Western thought,
from its inception, had conceived of Africa. "Perhaps," he writes, "this marginality could, more essentially, be understood from the perspective of wider
hypotheses about the classification of beings and societies."[28] Through the
discursive framing of Africa, configured as "invention" or "idea," Europe had
established its mastery over the African imaginary. In stating that this "discursive order" predicated on an "epistemological ethnocentrism" was a manifestation of "political power," Mudimbe observed that "colonialism becomes
its project and can be thought of as duplication and fulfillment of the power
of Western discourses on human varieties."[29] Mudimbe consequently identified medieval Christian thought as the foundation of a "missionary discourse"
authorizing Africa's territorial dispossession at the expense of an emergent
Western sovereignty. "The missionary," Mudimbe noted, "played an essential
role in the general process of expropriation and, subsequently, exploitation of
all the 'new found lands' upon the earth."[30] In structuring the colonial project,
"the missionary's objectives had to be co-extensive with his country's political and cultural perspectives on colonization, as well as with the Christian view
of his mission. With equal enthusiasm, he served as an agent of a political
empire, a representative of a civilization, and an envoy of God. There is no
essential contradiction between these roles. All of them implied the same
purposes: the conversion of African minds and space."[31]

Intent on excavating the full extent of the "colonizing structure," Mudimbe has repeatedly directed his readers to the fifteenth century and medieval
Christian thought. As Christians traversed primordial boundaries, the pope
fostered Catholic colonialism through "sacred instructions" and by sanctioning
discoveries, conquests, and enslavement. In doing so, Mudimbe writes, Christians obeyed

the "sacred instructions" of Pope Alexander VI in his bull *Inter Caetera* (1493): to overthrow paganism and establish the Christian faith in all barbarous nations. The bulls of Nicolas V—*Dum Diversas* (1452) and *Romanus Pontifex* (1455)—had indeed already given the kings of Portugal the right to dispossess and eternally enslave Mahometans, pagans, and black peoples in general. *Dum Diversas* clearly stipulates the right to invade, conquer, expel, and fight Muslims, pagans and other enemies of Christ wherever they may be. Christian kings, following the Pope's decisions, could occupy pagan kingdoms, principalities, lordships, possessions, and dispossess them of their personal property, land, and whatever they might have. The king and his successors have the power and right to put these peoples into perpetual slavery.[32]

For Mudimbe, an always already omnipotent Europe confronted and colonized Africa.

Intellectual subtlety seems insignificant to Mudimbe. The critical matter is that the "servant of the servants of God," Pope Nicholas V, promulgated *Romanus Pontifex*, on January 8, 1455, entitling the Portuguese king to "dispossess and eternally enslave Mahometans, pagans, and black peoples in general."[33] "*Romanus Pontifex*," writes Mudimbe, "shaped all subsequent agreements concerning rights to the newly discovered lands. It not only laid the foundation for the succeeding papal bulls, but over the years its basic tenets were faithfully maintained even as its politics were modified and transformed to fit concrete demands in the expansion of European projects."[34] For scholars of African but also Latin American and Asian studies, this bull simply established the modern colonial charter. "*Romanus Pontifex*," writes Mudimbe, "makes several points." It disavows property rights among non-Christians while sanctioning the violent enslavement of those unwilling to submit to the Christian invaders. "If the natives," according to Mudimbe, "failed to accept the 'truth' and, politically, to become 'colonized,' it was not only legal but also a required act of faith and religious duty for the colonizers to kill the natives." On the basis of Aristotelian ethics, "which, as we know, also justifies slavery," Mudimbe saw *Romanus Pontifex* regulating Christian interaction with the wider world.[35]

Mudimbe offers a stunning misreading, seductive in its simplicity, of the papal bulls. In the pope's eyes, insists Mudimbe, the state of grace—that is being a Christian and of good conscience—represented the theological grounds

on which rights, including the right to possession, rested. For this reason, heretics along with infidels and pagans lacked rights, prompting the pope, as
Mudimbe notes, to sanction violence against them. But the actual text, which
refers to non-Christian polities as "nations" and "kingdoms," calls into question Mudimbe's claims—which are widely shared—about dispossession.[36]
Instead of encountering land without a sovereign occupant, *terra nullius*, the
Portuguese confronted "enemies" wielding "temporal" authority that they
had to "vanquish" if they expected to "subject them to their own temporal
dominion."[37] In describing the intent of the "Catholic kings and princes,"
Nicholas actually acknowledges the "temporal" dominion of non-Christian
polities. Interestingly enough, *Romanus Pontifex* does not bestow the right of
possession to the Catholic lords:

> Fearing lest strangers induced by covetousness should sail to those
> parts, and desiring to usurp to themselves the perfection, fruit, and
> praise of this work, or at least to hinder it, should therefore, either
> for the sake of gain or through malice, carry or transmit iron, arms,
> wood, used for construction, and other things and goods prohibited
> to be carried to infidels, or should teach those infidels the art of nav-
> igation, whereby they would become more powerful and obstinate
> enemies to the king and infant, and the prosecution of this enterprise
> would either be hindered, or would perhaps entirely fail, not with-
> out great offense to God and great reproach to all Christianity, to
> prevent this and to conserve their right and possession, [the said king
> and infant] under certain most severe penalties then expressed have
> prohibited and in general have ordained that none, unless with their
> sailors and ships and on payment of a certain tribute and with an ex-
> press license previously obtained from the said king or infant, should
> presume to sail to the said provinces or to trade in their ports or to
> fish in the sea [although the king and infant, have taken this action,
> yet] in time it might happen that persons of other kingdoms or nations,
> led by envy, malice, or covetousness, might presume contrary to the
> prohibition aforesaid, without license and payment of tribute, to go to
> the said province, and in the provinces, harbors, and sea, so acquired,
> to sail, trade, and fish; and thereupon between King Alfonso and the
> infant . . . and the presumptuous persons aforesaid, very many ha-
> treds, rancors, dissensions, wars and scandals, to the highest offense
> of God and danger of souls, probably might and would ensue.

Romanus Pontifex acknowledges Portugal's discoveries and alleged "possession" of "some islands and harbors and the sea adjacent to that province," which enabled the Portuguese landing rights, access to trade, and the right to extol their faith. The bull even recognizes that the Portuguese had enslaved some of the inhabitants of Guinea that they have encountered:

> And so it came to pass that when a number of ships of this kind ("caravels") had explored and taken possession of very many harbors, islands, and seas, they at length came to the province of Guinea, and having taken possession of some islands and harbors and the sea adjacent to that province . . . war was waged for some years against the peoples of those parts in the name of the said King Alfonso and of the infant, and in it very many islands in that neighborhood were subdued and peacefully possessed, as they are still possessed together with the adjacent sea. Thence also many Guineamen and other negroes, taken by force, and some by barter of unprohibited articles, or by other lawful contract of purchase, have been sent to the said kingdoms. A large number of these have been converted to the Catholic faith.[38]

Even in view of the act of enslavement, *Romanus Pontifex*'s rationale resides in legitimizing the Portuguese as initial Christian arrivals. The bull ostensibly serves to mediate relations between Christians who have a right to land and trade with, but not to dispossess or possess, the inhabitants of Guinea. In *Romanus Pontifex*, Catholic authorities recognize, acknowledge, and record acts of dispossession and possession but do not preach for a crusade of conquest and enslavement. For modern observers, this might simply be a matter of semantics, but for contemporaries, such alleged subtleties reflected distinctions of theology, law (natural, divine, Roman, canon, and positive), and the force that accompanied expansive lordship. These distinctions, as we have seen and shall see again, subsequently delineated jurisdictional domains that brought sovereignty and subjects into relief.

Again, I posit that contextualized and close readings of *Romanus Pontifex*, among other alleged colonial charters, bring into focus a contested authority that enable us to tack a genealogy of pagan rights constitutive of African dominion. What is needed are subtle, not sweeping, readings of the corpus of texts issued during the fifteenth century that defined what has come to be called the colonial library. In practical terms, Iberians along the African littoral, on the Atlantic islands, and in the Americas recognized that certain pagan and Saracen princes wielded dominion over their subjects and territory and that these subjects, in turn, manifested a semblance of authority over their bodies and therefore their souls. In short, text and context underscore a far more layered reality than standard representations of the Christian colonial imposition. For one thing, Mudimbe's interpretive gloss anticipates a more recent colonial moment that he transposes on the earliest encounter between Europeans and Africans.[39]

Mudimbe's commentary on *Romanus Pontifex* broaches the central methodological concern informing this project. How might we approach descriptions of spectacles and ceremonies—those ritualized encounters—that I suggested, at the outset, represented political signifiers that divulge the existence of African sovereignty? "Ceremonial performances," writes Lawrence Bryant, a historian of early modern France, "were the heart of political life." For this reason, notes Bryant, "much of late medieval and early sixteenth-century public history consists of chronicles and lists of ranks, meeting places, forms of address, and procedures in a vast number of ceremonial assemblies."[40] Through textual production, scribes, chroniclers, and court historians brought into relief "early modern political culture, and with it the early modern state." An analogous reading—as we have seen and will continue to see—animates the methodological approach adopted here. Mining those familiar accounts and passages—though composed by Europeans—offers sightings of distinct political cultures and the associated state forms. Predicated on the politics of writing, the chronicles understandably privilege the political and in doing so have left us with countless performances of political life. Aimed at a variety of audiences, the most dramatic features of the extant political cultures—the rites and rituals—illuminated the glory yet rarely the substance of specific traditions. At best, we glimpse fragments of symbolic authority representing a claim, a counterclaim, and thus the semblance of sovereignty through which novel state forms arose. As Bryant observed for early modern France, although it is equally germane to Atlantic Africa, there flourished "significant attention on the tension between 'men in groups' and 'the practice of government' to shape 'the state in the sixteenth century'; how politics . . . were represented in communities and assemblies that were superior to the king or any individual group."[41] This interpretive framework, the one employed throughout this study, relies on a specific enactment: descriptions where Africans occupy the status as subjects, not objects, of the storyline. It is difficult to argue for African sovereignty when Africans appear in encounters as objects. From this perspective—a perspective that Mudimbe and numerous other Africanists share—there was often no recourse from wholesale dispossession, thereby engendering stylized renderings of first contact that already had foreclosed the possibility of agency. "When Christian Europeans—namely, Spanish and Portuguese people," Mudimbe observed, "met natives, they would invite the local king or chief and his advisors to a meeting. They would present to them a Christian interpretation of history that closely followed the Old and New Testaments. At the end of the meeting, the natives were invited to pledge submission and to convert. If the natives failed to accept the 'truth' and, politically, to become 'colonized,' it was not only legal but also an act of faith and religious duty for the colonizers to kill the natives."[42] Here Mudimbe projects the Requerimento—a text read out loud to Natives demanding that they surrender to Christian authorities, if not the blame for the ensuing violence would be solely attributed to them—into the African context, though it was specifically crafted for Spanish encounters with the inhabitants of the Indies. Such renderings, of course, stake considerable claim in how the public but also scholars represent the encounter between Africans and Europeans. On the basis of an equal number of contrary examples—especially over the course of the initial century of sustained contact—conveying ambiguity and dialogue but also the insistence on enactments of African sovereignty and the defense thereof, I question this flat reading of the past. The image of the abject native standing in contrast to renderings of courts, kings, and despots requires our attention but not necessarily resolution.

Acknowledging ambiguity in relation to the slave trade brings a political complexity to the fore in our historical imagination long dominated by modern configurations of economics and race. The hegemonic rendering of the slave trade is the story of the eighteenth century in which a romance with African nobles had long ceded to a perspective privileging black abjection and tyrannical black slave traders. In relation to both the black slave and the African slave trader, an emergent moral critique shaped representations of the slave trade that still govern modern histories of race relations. Before the eighteenth-century emergence of humanitarian sensibility, however, few questioned slavery and even fewer the enslavement process. For this reason, the slave trade represented the routine workings of African sovereigns and traders. In the absence of moral quandary, why would scribes, chroniclers, and travelers fabricate a political landscape resplendent with enactments of African sovereignty and African lordship alongside serial representations of African barbarism? Perhaps the answer resides in the historical reality but also the realism that resulted from the Renaissance optic. As depictions of African savagery

emerged ascendant, the Renaissance sensibility engendering an ethic of realism that acknowledged the political—on both sides—faded from framing
the African-European encounter.

Still, it should be said that in directing scrutiny at the papacy's imperial
rhetoric, Mudimbe brought into relief the popular conception that views
Christianity, but especially the missionaries, as a benevolent presence blunt-
ing colonialism's impact. The Christian veneer of eighteenth- and nineteenth-
century Anglo-American humanitarianism, discernible in the campaigns to
abolish the slave trade and the antislavery movement, fed the popular sensibility that paternal benevolence guided the clergy's relationship with Africans.[43] Such views were not only commonplace among the "public" but at
one time defined the scholarly consensus. In his classic *Slave and Citizen*, the
historian Frank Tannenbaum observed how "the slave trade had been condemned by Pius II on October 7, 1462, by Paul III on May 29, 1537, by Urban
VIII on April 1639, by Benedict XIV on December 1741, and finally Gregory
XVI on December 3, 1839. The grounds of the condemnation were that innocent and free persons were illegally and by force captured and sold into slavery, that rapine, cruelty, and war were stimulated in search for human beings
to be sold at a profit."[44] Conceding that "the Church did not interfere with
the customary institution where it derived from known practices in a given
community, such as born slaves, slaves taken in a just war, or those who had
sold themselves or had been condemned by a legitimate court," Tannenbaum
left the reader with an ambiguous impression of the Catholic Church.[45] Mudimbe, in contrast, focused on the "terrifying" aspects of Catholicism in the
form of papal bulls that authorized colonization, forced conversion, and enslavement, thereby constituting Christianity as a relentless force of colonial
domination.[46] Mudimbe's perspective disavows ambiguity. But even the concept of "just war" manifested a modicum of ambiguity since it implied an
(individual) experience with liberty, if not (a collective one in the form of)
sovereignty, preceding events whereby "innocent and free persons were illegally and by force captured and sold into slavery."[47] To ignore this ambiguity
means to forsake an acknowledged experience with African sovereignty. Indeed, by reducing the conflicting genealogies to a uniform constellation of European thought, scholars of African history and historians of the early modern
African diaspora have overlooked the complex articulation of politics and
political thought informing the early African-European encounter. In fabri-
cating a condensed, monolithic, and totalizing image of Europe capable of
imposing its will, Africanists and scholars of the African diaspora obviously

obscure a far more complicated European reality that simultaneously engendered African initiatives. African initiatives mediated through an existing corpus of African political traditions highlight the institutional dynamics with which Europeans had to contend and that, in turn, distinguished sovereign Africans and those ensnared in the social mechanism that engendered the formation of the diasporic subject. But even as expansion unfolded in the crucible of tradition, it also engendered novel experiences—Atlantic encounters—the specifics of which have been lost in the prevailing story that configures the African-European encounter. Europe, in this version and in its juxtaposition with Africa, appears as fully constituted—or at least as the entity associated with a later period. What is lost in this historical representation is the vibrant story of power that characterized the fifteenth and early sixteenth centuries propelling European expansion but that also occurred in tandem with the European-African encounter, which had an effect on the formation of power not only in Africa but Europe as well.

In offering this critique of Mudimbe, it needs to be acknowledged that he complicated the framing of the European past that has come to shape the postcolonial imaginary in African studies, circumventing both the reductive structural framings and the idea of a colonial psychology that animated the nationalist project. The cultural critic David Scott writes,

> In the anticolonial story, colonial power (or Western power, more generally) is understood as a force blocking the path of the colonized, a force that, having intruded, is standing—literally and metaphorically—in the way of the colonized. In this narrative, colonial power is conceived in the image of an obstruction, often a morally distorting obstruction, that seeks to materially dispossess the colonized, to exclude them from access to power, and to psychologically dehumanized them. Colonial power is therefore something to be overthrown, to be overcome, in order that the colonized can progressively retake possession of their societies and their selves. Frantz Fanon's *The Wretched of the Earth* is perhaps the paradigmatic instance of this conceptualization.[48]

Here then is an understanding of power, albeit totalizing, that seriously engaged Europe and its formation and, in turn, was shaped by an equally complicated African past. Like the body of work framing the black radical tradition, Mudimbe's writings not only took Europe and its history seriously but insisted

that colonies engendered critical aspects of Europe's formation, including capitalist development and the reconfiguration of state power. By means of this
perspective, the colonies stood for far more than a fertile laboratory for the
European imaginary. Africa and Africans embodied more than a wellspring
for envisioning racial alterity. For Mudimbe, the European encounter with
Africa constituted the earliest instantiation of what Scott has identified as
"modern power." "Modern power," Scott writes, "obviously, is a crucial aspect
of the story of historical change in the non-European world because the modern age unleashed forces that sought not merely to extract forms of tribute or
impose asymmetrical patterns of exchange, but to forcibly—and very often
violently—destroy old ways of social and moral and political life and build
up new ones. Unlike non-modern power, in other words, modern power has
been concerned precisely with systematically transforming the very conditions
in which life as a whole is organized."[49] From this perspective, modern power
engendered Africans and the subjects of the African diaspora.

Western theorists of power—philosophical, historical, sociological, cultural, and popular—have systematically eschewed any engagement with the
transformation of the African into a colonized native or slave, although, as
Mudimbe argues, that very process embodies one of the starkest expressions
of power in the emergence of the modern world. By ignoring slavery in their
formulations of modern power, Western theorists display a profound methodological conventionality on the subject configured around indifference and
silence. From their normative perspective, slavery constituted an antiquated
institutional relic unrelated to the formation of modern power. Ironically,
representations of captains and masters—admittedly from the eighteenth
century—render them as quintessential absolutists in their respective domains:
the slave ship and the plantation.[50] Even as theorists of power categorize slavery
as a primordial holdover, they also represent bondage and the accompanying
social relations in a decidedly modern manner. Centuries of specific human
experiences and distinct relations to power are lost in this static, bifurcated
conception of slavery. In the modern formulation, as we shall see in Chapter 6, the institution appears primarily as an economic phenomenon, thereby
confining the slave to the material realm. References to power assume a late
modern form where master and slave struggle for affirmation. In this scenario, the slave appears as the object under dominion of the master but now
untethered from the household, a locus and an affiliation that characterized
the ancient and medieval world's instantiation of slavery. In the classical world's
household (*oikos*) and the master's dominion over its occupants (slaves, wives,

offspring, and retainers), *paterfamilias* assumed the status as lord and master, affording him a public life and a say in the political realm (*polis*). Slaves figured prominently in this classical and medieval configuration of power that rooted dependents in the household and therefore at the foundations of lordship. Despite a lingering romance, the household and dependents did not play a similar role in power's modern incarnation where the market, the commodity, and difference prevailed in governing the institution of slavery. Now, slavery no longer cohered to the narration of power. Conceived as an institution rooted within society but confined to the economic realm, slavery flourished beyond the domestic crucible of power. For this reason, theorists have been able to configure sovereignty without acknowledging its foundational relationship to slavery. We need to acknowledge, however, that this representation is specific to the late modern period—the eighteenth century and beyond—but also contingent on the emergence of numeracy and the logos of the market. That being the case, how then are we to conceive of the relationship between slavery and power in the wake of the medieval era and before market ascendancy? In posing this as a question about the nature of early modern power, we glean how those theorists who pondered this issue configured a narrative of absolutism completely devoid of any consideration of slavery and colonialism. This theorization showcases the (re)production of indifference and silencing formulated explicitly in relation to a context in which colonial expansion and slavery not only represented actual experiences but played a considerable role in engendering the modern. In staging absolutism without colonialism or slavery, theorists of distinct ideological and intellectual persuasions offer at best a truncated history of absolutism illustrative of a methodological conventionality in depicting modern power. Stated differently, slavery and the slave trade remain remarkably undertheorized as a manifestation of absolutism.[51]

In narrating absolutism, theorists point to the sovereign as the embodiment of power who simultaneously transcends the source and authority of his power, the law. Characterized as the "state of exception," the sovereign and his office bear a striking resemblance to quintessential (modern) depictions of colonialism: the all-powerful foreign ruler who operated without limits.[52] For this reason, one could conceive how the abstraction that theorists have identified as power in the emerging age of absolutism would accompany mercantile Christian expansion and inform the subsequent encounter with natives in Africa, Asia, and the Americas. Arguably, absolutism constituted a constituent element of colonial expansion. As one modality of early modern power, absolutism found expression in the Portuguese and Spanish seaborne empires, refracting the workings and mysteries at court throughout the realm and its peripheries. The colonial experience, in turn, came to shape absolutism at the site of its origins. For Renaissance theorists of power, however (including Niccolò Machiavelli, Jean Bodin, and Thomas Hobbes), colonialism—configured as trade—was distinct from the history of the state and absolutism. Absolutism registered as power and the political while colonialism touched on the realm of the *oikos*. The inclusion of economic matters, observed the political theorist Istvan Hont, became the distinguishing feature of modern politics, a novelty that only acquired traction in the eighteenth century. Until then, writings on politics eschewed an engagement with the economic and, by implication, with colonialism. "It was the right to new territory and new productive resources, through 'first occupation' or conquest," writes Hont, that "commanded the attention of many natural jurists." For Hont, the evolving "theories of private property" among eighteenth-century natural jurists "provided a legal foil for post-Renaissance policies of global territorial expansion." [53]

But there may be another way to see matters altogether—a way that would not formulate early modern thought at the expense of Spain and Portugal while insisting on colonial slavery's exclusion. Building on the writings of Anthony Pagden and the various Latin American postcolonialists who have commented extensively on the marginalization of early modern Spanish thought and history, it is conceivable that the definition of colonialism as a form of trade or the configuration of the political shorn of the economic was peculiar to sixteenth-century Italy, England, and France but not generalizable to all Iberian polities. On the basis of their extensive experience in the evolving Atlantic world in which the Crown regulated trade, including the slave trade, the Portuguese and Spaniards pioneered a distinct understanding of colonialism with a peculiar relation to the social order. But a teleological privileging of early modern thought around Italian, French, and English thinkers—and particularly the stylized genre of the political treatises—obscures the vibrant debates that Iberian theologians, canonists, and civilians mounted on a vast array of subjects related to legitimate authority, Christian expansion, trade and *policía* (order), dominion, Christian duties, and the rights of the *extra ecclesiam*. These musings, alongside the *fueros* (rights granted by a sovereign to a municipality) and the surrender treaties that framed relations between Christian sovereigns and conquered Moors, composed a vast compendium of political thought and political practice, which both obliquely and explicitly underscore that fifteenth- and sixteenth-century thinkers conceived of (*maiestia*) sovereignty, (*protesta*) power, status, expansion, trade (*contracíon*), and rights (*derechos*) as organically linked.

Materialists theorizing the history of Western power have manifested a similar indifference to colonialism and slavery. The relationship between the rise of the absolute state and early modern colonialism has invited scant attention among Western theorists of the state. Among such theorists—past and present—there is a standing tendency to frame state power in an isomorphic universe, when in fact the state—the Christian state—in its absolutist phase exceeded the territorial boundaries of the modern nation-state. Theorists of early modern European state formation, building on this naturalized absence, have therefore rendered the state and modern power as an exclusively European invention, even though centralization and exploration represented concomitant phenomena. Understandably the writings of the sociological and political science pioneers come to mind, most notably the sociologist Norbert Elias, who, in *The Civilizing Process,* brilliantly delineated the emergence of absolutism. For Elias, like Max Weber, absolutism was a novel phenomenon emerging as the cornerstone of modern society until market logic and practice began its reign. But even with the appearance of a market in the form of a world economy, the state initially prevailed. Immanuel Wallerstein writes,

> It was in the sixteenth century that there came to be a European world economy based upon the capitalist mode of production. The most curious aspect of this early period is that capitalists did not flaunt their colors before the world. The reigning ideology was not that of free enterprise, or even individualism, or science or naturalism or nationalism. These would all take until the eighteenth or nineteenth century to mature as worldviews. To the extent that an ideology seemed to prevail, it was that of statism, the raison d'état. Why should capitalism, a phenomenon that knew no frontiers, have been sustained by the development of strong states? This is a question which has no single answer.[54]

Though Wallerstein privileges the state and a series of external referents in his formulation of the modern, the experiences that register involve the Spanish encounter with the Ottomans and American Indians by which time the Spanish monarchy had already assumed its embodiment as an absolute state. For this reason, the political experience a century earlier should also invite our attention since it underscores the political process that conditioned the emergence of the initial forms of absolutism. Obviously, the relationship admits to far more than temporal convergence. In the end, however, the manifest indifference to examining how the rationality of colonial rule was expressed in absolutism brings into relief the circumscribed perspective shaping our understanding of modern power. Equally questionable is the locus of agency that is always already embodied in Europe past and present. The theoretical consequences render the narrative of early modern European expansion as a relentless, unquestioned imposition, thus confining the histories of Africa, Asia, and the Americas as the long formation of the object. As a mode of representation, this narrative configures the object in the simplest manner while neatly packaging moral responsibility. This plot makes for simplified but also ill-conceived history in which the non-Western subject merely appears as historical backdrop. This storyline, as I have argued throughout, seems especially associated with African-European interaction, most notably in the history of the slave trade. Consequently, we do not have a complicated history of sovereign power in the framing of the African past and in the early modern African diaspora: such histories are of critical importance in narrating the story of power in which an assumed and complex African humanity played an important and historical role.

*   *   *

Africanists have focused on contemporary manifestations of sovereignty, resulting in an increasingly vibrant historiography of precolonial and colonial social formations.[55] My concern does not, however, reside with that body of scholarship focused on attacking or critiquing the ancestral permutations of the African state. This state's absence in a related field piques my interest. Even the most cursory reading highlights the lacuna of writings on the state in histories of the African diaspora.[56] This absence and the resulting representation of power, in turn, explain why sovereignty does not figure in histories of the early modern African diaspora.[57] In stating as much, I am not expressing a postcolonial disavowal of the anticolonial nationalism that occasioned independence throughout Africa. Sovereignty, which contemporaries referenced as "political equality," the "politics of independence," or simply "freedom," shapes the global landscape. Today, however, we have lost sight of the critique initially leveled at anticolonial nationalists by European defenders and critics of empire who asked on what basis—historical, political, and cultural—sovereignty could be erected and sustained. Largely intended to thwart independence, the supposition of this query was present in the earliest encounters between Europeans and Africans, eventually serving as the ideological ground for European dominion over vast parts of the continent and its numerous inhabitants. The anticolonial nationalists' response varied from a disavowal of the query to invoking the romance of a precolonial past associated with a heroic founding king. By crafting histories of the indigenous African past (or equating the creolization of Caribbean slaves with an indigenous authenticity), scholars contributed to the historical foundations of political independence.[58] In hindsight, however, we see how much of that writing offered a cultural response circumventing the narrow framing of the political around which the query about sovereignty's basis was initially raised. Now, long after the initial imperatives informing this war of positions have waned, we may argue that scholars ceded too much ground by avoiding the question of sovereignty on a then defined narrow terrain of the political. As a matter of concern occasioned by early modern encounters, principally configured through imagined hierarchically structured collectivities understood by all parties as polities, sovereignty played a defining role in the earliest interactions involving peoples from Europe, Asia, the Americas, and Africa. In arguing for sovereignty's importance in the inaugural encounters involving Africans and Europeans both in Africa and in the formation of the African diasporas, I am also insisting on an engagement with a history of the political and cultural politics in the early modern past that scholars have heretofore largely framed as the cultural and social transformation of dispossessed ethnics into slaves.

On reflection, it seems odd to think of the history of enslavement and slavery without an engagement with the political. But narratives configured around the slave trade—the enslavement process and the Middle Passage—generally privilege the military conflicts, ideologies, laws, and market structures that made Africans into chattel.[59] In turn, when referencing the "agency" of the enslaved, extant narratives privilege cultural forms. Cultural resilience stands in for a political social existence. Cultural recovery and resistance, in other words, sublimates for state destruction and exile. For this reason, the social memory that configures the African diaspora centers on a primordial past, the family, and the amorphous community. But the dynamic that engendered the collective sense of loss invariably resulted from warfare and territorial displacement alongside social stratification and debt settlement—acts that bring both the African and European state into relief in the very making of slaves. Few Africanists or black Atlantic scholars have taken on this dynamic of power in relation to the African diaspora. Yet as Paul Lovejoy noted, "The people who ended up in the Americas left areas that were frequently the scenes of disaster—the stuff of history." Commenting on another scholar's efforts to recover Haiti's African past, Lovejoy writes, "When John Thornton reveals the influence of the Kongo civil wars on the revolution in St. Domingue, he is not only addressing the issues of agency in the Americas but also uncovering new material on the Kongo civil wars themselves."[60] Here we glimpse a rare instance in which state formation, represented as military conflict, is linked to New World cultural formation. Usually, discussions of cultural formation only vaguely reference the state or the political traditions that created specific African diasporas. An implicit assumption flows from the absence of the African state in the historiography of the African diaspora: in the process of enslavement the political traditions informing African state formation ceded unconditionally to the cultural imperatives that arose in the face of adversity and that came to define African ethnicity in the New World. In other words, the act of dispossession that engendered the African diaspora provoked in the enslaved only a cultural response.

A strange irony has indeed arisen in writings on the African diaspora configured around the experiences of the enslaved: the diaspora, often configured around state destruction, dispersal, and the exile of its inhabitants whose collective memory privileges the idea of a homeland, eschews an engagement with the African state. Scholars of Atlantic slavery and the African diaspora generally represent the process of enslavement—a political process that was largely engendered by warfare, a polity's destruction, and the subjection of the newly vanquished—as an act of deracination that elicited a desire for cultural identification and quest for cultural autonomy?[61] At its core, the African diaspora has come to represent an engagement with culture as opposed to a theory of state and nation in which culture figured. So here was a people engaged in abstracted cultural survival, abstracted because the customary beliefs, norms, and practices were no longer concretely linked to state forms or institutional mechanisms. Framed in this manner, the African diaspora has emerged as a theory of culture or cultural engagement in a decidedly modern sense, with culture abstracted from its institutional moorings but in particular from the polis. For this reason, cultural practices predominate in histories of the diaspora and determine why cultural identification shapes our approach to race and ethnicity. "Acclaimed histories of slavery in the Americas," writes the historian Vincent Brown, "have refined our understanding of how different

New World contexts shaped black identities and generational experiences." Yet Brown also notes how "the cultural history of slavery in early America goes much deeper than characterizations of identity along a continuum from African to American (or, for that matter, assertions that identities are in fact hybrid) can capture. . . . This kind of analysis also leaves the mistaken impression that people's sole aim was to achieve a distinct cultural identity."[62] We need to add here that the focus on ethnicity in slave studies, while intended to complicate our understanding of the African past, seems far too concerned with framing ethnicity among the enslaved in relationship to the New World and the institution of slavery, thereby offering the mistaken impression that New World circumstances exclusively engendered the meaning that ethnicity assumed. But even a casual reading of African history underscores the centrality of ethnicity in the history of Africa and highlights how ethnicity was inextricably linked to a concept of the political that would seriously undermine the strictly cultural rendering of the slave community in which African survivors figured prominently. Not only would political animosity among Africans shape their senses of self, but according to anthropologist Andrew Apter, these African senses of self lingered indefinitely as a feature of social memory.[63]

In a prescient critique of the scholarship on enslaved people's ethnicity, the historian Alex Byrd notes how two prominent observers of diasporic cultural formation acknowledge the novelty of Ibgo as a cultural concept yet still gesture to some authentic past as the source for African cultural formation in the Americas. According to Byrd, though Douglas Chambers and Michael Gomez conceived of Igbo as "a social process," they do not develop the analytical implications that such a conception of culture would have for the representation of the African past in the New World. "Thus," concludes Byrd, "their work is more prone to describe being Eboe as possessing certain traits, performing certain actions, and practicing certain behaviors than it is to interrogate the process (or processes) of becoming Igbo."[64] The importance of Byrd's critique cannot be overstated. It underscores the conceptual fault line informing the study of African cultural formation in the Americas. Still, that contentious debate need not detain us here. What should invite our attention is Byrd's brilliant yet understated insight that both a cultural and social dynamic engendered the diasporic formation, resulting in the emergence of the Igbo. For Byrd, the very violence and the story of power that rendered thousands of Africans in the Biafran littoral into slaves demands as much attention as the alleged cultural properties associated with the people identified

as Igbo. "The origin of the Igbo nation in the diaspora," writes Byrd, "was
not simply a cultural imperative. At its base, it was also a social imperative
born of migration—in particular the violent, alienating dislocation that
characterized slave trading in the Biafran interior. In ways too important to
ignore, the Igbo of the Americas were made so through their migrations."[65]
Besides representing an epistemological critique of the authentic, the emphasis
on the social aspect of a diasporic formation offers an opening for conceiving
of the state and its role in fomenting both violence and African ethnicity.
Here the state functions less as an abstraction that monopolizes violence than
as a generative social form. State formation in its destructiveness is simultaneously constructive. But the valence Byrd accords to violence presses us to
theorize the state as the constituent element of diasporic ethnicity and in
doing so enables us to circumvent the exclusive cultural configuration that
has long dominated our analysis of African diasporic formations. What is
more, the process of ethnic formation represents one of the earliest manifestations of modern power since it entailed "systematically transforming the
very conditions in which life as a whole is organized."[66]

*   *   *

The anthropologist David Scott has offered a searing critique of postcolonial
projects and positions that he views as being mired in dated polemics. Scott
has forged a formidable history of Caribbean thought that, in turn, has resulted in a rewriting of colonial modernity and that should thus be of interest
to a disparate range of theorists. With subtle insistence, Scott has made a compelling case for the Caribbean as an ur-site of our political modernity. Much
of this critical work, of course, builds on a discussion initially formulated in
"colonial governmentality," where Scott offered an extended engagement
with the political philosopher Michel Foucault, who argued in his 1977–78
lectures at the Collège de France that a new modality of power arose in the
middle of the sixteenth century.[67] For Foucault, governance gradually supplanted sovereignty, thereby signifying a shift in the prince's political rationale
from territorial possession to population regulation. Scott takes up Foucault's
schematic to argue that a similar dynamic was discernible in the history of
colonialism, to which scholars of colonialism and postcolonialism should be
attentive in order to track the shifting nature of power. That which defined
colonial power as modern resided in its transformative capacity and rationale.
"My own view," writes Scott, "is there are more fruitful questions to be pur-

sued, questions that turn around a more constructive idea of the problem of
power, and the modern power of the New World slave plantation, more specifically."[68] Focused above all on the "constructive" features of power, Scott
maintains "it is this conception of power and historical change that ought to
command our attention in our contemporary discussions of modernity."[69]

In urging us to deconstruct "dead-ended modernities fabricated by the
postcolonial state," so as to delineate "the modern concepts and institutions
upon these resisting projects themselves depended," Scott has identified "the
regime of slave plantation power" as the crucible in which modern black cultural formation was initially forged. Here the relationship between cultural
formation and power gets accented in ways rarely discernible in writings on
African, slave, or black culture. Not only are Scott's claims critically important in historicizing modern power; his critique, I would argue, is equally
relevant to distinguishing between power across social formations. Oddly
enough, Scott obscures earlier incarnations of power's modern form embodied in distinct rationalities. By configuring power in relation to the regime
of New World slavery, Scott's formulation distorts the very historicity of
power—a historicity that even preceded the ascendance of governance over
sovereignty.[70] While I am in agreement with Scott's urging, it should be noted
that by constricting modern power to "the regime of slave plantation power,"
he forecloses an earlier and equally pervasive form of that phenomenon associated with countless experiences beyond what theorists of slavery still
identify as the *locus classicus*, the plantation.[71] In fact, a narrow focus on the
plantation (land, commodification, production, and discipline) obscures the
ways that a series of sites before and beyond the New World's *locus classicus*—
the process of enslavement, coastal enclaves, the slave ship, and urban com-
plexes, along with the long-neglected medieval Christian discourses—structured
the (political) lives of Africans throughout the early Atlantic. This structuring process, as we have seen with ethnicity and more generally with diaspora,
embodies modern power.

*   *   *

Despite the commonplace understanding that a series of momentous transitions, if not transformations, defined Europe's early modern formation, scholars and theorists have depicted Europeans and their institutional presence as
fully formed (or at best constituted in relation to a hermitically sealed "European" cosmos) while insisting on the contingency of the non-Western subject

and their institutional forms.[72] In this narrative, the Iberian Peninsula embodies an anomaly since theorists have rendered a series of regional events (1492) to mark modernity's emergence, although being reluctant to associate the iconic West with Spain and Portugal. The process of centralization manifest in the absolute monarchy, a defining event in the history of modernity, though initially associated with the Iberian Peninsula, engendered in part by the conflict among its various polities along with the fifteenth-century discoveries and conquests in North Africa and the Atlantic littoral, still remains an under-examined phenomenon in the story of the West. Spain thus appears as both the initial incarnation of the West and simultaneously an outlier to it. The literary scholar Barbara Fuchs captures the conventional framing: "The paradoxes in the construction of Spain in this period are striking: we are used to thinking of Spain's self-definition as a process whereby both Jewish and Moorish elements were excised from its culture; the conquest of Granada in 1492 and the concurrent expulsion of the Jews are taken as signal events in the emergence of Spain as a nation. Yet after 1492 Spanish culture retained and even celebrated the culture of al-Andalus."[73] If 1492 both represents a defining moment and highlights the centralizing tendencies of the Spanish polity, then clearly political and economic events in the fifteenth century played some role in state and economic formation. To acknowledge as much requires scholars to take into consideration the series of Iberian-African encounters in the Atlantic littoral where Spaniards and the Portuguese enacted ceremonies, rituals, and institutional practices derived from their medieval past and also as subjects of Muslim overlords. These enactments of power— symbolic and cultural—acquired new valence in relationship to Christian ascendance over the various Muslim polities and their subjects in the Iberian Peninsula and in light of the encounter with new peoples.

CHAPTER 5

Histories

In the decade after Antão Gonçalves's 1441 raid, the Portuguese in their continuing quest to circumvent the "Moors" established a Christian alliance with
Ethiopia's mythical monarch, Prester John; secured a new route to India; and
explored the Guinea coast for commercial opportunities.[1] By 1448, Portuguese
seafarers had encountered the inhabitants of the Niumi kingdom, located in
present-day Gambia, and imported nearly a thousand persons as slaves from
a vast area bordered by Mauritania in the north and the Gambia River in the
south.[2] The apparent ease with which the Portuguese expeditions acquired
chattel incited further interest in Guinea. Anxious to benefit from his labors
as patron, Infante Henrique had obtained a monopoly in 1443 from Portugal's regent prince Dom Pedro obligating his subjects and other Christians to
procure a royal license in order to trade with Guinea's inhabitants.[3] This
monopoly along with the *quinto* (royal fifth), the construction of a fort on Arguin Island, and the establishment of the Casa da Guiné (House of Guinea)
underscore the speed with which the Portuguese Crown imposed a corporate
structure on its purported discoveries.[4]

Directed at Portuguese and other Christian subjects, the institutional
practices introduced by Portugal's royal officials sought to regulate all European mercantile activity with Guinea—including the slave trade. In the fiercely
competitive era of discoveries, Portugal's rulers wanted to prevent other
Christian sovereigns, especially the Castilians, from enjoying their imperial
spoils. Though the Portuguese Crown often relied on military might to prevent
native and foreign interlopers from circumventing the monopoly, the rule of
law manifest in royal proclamations, diplomatic treaties, and papal bulls emerged
as the representative practice. As the Portuguese Crown imposed its authority
on potentially profitable discoveries, some royal and ecclesiastical authorities

appropriated rhetorical authority over Guinea and bestowed a subject status, derived from Europe's political lexicon, on the region and its inhabitants. The Portuguese, in short, ascribed Guinea's inhabitants a juridical subjectivity by means of the regulatory devices—royal charters, commercial contracts, and papal accords—designed to preserve the royal monopoly.[5]

As they bestowed juridical identities on Guinea's inhabitants, the Portuguese relied on their own representational lexicon to describe the polities and the inhabitants that they encountered—a lexicon that associated sovereignty alongside polity and ethnicity with feudal and mercantile references. As early modern European explorers scoured the Guinea coast for commercial possibilities, they searched incessantly for regional sovereigns. Zurara reminded his readers that until Gonçalves's expedition, Infante Henrique "hath toiled in vain in this part of the world, never being able to arrive at any certainty as to the people of this land, under what law or lordship they do live."[6] Longing for permanent, as opposed to haphazard, commercial ties, the Portuguese assumed that Guinea's sovereigns could best implement them. Having identified a "lord," the extent of his jurisdiction, and the inhabitants' *ethnos*, the Portuguese restricted themselves to establishing commercial patterns with local rulers—rulers they believed controlled the flow of goods, including human chattel. From the Portuguese and subsequent European perspective, the enslavement process resided with Guinea's sovereigns. Aware that canon law sanctioned specific avenues whereby the *extra ecclesiam* could be rendered into slaves, the Portuguese consciously depicted the act of enslavement as the sole provenance of Guinea's lords. By way of this representational strategy, the Portuguese defined some Africans as sovereign subjects while implicitly identifying those who entered their possession as individuals devoid of sovereignty. Since they ascribed full responsibility to Guinea's rulers for depriving individuals of their liberty, the conscience of Christians who acquired slaves remained unencumbered. They, after all, bore no responsibility for the enslavement process.

The search for sovereigns underscores that the Portuguese did not perceive Guinea as *terra nullius* whose inhabitants Christians could indiscriminately label as chattel. Even though some contemporary observers construe the imperial and papal rhetoric as sanctioning Christian dominion over Guinea, canon law and the specter of African military might limited the Portuguese and their Castilian rivals to struggling for the exclusive privilege of trading in the "land of the blacks." As the fifteenth-century travel accounts illustrate, Africa's sovereigns remained unaware of and subsequently appeared undaunted by Christian claims to Guinea. Despite competing imperial claims, the Portuguese and Castilian monarchs realized that their hopes of securing access to Guinea's resources depended on cultivating ties with the province's "lawful" authorities.

As sovereigns manifesting *dominium* over their jurisdiction and their subjects, the lords of the land actually dictated the terms and items of trade. In fact, Guinea's sovereigns regulated the slave trade, like all trade, and indeed during the earliest phase of the encounter with Europeans—the chronological focus of this project—bore responsibility for those deprived of their African mooring. Respectful of the customs vesting Guinea's lords with sovereignty, early modern Christian slave traders rarely questioned the enslavement process responsible for transforming sovereignless subjects into chattel despite the fact that canon law required them to do so. For Christians, enslavement conveniently represented the intricate workings of power and sovereignty. As the beneficiaries of an enslavement process residing among Guinea's inhabitants, Iberian slavers avoided having to scrutinize their Christian conscience. Slavery, paradoxically, failed to elicit the same scrutiny as the enslavement process. As a practice and as an institution, slavery thrived unquestioned in an emerging Europe just as it had flourished in early Christendom and Greco-Roman antiquity.[7]

* * *

On April 10, 1454, Castile's sovereign informed his nephew and Portugal's king, Afonso V, that a Portuguese caravel had attacked "our subjects and naturals" within sight of Cadiz, "our lordship and jurisdiction." Juan, king of Castile and Afonso's uncle, was a doddering intractable old man who strongly deplored this aggression against his subjects "coming with their merchandise from the land which is called Guinea." Basing his argument on Visigothic incursions across the Straits of Gibraltar, Juan insisted that "Africa" represented "our conquest." The Portuguese, he asserted, had committed an unjustified assault against "our said vassals, subjects and naturals" for which Juan demanded compensation and the Castilian captives' unconditional release.[8]

Later that year, anxious to resolve the matter in his favor, Juan sent a diplomatic delegation to Afonso, enjoining Portugal's sovereign to cease his "conquest of Berberia and Guinea." As the emissaries conveyed Juan's assertion that Guinea "was his own," they also leveled a threat. Through the communiqué, Juan cautioned his nephew that by not complying "it was certain that he would make war upon him with fire and blood as upon an enemy."[9] In response to his uncle's claims, Afonso insisted that his Portuguese predecessors had inaugurated Guinea's conquest. According to Afonso, this conquest and the recent discoveries in the "land of the Blacks"—for which he, along with the conquest of Morocco, was labeled "the African"—substantiated Portugal's claims. But he bid his uncle "not to break the truce . . . until he [Afonso] had ascertained whether it was true that the conquest pertained to him." Juan's death, in 1454, brought the kingdoms a brief reprieve that momentarily favored Portugal.

As Castilian and Portuguese exploration mounted in the fifteenth century, the subjects of the emerging absolutist monarchies engaged in a protracted contest for the symbolic, if not actual, possession of Guinea, especially the Atlantic islands.[10] Zealous in defense of their respective sovereigns' claims, royal officials acted in a manner that occasionally brought their kingdoms to the brink of war. Dom Henrique's former page, Diogo Gomes, recounted one instance during which the Portuguese captured a Castilian-sponsored interloper named De Prado. After his apprehension on the Guinea coast, Diogo Gomes ordered the hapless merchant sent to Oporto, where Portuguese officials paraded him "in a cart" through the streets, eventually burning him "with his sword and gold" for having "carried arms to the Moors."[11] In the second half of the fifteenth century, such acts occurred with some frequency. In an era when subjects, as corporate entities, embodied juridical boundaries and zealously defended territorial domains, Portugal's execution of a Castilian was tantamount to war.[12] Describing the terse exchange between Juan and Afonso, a contemporary Castilian historian observed that "the excesses of war . . . caused grave disasters by sea to the Castilians, must be abandoned, or reparation should instantly be made, if it was desired to observe the alliance agreed upon by the fathers of both princes; or, on the contrary, war would be declared."[13] Justice and its application were, in short, a sovereign's prerogative. The *pelourinho* (pillory) invariably brought the king's authority over his subjects' life and death into stark relief. As the persons with a monopoly on legitimate violence, sovereigns manifested their dominion through the whipping post and the dispensation of justice.[14]

Through these incidents, we glean how Hispania's Christian monarchs, thwarted in their efforts to eliminate the last Moorish stronghold, nonetheless strove to extend their dominion against rival Christian lords. Notwithstanding the Reconquista rhetoric, Hispania's Catholic princes steadily waged conflict with their Christian rivals. The exchange between Juan and Afonso simply highlights the long-standing conflict among Christians that had escalated into a rivalry over territorial possessions, imperial dominion, and lordship.[15]

During the course of the fifteenth century, as the tension between Hispania's Catholic monarchs escalated, it threatened more than Castile's and Portugal's ruling houses. Catholic competition eventually raised papal concerns and led to direct intervention by the "vicar of Jesus Christ." Such interference, in the form of mediation and adjudication, underscores the seriousness of the Catholic divide. In an era when Constantinople fell to the "Turks," the beleaguered pope viewed the conflict among Hispania's Catholic monarchies as a threat to Christendom. Successive fifteenth-century popes, in fact, promulgated bulls with the intent of settling the territorial disputes at the core of Iberia's Catholic divide.[16] On January 8, 1455, two years after Islamic armies sacked Constantinople and months after Castile's monarch threatened Portugal with war, Pope Nicholas V acted decisively to quell the rivalry in Hispania.

Though denying that Portugal's sovereign appealed for papal intervention, Nicholas V issued *Romanus Pontifex* at Afonso's behest, intending to bridge the Catholic divide. But by adjudicating in Portugal's favor, the pope presented Afonso with "suitable favors and special graces." Some observers, as we noted in the previous chapter, have surmised that *Romanus Pontifex* simply constituted an imperial charter sanctioning Portugal's dominion over Guinea that abnegated indigenous peoples' sovereignty.[17] Nicholas stipulated that Afonso and his successors could "in these [acquisitions] . . . make any prohibitions, statues, and decrees whatsoever, even penal ones . . . as concerning their own property and their other dominions."[18] Such language seems to affirm Portugal's imperial dominion. The pope, after all, granted Portugal the right to administer justice, sovereignty's penultimate manifestation. As defenders of the faith, Nicholas also insisted that Portugal's sovereigns represented the "true lords" of those "harbors, islands, and seas," which they have "explored . . . acquired and possessed." Portugal's dominion rested on efforts to "restrain," "vanquish," "subdue," and "subject" the "perfidious enemies." Here papal sentiments seemingly sustain assertions that *Romanus Pontifex* denied Saracens, infidels, and pagans "ownership rights to the land on which they are living."[19] Since territorial sovereignty constituted a necessary precondition for freedom, Christians could "invade and conquer" the inhabitants of *terra nullius*, expel them, "and when necessary to fight them and subjugate them in a perpetual servitude, and to expropriate all their possessions."[20]

Despite the bull's imperial tenor, indiscriminately extending *Romanus Pontifex* to Guinea belies authorial intent while occluding Nicholas's anxieties about the "Turk" who embodied Islam's latest vanguard. In the fifteenth century, the "Turk," not the "Moor," offered Christendom its greatest threat. Poised on Italy's border, Turkish armies reigned ascendant in the eastern Mediterranean region. Irrespective of the Islamic presence in Hispania and "Africa," throughout this period when Christians lamented the "savage excesses of the Saracens and other infidels," they generally referred to the "Turk" not the "Moor." But in *Romanus Pontifex*, Nicholas transposed his specific concerns with the "Turk" into a general apprehension about the Islamic faithful. By ruling in Dom Afonso's favor, Nicholas and Calixtus III, his successor, supplanted one Islamic foe with another since they rewarded the only Catholic sovereign who heeded their plea for a crusade against the "Turk" after Constantinople's fall.[21] These circumstances contextualize the imperial tone of *Romanus Pontifex*, which in actuality reflects the defensive tenor of an unfulfilled Christian crusade aimed at stalling another Islamic invasion of Western Christendom. The "Moor," Christendom's erstwhile nemesis and kin to the "Turk," represented Portugal's purported enemy. But in a transparent passage of the bull, Nicholas actually defined Guinea's inhabitants as "pagan peoples . . . who are entirely free from infection by the sect of the most impious Mahomet."[22]

By identifying Guinea's inhabitants as pagans, Nicholas and Calixtus manifested the same ambiguity characterizing the Moor-black African divide. Far from being ethnographically precise, this characterization underscores Guinea's shifting location and the fluid perception of its cultural geography. Predisposed to seeing Guinea through an Orientalist prism in a manner akin to the royal chronicler Zurara, the pope conflated "Guinea," the territory of black pagans, with "Africa," the continent's northern edge inhabited by Islam's various adherents. This confusion expressed itself repeatedly in *Romanus Pontifex* and in subsequent bulls, thus explaining papal insistence that certain items, including "iron instruments," "wood for construction," and "cordage, ships or any kinds of armor" could not be sold to "Saracens and infidels."[23] Prohibitions of this sort unmask papal anxieties about fifteenth-century Islam, suggesting that Roman authorities simply projected knowledge of the Moorish presence in "Africa" onto "Guinea," unaware that the referents gradually embodied distinct regions and persons.

Since the Moors, especially those aligned with the Turks, represented the subject of papal anxieties, it seems questionable whether the pope conferred more than a commercial concession manifested in the language of "harbors, islands, and seas" to the Portuguese.[24] Moreover, in light of Islam's expansion under the Moors, most of the territory Christians conquered represented *terra irredenta* (land formerly held by a Christian prince). Yet as we shall see, on the basis of treaties, contracts, and the rents paid to Guinea's sovereigns, neither the Portuguese nor the Castilians perceived the region as *terra nullius* or for that matter as *terra irredenta*. Despite the imperial overtones expressed in *Romanus Pontifex* and the successive fifteenth-century bulls, these texts referred to an imaginary landscape that the Moors supposedly inhabited. But specifically, these texts granted Portugal, as opposed to the other Christian monarchies, a mercantile monopoly over the Guinea trade. In the context of the imperial Christian charter, "Guinea" as opposed to "Africa" represented an aside. For reasons related to a familiarity with "Africa," the Reconquista legacy, and the Turkish threat, at the time that Nicholas V composed *Romanus Pontifex*, Guinea did not constitute a fixed discernible entity in the papal imaginary. The "Guinea" in *Romanus Pontifex* embodied an imprecise referent standing at odds with the experiences of those Portuguese who actually traveled and traded in the "land of the Blacks." This ambivalence, like the dearth of marvel in Zurara's chronicle, underscores the discursive overlap operative during Portugal's early modern encounter with Guinea.

Questioning the notion that *Romanus Pontifex* granted Portugal possession of Guinea should not obscure the central role that laws and treaties commanded in shaping the early modern encounters.[25] Until recently, the specter of violence associated with chattel raids has, in discussions of Europe's encounter with Africa, overshadowed the intrinsic violence embedded in the rule of law. In fact, soon after the initial chattel raids, the rule of law—in the form of proclamations, monopolies, accords, contracts, and performances—mediated the interaction between Africans and Europeans. Underneath this legal veneer protecting a shifting core of African and European elite, the law wreaked havoc on the lives of countless people.[26] *Romanus Pontifex*, as suggested, bore little if any responsibility for actual transgression toward Guinea's inhabitants. It neither granted possession nor legitimized enslavement. As a papal bull adjudicating on an intrinsically secular matter, *Romanus Pontifex* symbolizes the haste with which Europeans looked to the law in order to legitimize their respective imperial claims. The papal bulls did not supersede canon law in regulating Christian affairs with the *extra ecclesiam*.[27] By constituting Guinea and its inhabitants as objects, *Romanus Pontifex* did, however, initiate violence—violence very much in keeping with the colonial discourse's tradition and to which the papal bulls contributed in a significant manner.

As Christians processed Guinea's discovery, a multitude of overlapping discourses shaped their perception of the subject that they encountered. Guinea's inhabitants invariably emerged as "Moors," "Turks," "infidels," and "pagans." The fluid, if not contradictory, depictions reify the discursive juggling characteristic of colonial discourses that was constitutive of the Africanist archive's formation. Within this discourse, as one modern critic has noted, the imagined or invented referent reigned ascendant. "Underlying the idea of a colonial discourse . . . is the presumption that during the colonial period large parts of the non-European world were produced for Europe through a discourse that imbricated sets of questions and assumptions, methods of procedure and analysis, and kinds of writing and imagery."[28] In the texts invoking fifteenth-century Guinea, the region and its inhabitants embodied anything but stable referents.[29] In the litany of texts constitutive of the colonial discourse, Europe produced many Guineas.

Even as *Romanus Pontifex* embodied this discursive ambivalence, it endeavored to structure relations between Guinea and specific Christians for the latter's benefit. The principle of order, at the core of this regulatory process, played an important role in shaping the interactive process but also made assumptions about Guinea that simply reflected the content of the nascent imperial imagination. Even as we question the extent to which Guinea represented the object of *Romanus Pontifex*, this bull denied agency to the very entity it had accorded subjectivity. Though depicted as a self-conscious referent, the pope assumed that an amenable Guinea simply awaited the Christian arrival. By allowing the Portuguese latitude, for instance, to contract treaties, establish dominion, commence trade, and construct churches, Nicholas V took for granted the inhabitants' consent. Such a supposition unveils more than papal projection of a Christian psychology onto Guinea; it posits a series of social and cultural arrangements that would sustain the Christian presence in the "land of the blacks." Christian arrogance, of course, reigned supreme in this assumption, and yet it identifies a zeitgeist steadfastly refusing to acknowledge immutable differences. Guinea, though "situated in the remotest parts unknown to us," represented a knowable subject with distinctly identifiable if not familiar polities, mechanisms of exchange, and cultural practices.

*   *   *

In the face of a renewed Islamic offensive, Pope Nicholas V took the initiative with *Romanus Pontifex* to solve Hispania's Catholic divide. The Christian breach, as suggested above, revolved around imperial dominion largely over trade, a decidedly temporal concern. Crafted in part to reconcile Castile and Portugal, *Romanus Pontifex* and the plethora of papal bulls promulgated during the fifteenth century largely touched on secular matters associated with the expanding centralized monarchies.[30] In fact, from Ceuta's conquest in 1415 to the signing of the Treaty of Tordesillas in 1494, the Castilian and Portuguese monarchs repeatedly petitioned the pontiff, invariably after the fact, to sanction their temporal activities. "During the exploration and conquest of Africa and the island chains of the Atlantic," as one modern observer has noted, "the Portuguese and the Castilians informed the papacy of their activities in traditional rhetorical forms that stressed their desire to spread the word of God. They acted, however, according to their own dynastic interests, seeking papal approval for courses of action already taken."[31] Even though the "princes" cloaked their activities in crusading and conversion rhetoric, the petitions cannot obscure a shifting sensibility in favor of Hostiensis. The secular authorities' nascent nationalism gradually steered them away from Innocent IV's commentary granting *dominium* to the *extra ecclesiam*. But as late as the sixteenth century, Francisco de Vitoria, the prominent theologian at Salamanca, upheld Innocent IV's opinion, arguing that infidels and pagans legitimately maintained dominion over their possessions.[32]

In light of mounting imperial activity, secular rulers insisted that a Christian crusade sanctioned the subjugation of infidels and pagans. They steadfastly petitioned the pope, aware that the Schism of the West (1378–1418) had significantly weakened the pontiff's power but that his rulings still carried symbolic weight among Catholic sovereigns. Even as they deferred to the canonists, Hispania's Catholic lords sought to undermine the commentary granting infidels and pagans sovereignty by extracting successive papal bulls legitimizing their imperial expansion. Despite this imperial tenor, none of the fifteenth-century bulls superseded canon law. But in the words of a prominent medievalist, they do underscore the fact that "the initiative in dealings with non-European societies was passing to secular rulers."[33] Conceding as much when they mediated between Castile and Portugal, Nicholas V and Calixtus III adjudicated over a temporal matter while cloaking their anxieties about the "Turk" by siding with the monarch who was allegedly mounting an offensive against "Saracens and infidels."

In the final analysis, the various papal bulls deferred to canon law and the litany of commentaries on the *extra ecclesiam*'s rights. A contextualized reading of the fifteenth-century bulls calls into question the assertion that

Guinea had been bestowed on the Portuguese sovereign and, therefore, the Portuguese could justly "reduce" the indigenous population "to perpetual slavery."[34] Distinctions of faith simply did not valorize Portugal's colonization nor justify the random enslavement of Guinea's inhabitants. Despite their limited application, even in the realm of the law of nations, the papal bulls operated on the assumption of Guinea's familiarity—a symbolic manifestation of possession. From the beginning, however, ambiguity formulated around Guinea's subjectivity riddled the sense of possession expressed in the papal bulls. One modern observer has insisted "the level of practical intercultural understanding was considerably higher than the available texts would indicate. On the European side, where all the texts originate . . . what we see developing is a theory of African society that is to a considerable extent independent of actual experience, though it appears to be well grounded in ethnographic reporting, and which is implicitly revelatory of important features of European culture."[35] This discourse, according to the observer, marks the theoretical emergence of the fetish. The fetish derived etymologically from Portugal's encounter with Guinea, constituting "a pragmatically totalized and totalizing explanation of the strangeness of African societies and the special problems [Europeans] encountered in trying to conduct rational market activities with these benighted peoples."[36] Though present in the papal bulls, "strangeness" became increasingly prominent in the travel accounts' ethnographic descriptions. Predicated on wonder, ethnographic representations thrived on the notion of difference.[37] At the same time that travel accounts acknowledged alterity's presence, they also reveal that Christian explorers respected the rights of the *extra ecclesiam*—represented in a discourse on sovereign power—which they manifested in treaties, contracts, and tribute payments to Guinea's lords.

*   *   *

In 1455, the same year that Pope Nicholas V issued *Romanus Pontifex*, Alvise da Cà da Mosto, a Venetian merchant, embarked on the first of his two voyages to the "land of the Blacks." As his caravel under Infante Henrique's banner plied the Atlantic waves, Cà da Mosto reflected on the goods the prince's emissaries had exhibited earlier. An experienced merchant and keen observer, the young Venetian knew sugar's market price and the value of the diverse spices that the Infante's factors had displayed. Eager to reach his destination, Cà da Mosto anticipated the profit that he and his kinfolk would derive from his momentous voyage to "lower Ethiopia." As he crafted his narrative about the Guinea ventures a decade later, Cà da Mosto vividly recalled his earlier seduction. "I was young," he observed, thus "well fitted to sustain all hardships, desirous of seeing the world and things never before seen by our nation." Vivacious and daring, Cà da Mosto acknowledged that he sought glory and material rewards from his toils in "the lands of many strange races, where marvels abounded."[38]

Underscoring his zeal for adventure, distinction, and profit, Cà da Mosto proclaimed that his goals could readily be accomplished in the "land of the Blacks" since the region represented "another world." A cursory reading of Cà da Mosto's sentiments suggests that the Venetian perpetuated the Reconquista rhetoric characterizing Zurara's *The Conquest and Discovery of Guinea*. But a closer examination of the text brings a different understanding into relief. Cà da Mosto, in contrast to the royal chronicler, described seeing "many things new and worthy of some notice." He, in fact, repeatedly asserted having witnessed numerous marvels during his sojourn. A consummate trader who candidly acknowledged his encounter with "strange new places," Cà da Mosto focused closely on Guinea's *ethnos* and their respective cultural characteristics. As a result, Cà da Mosto's text embodied a discursive shift highlighting more than a merchant-chronicler divide. It underscored the fact that marvel constituted a precondition for ethnography's production.

By acknowledging the novelty of "the land of Blacks," Cà da Mosto represented one of Europe's initial early modern travelers to record ethnographic details about Guinea or "lower Ethiopia," as he often referred to the region. While marvel facilitated the text's ethnographic observations, Cà da Mosto's narrative cannot be said to present an unmediated representation of Guinea and its inhabitants. The themes, the concepts, and the very language with which he described the landscape—natural, cultural, and social—attest to differences but also obscure the extent to which he saw Guinea and its inhabitants symbolizing alterity. In the context of the Christian monogenetic universe secured on divine law and the patristic teachings, Cà da Mosto—like successive early modern travelers—could not bring himself to "other" Guinea's inhabitants.[39] Instead, he rendered them knowable while acknowledging their lack of civility.

This discursive phenomenon had serious implications for representations of Guinea's cultural geography and the manner in which the region's inhabitants entered Europe's early modern archive. Early modern ethnographers, like their twentieth-century counterparts, used analytical devices forged in and exclusively meaningful to the Christian West.[40] In the early modern phase of

Europe's encounter with Guinea, Christian travelers relied on feudal terms like *lords*, *vassals*, and *fiefdom* to map the landscape, define jurisdictions, and determine sovereignty. Aware of Christian military limitations vis-à-vis Guinea's inhabitants, Cà da Mosto understood that his commercial success depended on the region's sovereigns who lorded over merchants and markets. Europe's fifteenth-century travel accounts magnify this awareness through a relentless quest to identify Guinea's diverse sovereigns.[41] In the process, these accounts constituted states, nations, and ethnicities by means of a purported sovereign's territorial jurisdiction and commercial resources—a decidedly Christian European formulation of polity and corporate consciousness. As Europeans mapped Guinea's landscape in accordance with their cultural lexicon, a ruler's sovereignty played a decisive role in defining those individuals whom Europeans could legitimately deport as slaves.

After obligatory port calls on Madeira and the Canary Islands, Cà da Mosto's caravel entered "Ethiopia." From his initial landfall to his final departure from "the Gambra" the following year, the Venetian compiled an immense array of ethnographic details. Far from being random descriptions of the landscape and the inhabitants' customs, Cà da Mosto's gaze structured the narrative in accordance with classical and Christian tropes of *civitas*. Though purporting "to understate [rather] than to relate anything which exceeds the truth," Cà da Mosto inscribed what his Christian-European-merchant-male prism enabled him to see. The "truth" of his vista largely centered on lordship, the *polis* (city or town), and mercantile activity. Well into the early modern period and beyond, these and related sociocultural manifestations—including faith, language, writing, and money—represented tangible expression of Western Christian civility. As Europeans encountered "strange new places," the *ethnos* of each region and the state of their *civitas* emerged via this grid. Of course, "Europe," especially an imagined classical Greece and Rome, constituted the norm against which Christians judged "communities," thus ensuring that in rare instances non-Christians could match them in achievement but never actually surpass them. In Christendom's ethnocentric universe, a non-Christian community's best image constituted an imperfect replica of European institutions and cultural practices. Ironically, the naturalized standards European travelers upheld as universal composed an ideal rarely if ever manifest in Europe itself.

In the course of Europe's early modern period, the search for sovereigns and walled cities motivated commercially minded travelers who longed for specific commodities. Though Cà da Mosto referred to the reigning elite he encountered as "lords" and "dukes," the Venetian clearly discerned subtle distinctions between law-based lordship and dominion contingent on might. The latter represented uncivilized and impoverished despots prone to slave raiding and warfare and their destabilizing effects.[42] In the Canaries, Cà da Mosto found lordship in such disarray that he linked the islands' inhabitants to brute animals. The native inhabitants and their rulers accordingly resided in a civil state akin to nature since the "princes" did not reign on the basis of "natural law, where the son succeeds the father, but by right of the strongest." The physicality of the rulers' dominion and the absence of primogeniture led the heirs of the purported nobles to "continually wage war among themselves, slaying each other like beasts." These "beasts," of course, lacked iron weapons, clothing, "walled houses," and the essentials of civility. For Cà da Mosto it seemed fitting that they flourished "in caves or caverns in the mountains" confined to a simple diet of "barley, flesh and goats' milk of which they have plenty, and on fruits, particularly figs."[43] But nothing underscored the Canary Islanders' baseness more than their lack of attire. "They always go naked," Cà da Mosto insisted, though "they anoint their bodies with the fat of goats mixed with juice from some of their herbs." Recalling that this custom "thickens the skin," Cà da Mosto implied that the Canary Islanders transformed themselves into a distinct race.[44] Manifesting this distinction through their bodies, the Canary Islanders could easily "leap from rock to rock, barefooted like goats," convincing Cà da Mosto "that this is the most dexterous and nimble race in the world."[45] For Cà da Mosto, like many of Europe's early modern travelers, the body often manifested distinct customs. Even after his encounter with "the Blacks of lower Ethiopia," whose bodies fascinated him to no end, Cà da Mosto positioned the Canary Islanders on the lowest rung of his genus.

Though their primary commercial center was "not walled," even the Arabs Cà da Mosto encountered at Arguin Island occupied a more elevated status than the Guanches (inhabitants of the Canary Islands). Irrespective of their faith, which made them "very hostile to Christians," Cà da Mosto valued the Arabs' ability to cultivate and raise livestock. He also approved of their attire—a salient index of civility—noting that the residents "wear white cloaks edged with a red stripe," though "they always go barefooted." This deficiency and the lack of wine, which confined Arabs to drinking "the milk of camels and other animals," represented glaring cultural omissions. But the Arabs "trade for merchandize" more than compensated for these deficiencies.[46]

The trade in "slaves . . . from the land of the Blacks and gold *tiber*" truly distinguished the Azanaghi (now the Sanjalas) as sovereign if not superior people who warranted peace with Christians and a permanent Portuguese presence. In his description of the Azanaghi, Cà da Mosto also acknowledged the explicit relationship between commercial potential and peace. He noted how "before this traffic was organized, the Portuguese caravels, sometimes four, sometimes more, were wont to come armed to the Golf d' Arguin, and descending on the land by night, would assail the fisher villages, and so ravage the land. Thus they took of these Arabs both men and women, and carried them to Portugal for sale."[47] Peace descended, however, once the Portuguese understood the region's commercial importance. Having acquired human chattel and gold dust from the region's inhabitants, Cà da Mosto reported how Dom Henrique "will not permit further hurt to be done to any." Under the pretext of "not yet being firmly attached to the tenets of Muhammad," Infante Henrique protected the Azanaghi, though in actuality he sought to preserve the lucrative trade. Cà da Mosto remained less sanguine about the Azanaghi, whom he describing as having "no lords among them, save those who are richer." "These are honoured and obeyed to some degree," he observed but then rehearsed Zurara's sentiments that they represented "very poor people, liars, the biggest thieves in the world, exceedingly treacherous."[48] Despite these alleged characteristics, Cà da Mosto retracted his earlier condemnation, noting that Azanaghi "are the best slaves of all the Blacks."[49] In making this assertion, Cà da Mosto, like countless other travelers, perpetuated the ambiguity surrounding the nascent Moor-black African divide.

In line with Zurara, Cà da Mosto attempted to distinguish between Moors and black Africans. As his caravel entered the kingdom of Senega, Cà da Mosto observed how he finally reached "the beginning of the first Kingdom of Ethiopia."[50] Fourteen years after Antão Gonçalves's momentous raid, Cà da Mosto underscored the growing subtlety that Europeans discerned among "Ethiopia's" inhabitants. "We sailed on our journey to the river called Rio de Senega," which according to Cà da Mosto represented "the first river of the Land of the Blacks." As he crossed the territorial divide, Cà da Mosto discerned corporeal distinctions between Moors and black Africans, which subsequent Europeans harnessed to their most recent incarnation of the master-slave divide. For the time being, Cà da Mosto rendered physical differences culturally meaningful by relating them to topographical fertility, political organization, and commercial potential. The Venetian observed that "this river separates the Blacks from the brown peoples . . . and also the dry and arid land, that is . . . dessert, from the fertile country of the Blacks." Cà da Mosto noted that this distinction "appears to me a very marvelous thing" and then described how "beyond the river all the men are very black, tall and big, their bodies well formed; and the whole country green, full of trees, and fertile: while on this side, the men are brownish, small, lean, ill nourished, and small in stature: the country is sterile and arid."[51] Cà da Mosto associated topographical bareness with a social formation's lack of complexity. This explained why the desert dwellers, for instance, "have no religion, nor any natural king." Though acknowledging "that they recognize and do reverence to one more than to another," Cà da Mosto insisted that such individuals "are not lords."[52]

In Senegal, according to Cà da Mosto, "the country of these first blacks," a king named Zuchalin (Zucolin) reigned over the Jolofs. Though identifying Zuchalin as the Jolofs' sovereign, Cà da Mosto cautioned his readers that this prince lacked true dominion since "there are divers lesser lords . . . [who] agree among themselves, and set up a King of their own." Zuchalin's tenure, therefore, rested on being "pleasing to the said lords." Thus, Cà da Mosto concluded his inaugural remarks about the "first Kingdom of Ethiopia" with the observation that sovereignty in Guinea was far from being "stable and firm."

For Cà da Mosto, this lack of stability reflected the kingdom's improvised state and the absence of walled cities. "You must know," Cà da Mosto noted, "this King is lord of a very poor people, and has no city in his country, but villages with huts of straw only. They do not know how to build houses with walls: they have no lime with which to build walls, and there is a great lack of stones."[53] With a kingdom structurally deficient and devoid of a mechanism that could guarantee the sovereign a fixed revenue, Cà da Mosto insisted that slave raids represented the Jolof monarch's only recourse. "The King supports himself," Cà da Mosto maintained, "by raids, which result in many slaves from his own as well as neighbouring countries." Though Zuchalin employed some chattel "in cultivating the land allotted to him," Cà da Mosto noted how he sold most to the Arabs and the neighboring Azanaghi "in return for horses and other goods" but also to "Christians, since they have begun to trade with these blacks."[54] Christians, in other words, legitimately acquired their chattel via the transgressions of Guinea's sovereigns. Symptomatic of the predatory but weak monarchy manifest in "lower Ethiopia," the slave trade simply shuttled individuals that infidels and pagans deprived of their freedom into Christian hands. In fact, Cà da Mosto absolved Christians for acquiring slaves since they bore no actual responsibility for enslaving sovereign subjects. This responsibility resided with the "negro chiefs" who incessantly warred against one another.[55]

Critical of Zuchalin and "the lords of the country," Cà da Mosto concluded that the inhabitants of Senega acted in such an abhorrent manner as
do people who exist "without laws." Since the Jolof sovereign relied on slave
raids to obtain revenue, the rule of law represented a distant reality limiting
the kingdom to trafficking in human chattel. As "great liars and cheats" prone
to war and polygamy, Cà da Mosto insinuated that the "kingdom of Senega"
constituted an unstable domain devoid of all but slaves. For these reasons, Cà
da Mosto made haste to the "country of Budomel," where "a notable and an
upright ruler, in whom one could trust" presided.[56] Entering "the land of
Budomel" where slaves, like in the "kingdom of Senega," constituted the
sole commodity, Cà da Mosto nonetheless felt confident enough to contract
trade and discard his cargo of "Spanish horses," woolens, and "Moorish silk."
Trade flourished in a stable context, imagined and real, in which local sovereigns could on the basis of their hegemony protect the new arrivals from
Europe. Budomel, in contrast to Zuchalin, could be trusted since his authority offered Christians greater security.

    Despite his favorable initial impression of Budomel, Cà da Mosto later
amended this assessment on the grounds of "what I was able to observe of this
lord, and his manners and his house."[57] Manifesting a dearth of civility—
cities, stone houses, and wealth—the material state of Budomel's kingdom
tempered Cà da Mosto's initial exuberance, leading him to make a general
pronouncement about lordship in Guinea. "I saw clearly that, though these
pass as lords, it must not be thought that they have castles or cities. . . . The
King of this realm had nothing save villages of grass huts, and Budomel was
lord only of a part of this realm—a thing of little account. Such men are not
lords by virtue of treasure or money, for they possess neither . . . but on account of ceremonies and the following of people they may truly be called
lords: indeed they receive beyond comparison more obedience than our lords."[58]
In contrast with the discrete manifestations of *senhorio* (lordship) in Christian Europe, Cà da Mosto ascribed more ephemeral and despotic qualities to
Guinea's sovereigns. This explains Cà da Mosto's recurring observation that
Guinea's sovereigns "are not lords by virtue of treasure or money." In making
this assessment, Cà da Mosto implied that Christian lords had evolved from
relying on naked violence in order to acquire revenue. But even as the ancestral embodiment of the European secular states emerged from the territorial
monarchies of the twelfth century, Christian lordship still derived its authority from ecclesiastical rituals while relying increasingly on temporal trappings,
including taxation to bolster royal authority. Despite his keen ethnographic

gaze, Cà da Mosto, like other Christian observers, confused form with content. Indeed, at the very moment that Cà da Mosto sought to identify Guinea's sovereigns and discern the basis on which their dominion rested, Europe's monarchies drew on more ecclesiastical rituals and pomp as they asserted their absolutist authority over their jurisdictions and subjects.[59]

While Guinean sovereigns' impoverishment prompted Cà da Mosto to question the extent of their dominion, the pomp and elaborate rituals surrounding rulers left him with no doubt. Cà da Mosto often insinuated that these sovereigns' authority resided in the ornate ceremonies and kingship performances. After staying with Lord Budomel for a brief stint, Cà da Mosto declared that "such lords as he . . . display much ceremony." Deeply impressed by the reverence that Guinea's inhabitants extended toward their sovereigns, Cà da Mosto described an audience in minute detail. He intoned that "however considerable he who seeks an audience may be, or however high born, on entering the door of Budomel's courtyard he throws himself down on his knees, bows his head to the ground, and with both hands scatters sand upon his naked shoulders and head. This is their manner of greeting their lord."[60] According to Cà da Mosto, respect and especially fear made all subjects obsequious. He added,

> No man would be bold enough to come before him to parley, unless he had stripped himself naked save for the girdle of leather they wear. The client remains in this posture for a good while, scattering sand over himself; then, without rising but groveling on hands and knees, he draws nearer. When within two paces, he begins to relate his business, without ceasing to scatter sand, and with head bowed as a sign of greatest humility. The lord scarcely deigns to take notice of him, continuing to speak to others: then, when his vassal has done, he replies arrogantly in few words: thus by this act he shows much haughtiness and reserve.[61]

By these symbolic means, Guinea's sovereigns extracted a reverence from their subjects that verged on tyranny and terror, thus enabling the despots to ruthlessly maintain their hegemony. Justice in Guinea was swift and arbitrary and always raised the specter of enslavement. "Thus it appears to me," Cà da Mosto observed in relation to Budomel, "his power exacts obedience and fear from the people by selling their wives and children."[62] Asserting that the enslavement process resided in Guinean sovereigns' hands, Cà da Mosto insinuated that dominion in "the land of blacks" was totalizing since the king alone determined his subjects' status. Cà da Mosto then surmised how "if God himself came to earth I do not think that they could do Him greater honour and reverence."⁶³

Cà da Mosto left "Terra de Budomel" in search of that "kingdom called Gambra," where former inhabitants of the region who now resided in Portugal "said there was gold in large quantities." As he traveled to the southern edge of the "empire of Melli," he identified a paucity of despotic lords. Further south, Cà da Mosto found Cabo Verde's gulf "inhabited by two races, the one called the Barbazini, the other, Sereri," where sovereignty's absence was intentional. "They have neither king not lord of their own," Cà da Mosto declared, but "they will not recognize any lord among them, lest he should carry off their wives and children and sell them into slavery, as is done by the kings and lords of all the other lands of the negroes."⁶⁴ Since despotism resulted in slavery, Cà da Mosto attributed the lords' absence to resistance on the part of the Barbazini and Sereri. Kingship's rapacious nature, in other words, represented the true threat to Guinean inhabitants' liberty. But enslavement not only reflected the sovereigns' avarice. In the Gambia, Cà da Mosto's informants told him that the people rarely left their domain "for they are not safe from one district to the next from being taken by the Blacks and sold into slavery."⁶⁵ By representing Guinea's inhabitants as the culprits, Cà da Mosto absolved his fellow Christians from having violated canon law, which expressly forbade the enslavement of the *extra ecclesiam*. Nonetheless, the political disputes and greed that rendered Guinea an ominous landscape for the inhabitants proved quite propitious for Christians seeking human chattel. "These negro chiefs," Cà da Mosto observed, "are continually at war, the one with the other, and also frequently with their neighbors."⁶⁶ From such conflicts, however, the Portuguese derived their chattel.

Mindful of the political landscape and the diverse ways in which despotic rule fueled chattel slavery, Cà da Mosto favored diplomacy and solicited ties with local sovereigns. As an astute merchant, Cà da Mosto knew that in this allegedly volatile political context, Christians needed alliances with Guinea's powerful sovereigns to obtain the objects of their desire. Even after the inhabitants of the Gambia had repeatedly attacked his caravel and his advance party's canoe, Cà da Mosto instructed the crew to avoid armed conflict at all cost. "Because we had come thither to trade in the country peacefully and with their approval," Cà da Mosto insisted that it "would be more fittingly accomplished by tact than by force."⁶⁷ Following several deadly and near fatal skirmishes, Cà da Mosto—through his interpreters—finally initiated a dialogue with the Gambia's defensively minded inhabitants.[68] Informing his adversaries that "we were men of peace, and traders of merchandize" who maintained "peaceful and friendly relations with the negroes of the Kingdom of Senega," Cà da Mosto petitioned for peace with sundry gifts. On presenting the trifles, he asked his nemesis "to tell us in what country we were, what lord ruled over it, and the name of the river."[69] Through diplomacy and the standard ethnographic refrain "who were the lords of that country," Cà da Mosto underscored an opinion common to early modern Europeans travelers: Guinea's sovereigns represented the most effective conduit for trade.[70]

After his turbulent search for "el Dorado," Cà da Mosto finally landed in the Gambia. He immediately attempted to discern the Gambia's political morphology on which trading would rest. Trade in general but the slave trade in particular brought Guinea's diverse polities into relief. With his interpreters' assistance, Cà da Mosto queried a local resident about the Gambia's social structure. Cà da Mosto recalled how "at last I ascertained that this was the land of Gambra, and that the principal lord was Farosangoli." "This Farosangoli," he ascertained, "was subject to the Emperor of Mellie, the great Emperor of the Blacks, but nevertheless, there were many lesser lords who dwelt near the river."[71] Anxious to trade, Cà da Mosto opted to meet Batimaussa, one of the "lesser lords" who resided nearby, sending an advance party that included an interpreter and the local informant ahead "with a present" accompanied by an elaborate message. Premised on the perceived relationship between sovereignty and trade, the message for Lord Batimaussa magnified Portugal's recognition of African sovereignty. "He was to say," Cà da Mosto recalled, "that we had come by command of our lord King of Christian Portugal, to establish firm friendship with him and to inform him that if he had need of the products of our country, our King would send them to him each year."[72] Even before ascertaining Batimaussa's or Mali's emperor's strength, Cà da Mosto as a merchant sailing under the banner of Infante Henrique adhered to the protocol that the Portuguese extended toward Guinea's sovereigns. Irrespective of the imperial tenor of *Romanus Pontifex*, Dom Henrique clearly had instructed his subjects about the appropriate protocol, while some intuitively knew to acknowledge the sovereignty of Guinea's lords.

The incessant search for Guinea's sovereigns, the language and enactment of protocol, and the desire for treaties belie the idea that Portugal's sovereigns perceived Guinea as *terra nullius*. Trade in a land without sovereign power was at best precarious for it did not offer the securities and certainty preferred by merchants. The respect for sovereignty brings the morphology shaping

Portugal's fifteenth-century trade in Guinea into focus while underscoring the
ways in which the rule of law forged the early modern slave trade. Despite—or
perhaps because of—the alleged despotic nature of sovereignty in Guinea,
the Portuguese accorded the lords in the "land of the Blacks" diplomatic
recognition. Symbolizing the feudal corporate structure informing the early
Guinea trade, the Portuguese vis-à-vis this gesture ascribed Guinean inhabitants' distinct juridical identities. By deploying a feudal corporate structure in
their encounter with Guinea, the Portuguese imposed specific subjectivities
on the region's inhabitants that had been implicitly framed around the concepts of sovereignty or the lack thereof.[73] Intended for the regulation of Christians, the very terms of this corporate structure became the referents whereby
Europeans inscribed Guinea's inhabitants into the colonial and diasporic archives. Trade then and now brought nations and polities into relief. Those
without resources lacked representation, sovereignty, and by implication a
history. The Portuguese deemed sovereignless subjects as objects for enslavement.
Since the enslavement process resided in the hands of Guinea's sovereigns,
even vanquished subjects passed into Portuguese hands already transformed
into the sovereignless. This then would explain the incessant Portuguese focus
on wars, raids, and Guinea's inhabitants enslaving one another.

In 1455, at the time of Cà da Mosto's first voyage to Guinea, the Portuguese had introduced a corporate structure in "Africa's" northwestern regions
rich in the commodities that they desired. "You should know," Cà da Mosto
informed his readers, "the said Lord Infante of Portugal has leased this island
of Argin to Christians [for ten years], so that no one can enter the bay to trade
with the Arabs save those who hold the licence."[74] Having obtained a royal
monopoly, Dom Henrique issued licenses with the intention of structuring
the Guinea trade and restricting Christian interlopers from establishing a foot-
hold in Guinea. By erecting a permanent Christian settlement on Arguin Island, Dom Henrique sought both to restrict Christian rivals from the Guinea
trade and to redirect the infidels' inland trade into Portuguese hands, thereby
eliminating the North African middlemen. Interestingly enough, the presence
of Portuguese "factories where they buy and sell with the said Arabs who come
to the coast to trade" underscores the transforming effects of trade. Even in
the Reconquista milieu and with heightened anxieties about the "Turk," the
Portuguese willingly traded with infidels. By the time that Cà da Mosto landed
on Arguin Island, the Portuguese transformed the meaning of Arab from "perfidious infidel" into a synonym for trader. Earlier, Cà da Mosto had even
noted how years after the initial Portuguese expeditions in Guinea, Christian

explorers conceived of the Azanaghi, purportedly the "best slaves of all the Blacks," as traders and potential Christian converts. As the Portuguese ventured south into the "land of the blacks," their trepidation about the Azanaghi ceased since as traders and potential Christians they constituted allies. "For some time," Cà da Mosto observed, "all have been at peace and engaged in trade." Thus, he observed, the Infante forbade his subjects from enslaving or in any way harming the Azanaghi.[75] Trade, a meta trope for *civitas*, distinguished enemies from allies, black Africans from Moors, the savage from the semicivilized, dark from light, and the slaves from the free. While this Manichaean ontology informed successive Portuguese encounters with Guinea's inhabitants, alterity's object remained anything but fixed.

*   *   *

With Dom Henrique's death in 1460, the monopoly reverted to the Portuguese Crown. During the next twenty-one years (culminating with Dom Afonso's death), the Portuguese steadfastly explored and traded in Guinea, though they did so without their earlier zeal. Preoccupied with possessing the Castilian throne and his North African conquests, Dom Afonso (1449–81) distributed the monopoly between his son, João, and several court favorites.[76] Two years after Henrique's death and twenty years after the Portuguese ventured beyond Cabo Blanco, they had christened the region south of the Senegal River to present-day Sierra Leone the "Guinea of Cape Verde." The Portuguese quickly established their administrative center, Santiago, in the Cape Verde archipelago, from which they explored but only occasionally settled the mainland of the Upper Guinea Coast—a riverine region named the "rivers of Guinea" that soon constituted Portugal's principal source for trade, including human chattel.[77] Despite Dom Afonso's lack of interest in Guinea, he and his representatives asserted royal authority over the concessions his predecessors had granted Dom Henrique, most notably in matters related to justice.[78] In subsequent grants and privileges, the Crown restricted the beneficiaries' juridical authority, which had been part of the "colonial concessions" extended to explorers, discovers, and conquerors. According to one astute student of colonization, sovereigns during the early modern period consciously sought "to reduce that autonomy to proportions fitting the prestige and authority of the centralized and increasingly absolute monarchy."[79] Yet even during Dom Afonso's reign, some notable exceptions prevailed. On June 12, 1466, Afonso granted Cape Verde's Christian inhabitants a royal charter over the Guinea trade except Arguin Island. Declaring that "people are unwilling to go live there, unless they are given very wide privileges and franchises," Afonso bestowed "civil and criminal authority over all the Moors, black and white, free and captive, and over all their descendants, who are in the said island, although they be Christians."[80] While granting his vassals juridical authority "over all the Moors, black and white, free and captive," Afonso carefully worded this privilege to apply only to those "who are in the said island." By his actions, Afonso did not arbitrarily extend his dominion over Moors. Moors and black Africans either willfully attached themselves to Cape Verde's nascent Christian *república* or represented enslaved persons who on the basis of their sovereignless subjectivity entered Christian dominion. This grant did not imply that the king's authority or that of his vassals extended to the mainland or its inhabitants. This decree and the grant bestowed on Fernão Gomes (who in exchange for a monetary settlement along with the annual exploration of an additional hundred leagues of the Atlantic littoral received exclusive rights over the Guinea trade) magnifies Portugal's regulatory practices aimed at safeguarding their monopoly from Christian interlopers. Such practices assumed greater importance in the last decades of the fifteenth century but especially during the War of Spanish Succession (1475–79) in which Afonso played a prominent role.

In the context of Hispania's escalating rivalry complicated by the Castilian succession dispute, Dom Afonso's Castilian opponents carried their conflict into Guinea, thereby defying *Romanus Pontifex*. As they transgressed the bull granting Portugal a commercial monopoly with Guinea, the Castilians directly challenged papal authority. The Castilians did not, however, intend to question papal jurisdiction in temporal affairs.[81] Instead, they objected to the opinion that favored Portugal at their imperial expense. Yet in violating Portuguese dominion, the Castilians relied on the same corporate structure to facilitate trade in Guinea. In doing so, they also discerned a difference between Guinea's sovereign and sovereignless inhabitants.

On August 19, 1475, the year in which Dom Afonso invaded her kingdom, Queen Isabel informed her subjects that she and her predecessors had "always enjoyed the right of the conquest of the parts of Africa and Guinea, and levied the fifth on all merchandise which was purchased in the said parts . . . until our adversary of Portugal intruded by engaging as he has . . . to the great damage and detriment of my said kingdoms and my revenue therefrom."[82] To stem the loss of revenue and recover possession of the "said parts," Isabel ordered Seville's customs officials not to permit anyone to "go or send, any person or persons with your ships to the said parts of Africa and Guinea, without license and specially command of my said receivers . . . under the penalty of death."[83] With this dire proclamation, Isabel reinaugurated Castile's imperial rivalry with Portugal for dominion of the Atlantic world.[84] Though twenty years earlier Pope Nicholas V had adjudicated in Portugal's favor, a defiant Isabel asserted Castile's claims to Guinea and various Atlantic islands, risking papal excommunication as she transgressed the *Romanus Pontifex*.

Before Isabel's ascendancy, Castilians had, however, repeatedly violated the papal accord by trading with Guinea's inhabitants. Andalusians frequently sailed "to the coasts of Africa and Guinea, whence they were in the habit of bringing back negro slaves, of which there were a great number in this city [Sevilla]."[85] While Andalusian raids bore the same effect as Queen Isabel's stated policy, Castile's sovereign did not condone the interlopers' activities. Since *cabalgadas* (unsanctioned raids against the sovereign's enemy) diverted the revenue that she badly needed, the phenomenon actually undermined her sovereignty. Yet Isabel's concerns with raids extended beyond the domestic domain since interlopers invariably threatened both Crown revenue and the imperial diplomacy on which the Guinea trade rested.[86] As she sought to wrest the Guinea trade from the Portuguese, Isabel insisted that the rule of law, embodied in the Crown and its legitimate representatives, should regulate relations between Castilians and Guinea's inhabitants. Despite the civil war pitting her against Afonso, Isabel refused to suspend the letter of the law governing Portugal's relations with Guinea. In fact, when her subjects raided the Guinea coast, undermining both the Portuguese monopoly and the sovereignty of the Niumi kingdom, Isabel acted swiftly to curtail this diplomatic breach.

On May 15, 1476, Queen Isabel chastised residents of Santa Maria and Palos, port towns on Castile's Atlantic coast, for having successfully launched a slave raid against Guinea's inhabitants. In her communiqué, Isabel condemned the raid as a "disservice" and "contrary to the letters and commands" that she had issued. By pointing to the *cabalgadas'* unlawfulness, Isabel unwittingly valorized Portugal's claims to the Guinea trade and used language implying that Guinea's monarchs did, in fact, manifest sovereignty. "It is said," Isabel intoned, "that they took one, who is called the king of Guinea and certain other person, relatives and dependents of the said king of Guinea."[87] In order to repair the breach, Castile's beleaguered monarch commanded her subjects to turn over the captured Niumi king and his entourage to her representative in Seville. Even though Castilians with the Crown's consent "were in the habit of bringing back negro slaves," Isabel, like her Portuguese counterparts, distinguished among Africans on the basis of sovereignty. Niumi's king and his subjects represented sovereign subjects with whom the Portuguese and, therefore, Castilians contracted treaties and trade. Though at war with Portugal, Castile's monarch respected and embraced the protocol distinguishing the sovereign from those who legitimately could be enslaved. War in Hispania did not suspend recognition of dominion elsewhere. Sovereignty transcended Iberia's Catholic divide. For centuries, Christian theologians, canonists, and Europe's nascent lawyers postulated that *senhorio* (*señorio* in Spanish, literally *lordship*) represented a universal phenomenon. As Christians, Castilians shared the conceptual grid enabling the Portuguese to discern sovereignty, dominion, and the related *ethnos*. A consensus among early modern authorities restricted slavery to those devoid of dominion.[88] In contrast, the Niumi, with whom the Portuguese had a trading relationship, represented sovereign subjects, a juridical status that in early modern Christendom proved translatable across vernacular nationalism's nascent absolutist divide.[89]

The royal decree issued on March 4, 1478, underscores Queen Isabel's objection to *cabalgadas* and similar such transgressions. But even after Palos's residents had mounted an unlawful raid against Niumi, two years later Isabel declared that "it is my pleasure that the inhabitants of the said town of Palos and of other parts of my kingdoms, who by my command thus go to Mina."[90] Though she had condemned their unsanctioned raid, Isabel now granted Palos's residents permission to carry on a lawful trade with Mina's inhabitants irrespective of the Portuguese sovereign's objections. Even as this and similar decrees threatened Isabel and her subjects with excommunication as it violated *Romanus Pontifex*, these proclamations paradoxically manifest Castile's scrupulous attention to the rule of law. In this instance, Isabel and Ferdinand sanctioned the violation of papal authority and Portugal's imperial dominion as long as their approval was forthcoming.[91]

Several years after the Niumi incident, Isabel and Ferdinand sued their Portuguese rival for peace, acknowledging his suzerainty over the Guinea trade.[92] Hispania's Catholic divide radically subsided when both sides signed the treaty of Alcàçovas (1479) granting Portugal exclusive access to Guinea in exchange for Castilian possession of the Canary Islands.[93] Presented with this treaty, Pope Sixtus IV issued the bull *Aeterni Regis* on June 21, 1481, that both sanctioned the Catholic sovereigns' accord and affirmed *Romanus Pontifex*.[94]

While imperial rivalry sporadically plagued Iberia's dominant households until signing the treaty of Tordesillas (a 1494 accord prompted by Columbus's discovery in which Castile and Portugal conceded to each other distinct ocean lanes), Portugal's dominion over the Guinea trade was firmly secured in the last decades of the fifteenth century.[95]

In 1481, two years after the signing of the treaty of Alcàçovas and the year of Dom Afonso's death, the newly crowned João II directed royal interest toward Guinea. During his fourteen-year reign (1481–95), João actively pursued the Guinea trade, notably gold, slaves, ivory, and pepper, even as he exhorted his vassal to find the coveted route to India. Despite the law and accords, Castile's imperial ambitions alarmed João—ever vigilant about protecting his patrimony, Portugal's imperial claims, and the lucrative Guinea trade. He thus ordered the construction of several forts along the Guinea coast, designed to protect Portugal's commercial interests. During this period, João also aided a deposed Jalof prince who had advanced Portuguese interests. As with all requests for military assistance from Guinea's rulers, João made conversion a precondition for such aid. Finally, João added "Lord of Guinea" to his list of titles while instructing his vassals to employ *padrões* (stone markers)— as opposed to the wooden crosses previously used—thereby signifying his kingdom's preeminence and permanence in Guinea.

Though João's actions and ambitious policy had an imperial air, the Portuguese presence, in the guise of *padrões*, forts, and permanently stationed soldiers, relied on the hospitality extended by Guinea's diverse lords. In practice their dominion over territory, subjects, and trade remained steadfast. As the rightful landlords, the Portuguese had to propitiate and respect—ritually and in actuality—Guinea's sovereigns if they hoped to trade. As a precondition for imposing a corporate structure on their end of the Guinea trade—in this instance *padrões*, forts, and soldiers that kept other Christians at bay—the Portuguese, including João II, had to respect the sovereignty of Guinea's lords. The chronicles, narratives, and official reports of the period reveal how the Portuguese continued to respect Guinea rulers' dominion, even during João II's ambitious reign.

Months after his father's death, João launched a new policy toward Guinea. Against the advice of his royal council, he ordered Diogo de Azambuja to erect a fort "in the land through which ran the traffic of gold." As commander, Azambuja led the most illustrious gathering of Portuguese nobles ever to land in Guinea. João also placed at his vassal's disposal a sizable fleet carrying one hundred craftsmen and five hundred soldiers. Two *urcas* (supply ships) loaded with "hewed stone, tiles, and wood, as well as munitions and provisions" accompanied the caravels. After stopping in Cape Verde for additional provisions, this massive Portuguese expedition anchored on January 19, 1482, adjacent to Mina's coast. After scouring the coast for a suitable site, Diogo de Azambuja elected a spot subsequently christened as Duas Partes (literally, *two parts*). João Bernandes, a factor trafficking in gold with the local sovereign before the expedition's arrival, advised Azambuja on how best to proceed with João's plans. Just hours after their arrival, Azambuja instructed the factor to ask the local king, the Caramança, for an audience and permission to land. In doing so, he acknowledged the Caramança's territorial jurisdiction. Even after a decade of contact, Mina's sovereigns exacted respect for their position as lords and landlords—respect that the Portuguese customarily accorded.[96] Rigid adherence to a diplomatic protocol facilitated trade but also implicated the Portuguese in local kingship rituals directed at both the strangers and the local inhabitants.

The next day, after the Caramança granted Azambuja's request, the Portuguese expedition "landed . . . smartly dressed but with hidden arms in case of need."[97] The diverse rituals, pomp, and cultural displays surrounding Azambuja's landing and his subsequent interaction with the king offer invaluable evidence that the Caramança insisted that the strangers from the sea respect his dominion. Of course, the Portuguese commander complied. Portuguese protocol, in fact, offered the Caramança this assurance, ritually and rhetorically, thereby acknowledging that even in João II's reign the Portuguese did not think it possible or even feasible to usurp Guinean sovereigns' authority. On landing, Azambuja ordered his men into formation as he approached a large tree on which he planted his sovereign's insignia. Following this act of possession designed for the consumption of subsequent Christian arrivals, the Portuguese expedition said mass before a makeshift altar whereupon they proceeded to eat.[98] Afterward, the carpenters erected a platform on which the noblemen assembled in their finest clothes and most elaborate jewels, accompanied by trumpeters and drummers. Meanwhile, the soldiers stood in formation, marking a path from the hastily constructed scaffolding in the direction of the Caramança's village.[99] Soon thereafter, the lord Caramança arrived in a procession accompanied by an escort of nobles and servants.

Following gestures of peace and goodwill, Diogo de Azambuja addressed the Caramança through an African interpreter "familiar with the language," whom a previous Portuguese expedition either captured or purchased.[100]

Azambuja informed the king that his lord knew of the "good treatment" that the Caramança extended toward "his vassals, who were accustomed to come to trade there." According to Azambuja, such goodwill convinced João to "secure peace and friendship; in such a way that in that place rather than in any other of that territory there might be made, and should be, a permanent centre for much, very rich merchandise." Wanting the Caramança to interpret João's offer as both beneficial and desirable, Azambuja intoned that "other kings and lords of that land . . . had already with many gifts begged him for such a centre the king, his lord, did not wish it save with them, because of the great trust and good credit, which already he specially reposed in them."[101] Though initially hesitant to allow the construction of a permanent structure, the Caramança consented after Azambuja's subsequent appeal during which the commander extolled João's commercial and military strength.

Yet in granting João's request, the Caramança insisted "that peace and truth must be kept." If the Portuguese acted to the contrary, the king declared before the assembled crowd "they would cause more harm to themselves than him." Caramança then warned Azambuja that at the slightest breach, he and his subjects would abandon and thereby isolate the Portuguese. This stern counsel underscored the Caramança's awareness that he wielded dominion vis-à-vis the Portuguese. By expressing it openly, the king displayed his authority for both his subjects' and the assembled Portuguese. Perpetuating the ritual the next day, Azambuja sent the Caramança and his nobles gifts representing both tribute and rent "which was to be given to them first before all else to ensure their goodwill." Unfortunately, the trader João Bernaldez did not deliver the goods before the Portuguese laborers broke ground. This oversight elicited a hostile response from the Caramança's men who lashed out against the Portuguese, ultimately forcing them back into their boats. "Learning from the interpreter that the main cause of the tumult of the negroes was that they had not received the gifts as expected," the Portuguese commander acted swiftly and decisively. Azambuja doubled the size of the gift that João Bernaldez was to deliver but not before publicly chastising the factor for his delay. By these actions, calm prevailed. The Portuguese commander then personally proceeded to break ground without further incident. Twenty days later, the Portuguese raised the walls around their newly erected tower and houses. In keeping with João's imperial pretense, Azambuja named the fortress O Castello de São Jorge da Mina in honor of St. George, Portugal's patron saint.[102] With the castle's defenses in place, Azambuja dismissed most of the expedition while remaining on the el Mina coast for more than two-and-a-half years,

supervising the gold trade while presiding over the erection of gallows and a
pillory. On March 15, 1486, with these symbols of his dominion in place, João
II granted São Jorge a municipal charter "with the privileges and preeminences
[sic] of a city," simultaneously adding "Lord of Guinea" to his titles.[103]

Such acts, of course, symbolized dominion. But Portuguese tribute payments, which continued well into the sixteenth century, tempered João's imperial claims.[104] Though royal officials served justice in the confines of São
Jorge da Mina, they generally applied it to the Portuguese and the occasional
Christian interloper from Europe. As subjects of their kings, Mina's indigenous inhabitants wielded immunity from Portuguese law. While the occasional slave, who by definition constituted a deracinated subject, felt the sting
of the lash, the Portuguese viewed most Africans, including the Christian converts, beholden to local laws. An incident involving Afonso de Albuquerque
forty years after the erection of El Mina represents a notable exception. In 1523,
a year after Albuquerque's appointment as commander of the city of São Jorge
da Mina, João III warned his subordinate that his zealous actions constituted
"a matter very prejudicial to our interest." The king ordered his commander
to moderate his tone and desist from administering physical punishment, but
"should they deserve punishment, they are to pay a fine to that church, or
something similarly adequate." Though the Portuguese sovereign referred to
Albuquerque's victims as "our vassals," thereby subject to his justice, he noted
that their strategic importance warranted patience not punishment. As Christians, João III insisted, "they must be defended, protected and instructed,
and not banished."[105] Highlighting Portuguese dominion over free persons of
African descent in Guinea, this incident stands out as an exception. After
all, as Christians, those Africans owed allegiance to Christ's nearest representative. In this case, that meant Portugal's sovereign and his representatives on
the spot.[106]

Perhaps the Christian inhabitants of the indigenous village constituted a
juridical oddity, having discarded their preexisting residential ties. As Mina's
residents, they were subject to Portuguese laws even though the Portuguese
Crown paid the local king rent for using his land. Merchants the world over
established the precedents for this phenomenon whose logic continues to inform the existence of embassies in the context of international law. By means
of this exceptional incident, we glimpse a distinct manifestation of the subjectivities that the Portuguese accorded to the persons of African descent.
Alongside the savage-to-slave trajectory, a parallel circuit of meaning, derived
from feudalism and Christianity, constituted Africans as "vassals," "knights,"

"friends," and even as "brothers." Such terms highlight favorable Portuguese perceptions of Guinea's inhabitants, but also much more. The very rhetoric identifies a representational domain whereby the Portuguese ascribed diverse subjectivities to Africans—a status encumbered by both privileges and obligations. Attention to such language tempers perceptions of João's imperial pretension and precluded Guinea from being defined as *terra nullius*. Sovereignty prevailed in Guinea, and those who lost it, according to the various merchants, officials, and chroniclers, could find blame in the region's rapacious kings.

Even Portugal's sovereign João II acknowledged that Guinea's lords had standing in the realm of nations. The protocol, courtesy, and military assistance he extended to "Prince Bemoy," the deposed Jolof ruler, magnifies this recognition. In 1488, soon after the Abyssinian priest Lucas Marcos left his court, "another Ethiopian" delegation landed in his realm. On learning of Bemoy's arrival, João instructed his officials to escort the "prince" and his entourage of nobles and relatives to an estate just beyond Lisbon. There in the town of Palmela, the Jolof delegation received Portuguese attire and horses in anticipation of their audience with João. João de Barros recorded that "he was treated in every respect as a sovereign Lord, accustomed to our civilization, and not as a barbarous Prince outside the Law."[107]

In their reception at court, both the king and queen extended Bemoy the highest honors of state. They commanded Francisco Coutinho, Count of Marialva, to escort Bemoy to the court in the company of noblemen. According to Barros, Portugal's sovereigns greeted Bemoy's arrival with "great ceremony and pageantry, each of them with their household: the King in the state room on a high dais with a canopy of rich brocade, accompanied by the Duke of Beja, D. Manuel, brother of the Queen, counts, bishops, and other notable persons; with the Queen were Prince Afonso her son, and many noblemen of the Court and their ladies in ceremonial dress." On entering the stateroom, João ventured in Bemoy's direction, and Bemoy, in turn, assumed a prostrate position at the Portuguese king's feet, "making as though he took the earth from under them and threw it over his head in token of humility and obedience." Moved by this display, João motioned Bemoy to stand while he walked back and leaned on his throne, a ritual gesture in its own right. Then João instructed the interpreter that Bemoy should state what brought him to Portugal. Barros observed that Bemoy delivered his speech with such poise and elegance that "he did not seem a negro, but a prince worthy of all respect."[108] Evidently, João thought so as well. Though João made Bemoy's Christian conversion the condition for military assistance, he eventually placed twenty caravels at the Jolof sovereign's disposal. The expedition ended in failure, however, since the Portuguese commander Pedro Vaz da Cunha coldly assassinated Bemoy on the Guinea coast. But this episode, filled with the ceremonial affairs of state, underscores how even João II, the purported "Lord of Guinea," recognized that the laws of nations extended to the region's actual rulers.

The year 1488 marked a turning point for João's Guinea policy for reasons other than Bemoy's death and the ill-fated Portuguese mission to establish an additional fort. Bartolomeu Dias's circumnavigation of Guinea in 1488 channeled Portuguese attention back to the objective that led them into the South Atlantic—India. The Portuguese maintained their interest in Guinea, but the principal focus shifted to India. Columbus's landfall in 1492 truly signaled India's ascendancy in the Portuguese imagination. The naming of Cabo de Boa Esperanca (Cape of Good Hope), in fact, brings India's prominence into focus. Duarte Pacheco Pereira, who greeted Dias on his return, related how when Dias "saw that the coast here turned northwards and northeastwards towards Ethiopia under Egypt and on to the Gulf of Arabia, giving great hope of the discovery of India, [he] called it 'Cape of Good Hope.'"[109] Even the kingdom of Kongo's earlier discovery in 1483 by Diogo Cão could not sustain Portuguese interest in Guinea. In fact, the placing of *padrões*, which João inaugurated with Cão's 1483 voyage, came right before the Portuguese shift in focus.[110] Conceived as signs of possession, the *padrões* eventually just served as wayside markers for the route to India until interest in Guinea, especially the slave trade, again increased in the second half of the sixteenth century. For the Portuguese, the Kongo's commercial limitations were symptomatic of those regions discovered during João's reign. "It so happens," Pacheco Pereira lamented, "that in the part discovered by the most serene King John the country from Cabo de Caterina is mostly deserted or if inhabited has little or no trade." Candid about the relationship between commercial possibilities and ethnographic descriptions, Pacheco Pereira remarked that "had it been rich in trade as the preceding region I should have had much greater pleasure in describing the advantages to be derived from it."[111] This link between commercial potential and ethnographic description shaped the Africanist's archive in fundamental ways. The trajectory from sovereigns and sovereignty to trade and then into the historical record represented the standard formula for traveler accounts on Guinea.[112]

Manuel's ascension after João II's death in 1495 marked the official end to Portugal's aggressive Guinea policy. Thereafter, the Portuguese relied on ex-

isting commercial channels until Luanda's conquest in 1575, making Angola
a Portuguese colony.[113] Yet even during João's reign, the Portuguese depended
on Guinea's rulers to facilitate trade. Portuguese acknowledgment of Guinean rulers' dominion accompanied this reliance, manifesting itself in the
elaborate protocols, rent and tribute payments, and adherence to customary
laws. Guinea's rulers insisted on the recognition of their landlord status, along
with desired goods, as a precondition for trade. Portuguese compliance
highlights the existence of sovereign domains in "the land of blacks," which
European merchants and officials alike respected. From this juridical configuration, nonetheless, emerged the sovereignless. They entered Portuguese
possession as slaves but through channels constructed by Guinea's rulers. Even
when travelers reported the existence of cannibals, the penultimate transgression against natural law that sanctioned enslavement by Christians, the Portuguese refused to violate Guinean rulers' domain.[114] Trade, including the slave
trade, represented Guinean landlords' provenance. Thus, in the quest for trade,
the Portuguese invariably sought out the lords of the land.

CHAPTER 6

Trade

In 1546, the Dominican theologian Francisco de Vitoria, though gravely "ill," entertained a query about the slave trade.[1] Fray Bernardino de Vique had written Vitoria as the acknowledged "master" of the School of Salamanca—a loose collection of theologians, both Dominicans and Jesuits, whose moral philosophy (Scholasticism) rested on the teachings of Saint Thomas Aquinas, in which Aristotle's rediscovered writings occupied a central role—with concerns about the trade's legality.[2] "Anyone who takes it upon himself to examine this question of Portuguese trading [*contratación*]," conceded Vitoria, "will find no lack of things to criticize." Candor aside, Vitoria assured "your Reverence" that the traffic in Africans did not violate Christian precepts. Addressing Fray Bernardino de Vique's specific concerns, Vitoria not only acknowledged the trade's vibrancy in fostering slavery "here in Spain" but obliquely alluded to African sovereignty.[3] The correspondence, in fact, referenced the symbiosis of African and European royal justice whereby Portugal's king governed aspects of the trade beyond the "justice" and "laws" of the "barbarians." Even though the exchange between Fray Bernardino and Vitoria touched on the issue of legality, both men insinuated that the trade had instilled a novel and, by implication, a more voracious commercial sensibility throughout the Iberian Peninsula. Deliberating over the purchase and to a lesser extent the ownership of slaves "here in Spain," the clergymen concurred in their critique of unruly commercialism.

Vitoria characterized the deceitful practices resulting in capture as a "cowardly ruse," bringing the status of the victims into question. "I can see no justification for considering them proper slaves," observed Vitoria, who then remarked, "I do not suppose this trick is common . . . though it may sometimes have occurred." As for the second concern (the status of captives "enslaved in their own countries in war"), Vitoria simply noted that "the

Portuguese are not obliged to discover the justice of wars between barbarians. It suffices that a man is a slave in fact or in law, and I shall buy him without a qualm." Enslavement, not slavery, was a matter of concern but only if Christians bore responsibility for the very act of transforming a free person into a slave. If "barbarians" alone enacted the transformation—a tacit recognition of sovereignty—then the Christian conscience could rest. Pondering the ethics of purchasing a condemned person, Vitoria stated flatly, "I do good business. . . . In my view he can be considered a slave for the duration of his life." As a rejoinder to Fray Bernardino's final concern ("can we rest easy in conscience on the assurance that the king of Portugal and the members of his Council will not permit unjust trading?"), Vitoria concluded that "Kings often think from hand to mouth, and the members of their councils even more so," yet deception rarely informed the trade. Since African agency—obliquely referenced as "those who were enslaved in their own countries in war" or "in a country where one can be enslaved in numerous ways"—engendered the act of enslavement, Vitoria exonerated both merchants and buyers of slaves. For Vitoria, the issue revolved around the nexus of exchange; slavery did not invite scrutiny.

In voicing his concerns, Vitoria touched on far more than the ways that commercialization fostered novel economic norms. Even if we acknowledge the role that rationalization played in Vitoria's thinking, his alleged ideological subterfuge underscored how enslavement and slavery engaged matters of the realm and thus represented the prince's affairs. As a theologian, and by implication a theorist, he perceived "traffic," "justice," "law," "enslavement," and "slavery" as indivisible. Indeed, Vitoria's pronouncements require us to think broadly about the social order and how the slave trade simultaneously effected change in an allegedly organic universe. In the sixteenth century, both the slave trade and slavery composed more than a commercial phenomenon; engendered by trade but also conquest and defeat, which collectively entailed the regulation of people, the slave trade touched on sovereignty and the loss thereof. For Vitoria and his early modern contemporaries, the shifting origins of the enslaved—a transition from subjects defeated by Christians to persons vanquished by barbarian lords—was accompanied by a critique of commercialization that was associated with the Africanization of the slave trade. Building on the *Etymologies*, the writings of the seventh-century cleric Isidoro de Sevilla, Vitoria saw enslavement through the prism of the Roman experience with "war slavery," whereby "slavery (*servitus*) is named from saving (*servare*), for among the ancients, those who were saved from death in battle were called

slaves (*servi*)."[4] While the Spanish historian William Phillips directs our attention to this genealogy, he overlooks how Vitoria, through his engagement
with classical authorities, conjoined conquest, enslavement, and sovereign
power. For Phillips and other early modern historians, the focus rests on cir-
cumscribing the process of enslavement to commercialization, the singular act
or transaction that made a slave rather than the political histories resulting in
slavery. In doing so, early modern scholars of slavery have taken up a particular genealogy related to slavery: the history of a separation in which the slave
is divorced from the politics informed by war and conquest, thereby enabling
difference and materiality to appear as autonomous, if not completely unhinged, from the very process that deracinated the defeated, making them
into the living death (i.e., diasporic subjects) and slaves. Stated differently, the
economic practice that acquires an ethnic inflection defines early modern
slavery—an institution that has been severed from the political formation.
Though slavery remains associated with such terms as *lord, master, despot,* and
tyrant that carry political valence, scholars of early modern thought and political economy use this language to reference the owner's authority and comment on the coercion required to ensure the institution's productivity. But this
dominion over the slave is decoupled from the working of the *polis.* For this
reason, Italian-, French-, and English-inflected political theory, notably the
contract theorists of the seventeenth and early eighteenth centuries, position
slavery as a form of trade but also as a phenomenon related to the economy
and its productive capacity. Francisco de Vitoria, Domingo de Soto, Tomás
de Mercado, and Francisco Suárez, however, saw matters differently, thereby
pointing us to the overlooked nature of early modern Spanish thought and a
lost genealogy that fused slavery, dominion, and sovereignty. In the face of a
nascent mercantile challenge, Vitoria and his contemporaries sought to shore
up a dominant yet diminishing discourse that underwrote the existing social
order. By sublimating slavery and commercialization, they signified how the
master-slave relation was related to the *oikos* and, in turn, to the *polis,* making
it an indivisible feature of sovereignty tied to the regulation of territory and
its inhabitants.

*   *   *

In the sixteenth century, the regulation of people played a considerable role
in defining sovereignty. As proof, we need only examine Iberian history. Indeed, what are we to make of the fact that King Ferdinand, as opposed to his

wife Queen Isabel of Castile, promulgated some of the most significant legislation related to the establishment of slavery in the Indies, including the royal
sanction in 1518 that allowed for the direct importation of *bozales* (unassimi-
lated Africans) into the New World? In view of the early development of New
World slavery, which saw Amerindians and African-descendant peoples being simultaneously enslaved in the Indies and Iberia before the direct importation of Africans into the Americas and the decline of the indigenous
population resulted in the mid-sixteenth-century Africanization of slave
labor, this question takes on an importance beyond demographics linked to
the economy.[5] Framed exclusively as a Castilian dynamic in which Spain is
synonymous with the Crown of Castile makes juridical sense but seems theoretically and conceptually problematic in view of the fact that Ferdinand
acted as the Castilian regent-sovereign for much of the period after 1497 but
in particular after Isabel's death in 1504. In short, Ferdinand presided over
the earliest developments in the Indies, including its social legislation related
to labor, the establishment of slavery, and the direct importation of enslaved
Africans. As king consort and subsequently regent for his unstable daughter,
Ferdinand may have implemented policy from his perch as the sovereign of
Aragon whose Mediterranean orientation brought a long history of ethnic,
racial, and religious conflict and coexistence to bear that was most notably
channeled through the institution of slavery. Even a cynical reading of this
development cannot obfuscate the link between fiscal policy and monarchial
sovereignty. Since demographics fueled the royal treasury, regulating populations represented an instrument of rule and a feature of sovereign power.

To suggest that population regulation wielded primacy in the framing
of sovereignty positions one at odds with a canonical position in contemporary
political theory. For the French political philosopher Michel Foucault, sovereignty's rationale resided foremost in the dominion over territory. Accordingly,
he notes that "from the Middle Ages to the sixteenth century, sovereignty is
not exercised on things, but first of all on a territory, and consequently on the
subjects who inhabit it. In this sense we can say that the territory really is the
fundamental element both of Machiavelli's principality and of the juridical
sovereignty of the sovereign as defined by philosophers or legal theorists.
Obviously, these territories may be fertile or barren, they may be densely or
sparsely populated, the people may be rich or poor, active or idle, but all these
elements are only variables in relation to the territory that is the very foundation
of the principality or of sovereignty."[6] Eventually, governance superseded
sovereignty, thus shifting lordship's objective to the regulation and control

of the populace. "Well, a new science called 'political economy' and, at the same time, a characteristic form of governmental intervention, that is, intervention in the field of the economy and population, will be brought into being by reference to this continuous and multiple network of relationships between the population, the territory, and wealth. In short, the transition form an art of government to political science, the transition in the eighteenth century from a regime dominated by structures of sovereignty to a regime dominated by techniques of government revolves around population, and consequently around the birth of political economy."[7] Acknowledging that lordship exhibited a new momentum, if not urgency, in the sixteenth century, Foucault focused on the burgeoning volume of "political treaties" concerned with "art of government." "Government as a general problem," writes Foucault, "seems to me to explode in the sixteenth century." Though sovereignty's rationale was largely restricted to territory until the ascendance of governmentality, it presided as the ruling technology over the transition and successive transformations that characterized the early modern period.

Yet it could be argued that Vitoria and his contemporaries, in noting how Africans symbolized the encroachment of a new commercial sensibility—associated with the fungible slave—had already taken up the issue of population as a concern of the sovereign. In the medieval and early modern Iberian world, the presence of Africans and Indians along with Muslims and Jews called forth policies to safeguard the Christian *república* and the king's various realms by regulating the *extra ecclesiam*. In the case of Muslims, Africans, and Indians, they were conjoined as the vanquished, chattel, and subjects while Jews, as aliens, were exiled: in both instances, this comprised the regulation of populations. To view matters in this manner underscores how population control, despite Foucault's claims, was a constitutive feature of *el señorio*, notably imperial sovereignty. Indeed, one of the clearest expressions of imperial sovereignty was how the Spanish monarchy regulated Africans (*bozales* [Spanish], *boçales* [Portuguese]), thereby superseding the master's authority. Early modern sovereignty entailed the regulation of persons and people—including slaves—but it also brought into relief the limits of sovereign power—constitutionalism—that, in turn, bestowed rights on subjects regardless of their status. In expounding on the critique of commercialization, Spanish theologians refuted the nascent specter of Protestant sovereignty only to bring the natural (sovereign) rights of Africans and Native Americans to the fore. But Spaniards and Portuguese did not perceive all natives—African or Indian—as bearers of sovereign rights and categorized those without such rights as slaves. By viewing the slave trade simply as trade, theorists and historians of political thought have overlooked the extent to which the transformation of subjects into chattel mobilized concepts of *dominium* and sovereign power, both of which also occupied a prominent role in key early modern transitions—the narrative of early capitalism, the rise of absolutism, and the emergence of sovereign Protestant polities. Consequently, the political is equated with sovereign power, which like the relation between master and slave found sanction in Roman law; however, until the German political philosopher Georg Wilhelm Friedrich Hegel positioned the master-slave dialectic as the central epic of the political, it remained relegated to the domain of the social in modern European thought. But for Vitoria and his contemporaries, the slave trade, as evidenced by their critiques, touched on human trafficking and, by implication, the political.

*   *   *

A century after the Portuguese, and to a lesser extent Spaniards, had acquired ever more enslaved Africans, the trade Africanized parts of the Iberian Peninsula. In Lisbon alone, Africans numbered 10,000 out of a population of 100,000, while their percentage total (10 percent) was manifest in many of the principal cities and towns of the Iberian Peninsula.[8] Even with such a sizable African presence, the implicit concern of those concerned with *policía* (order) resided with the ways that the trade engendered commercialization— which numerous canonists, theologians, and even popes voiced in the second half of the sixteenth century. As the trade in Africans and remittances of New World gold transformed the Iberian economy, thereby fostering distinctions in consumption, taste, and affect, priests and theologians extolled the virtue of a social order formulated around the symbiosis between *polis* and *oikos*, whereby household dominion prevailed over market relations.[9] In defending an order that seemed to recede as the African presence mounted, Christian commentators referenced how commercialization via the presence of the slave exacted its toll on the social order.[10] Understandably, the critics of commercialization exaggerated the extent of the transformation.

Even after a century of trading in Africans, of transforming people— different yet not avowed enemies—into chattel, to equate this act with the ascendancy of a new commercial sensibility seems exaggerated, if not fantastical. Indeed, this mythic belief informs contemporary histories and representations of the Atlantic slave trade that still privilege a decidedly modern conception of the economy. Within the prevailing formulation of (political) economy, the slave trade along with the *oikos* (economic life) and the commodity, constitute discrete realms of social life. In short, the economy and its constitutive elements—the market and commodities, trade and trading relations, property and private life—are represented as sovereign entities.[11] But the assumption that economic life exhibited complete autonomy belies the historical process whereby "the economic" as a phenomenon was distinguished from and eventually came to triumph over other realms of social life. Attention to the historical process, in this case to the earliest encounter between Africans and Europeans, underscores the manner through which cultural effects linked to "economic" practices inaugurated a transition in and against the very cultural order that organically defined social life. Of course, the pursuit of ascendancy prevailed and so did the threat to the existing order, but commercial hegemony in and over the social domain had to wait (two long) centuries before its triumph.[12]

Commercialization as the vehicle and symptom of this transformation, in that it accorded merchants means and confidence, threatened the sovereign's authority. In the age of absolutism, the slave trade and slavery emerged as sources of real concern for sovereigns and their supporters. In this respect, slavery constituted more than a metaphor referencing social relations among the ancients; slavery afforded nobles and commoners the wherewithal to contest sovereign authority. Since contemporary theorists tend to overlook these vibrant critiques, they have implicitly characterized colonial enslavement as a social phenomenon, the state of exception that did not influence the formation of absolutism. From this perspective, colonial enslavement did not inform the political or shape the early modern history of power.[13] For the reasons outlined above but also owing to the conceptual burden associated with 1492, the concerns about the slave trade along with its acknowledged discourse on African sovereignty—which Vitoria framed as "those who were enslaved in their own countries," "the justice of wars between barbarians," and "those others who are condemned to death"—remain mired in historical neglect. In their deeds and writings, however, sovereigns, theologians, and jurists expressed a different view.

In conceiving of colonial enslavement as a metaphor of human dominance and by configuring slavery solely as a property relationship governed by Roman law, historians of political thought have, in reference to Africa and the black slave, rendered a narrow formulation of "context." Even though some of the most prominent early modern theorists (Francisco de Vitoria and Jean

Bodin) addressed the ways in which colonial enslavement engendered novel social forms and corresponding expressions of the political, historians of political thought have generally elided the subject. In so doing, they not only confine all early modern slaves but particularly enslaved Africans, as property, to the realm of the social, thereby projecting a Kantian formulation of the political onto an earlier era—an era still associated with political Aristotelianism, which valued embodied ethics and the experiential.[14] Slavery rarely figures as a subject in modern political thought, but when it does, the slave generally appears embedded inside the household, which in the modern period remains so thoroughly removed from the public and political realm, thereby according it little role in narratives of territorial conquest. Stated differently, as a form of domesticity and therefore a base matter, modern theorists assign slavery to the domain of the social, which by definition excludes the slave from consideration in the formulation of sovereignty situated in the *polis* or its destruction. What remains in the slave trade's relation to Western power represents little more than an abstracted early modern period tethered to a fabricated *telos*. In other words, we are simply left with a representation of Western power divorced from its past.

By means of their formulations, the theorists who persistently invoke Jean Bodin and Thomas Hobbes—as the architects of absolutism—overlook the ways that absolutism as a theory of sovereign power, as the historian of political thought Julian H. Franklin pointed out years ago, resided in Roman law. In *Jean Bodin and the Rise of Absolutist Theory*, Franklin writes,

> We need only observe that Roman legal concepts, as elaborated by the medieval commentators, had long been accepted by French jurists as the ordinary form of learned discourse. In this process the basic equation of the position of the king of France with that of the Roman *princeps* became the tacit starting point for all reflections. Toward the end of the thirteenth century, the legists had relied on this idea to articulate the independent status of the king with respect to the Pope and German Emperor. According to their celebrated formula, the King of France within his kingdom was its emperor (*Rex Franciae in suo regno est imperator sui regni*). At least in this sense, therefore, he was "absolute."[15]

The very law, as we saw earlier, that scholars of slavery and colonialism insist granted masters an authoritative status over slaves had for centuries legitimized

the French sovereign's claims to imperial status in his domain vis-à-vis the pope
and the Holy Roman emperor. In this respect, the master's alleged dominion
over the slave was analogous to the sovereign's power over his subjects. Stated
differently, Roman law bestowed a common absolutist lineage on both sovereign authority and mastery.

Though lost on contemporary theorists, this shared genealogy underscores
an observation that the sociologist Orlando Patterson made in reference to slavery, noting how "the master-slave relationship cannot be divorced from the
distribution of power throughout the wider society in which both master and
slave find themselves."[16] For Bodin, this realization served as the basis of his
antislavery sentiment. Cognizant that "total power or property in the slave
means exclusion of the claims and power of others in him," Bodin opted in
favor of the absolute sovereign. By means of his critique expressed through
antislavery rhetoric, Bodin voiced opposition to the privatization of power that
in principle and in practice threatened both sovereign authority and the existing social order. Bodin, Vitoria, and their respective followers viewed the
slave trade as the conduit of commercialization threatening their sovereign
and his realm.

In voicing their critique that linked slavery to commercialism, theologians
underscored the ways in which the slave trade (and slavery) figured in the early
modern political imaginary. Simply put, the slave trade represented more than
a "metaphor" that had to await the Enlightenment before emerging as a matter
of philosophical concern. In the fifteenth and sixteenth centuries, the slave
trade facilitated a critique of commercialization on the Iberian Peninsula, but
in relation to Africans, it also brought into relief their natural rights and the
authority on which sovereign rights prevailed. For this reason, we glean how
theologians and jurists used the slave trade and slavery to comment on both
their own social order and the distinct polities that Christians encountered
in the early modern period. The slave trade and slavery carried a larger (political) valence in the early modern period than scholars of thought presently
acknowledge.

Making claims about the early modern era with the future (abolition and
emancipation) in mind has resulted in the conflation of motives. Historians
simply assume that a critique of the slave trade—"this question of Portuguese
trading [*contratación*] will find no lack of things to criticize"—expressed an
abolitionist sentiment. Writing from the vantage point of the early modern
period, one obvious explanation for this intellectual tendency resides in the
reasoning associated with "the problem of slavery in Western culture." But

critique of the trade need not position the individual in the genealogy of abolitionism. Working from this assumption has often foreclosed the possibilities that what modernists identify as "political" and "economic" concerns, as opposed to moral sentiment, informed the critique of the slave trade and slavery. Here the intellectual historian David Brion Davis's masterful *The Problem of Slavery in Western Culture* offers a telling example. "If for some two centuries no Las Casas actively fought for the Negro's liberty," writes Davis, "there were at least a few men who questioned the legitimacy of the African trade." In a description reminiscent of Vitoria's exchange with Fray Bernardino, Davis observed how "by the mid-sixteenth century Fray Domingo de Soto who was a friend of Las Casas, took note of rumors that Negroes were being seized by illicit means. While there would be nothing wrong, he said, with buying men who sold themselves into slavery, one could not in good conscience keep a man who had been born free and enslaved by fraud or violence, even if he had been purchased in good faith."[17] Davis then proceeds to argue that Tomás de Mercado extended Domingo de Soto's critique with the publication of *Suma de tratos y contratos*, which "provided a critical scrutiny of the disruptive effects of American colonization on prices, contracts, and business ethics." "He [Mercado] found," Davis observed, again reproducing the concerns informing the exchange between Fray Bernandino and Vitoria, "that a large number of slaves were being obtained by trickery, force, and robbery. Because the Africans were wild savages their actions were governed by passion rather than reason. The Portuguese and Spanish offered such high prices for slaves that the Negroes hunted each other like deer, raiding villages and kidnapping unprotected persons, even when they lacked the excuse of war. Incited by greed, princes and judges condemned their rivals and convicted countless others on trumped-up charges. Fathers sold their children out of spite or the slightest disobedience."[18]

"Mercado," writes Davis, "anticipated eighteenth-century abolitionists in his conclusions as well as in his descriptions of slaving raids and the Middle Passage." By reading Mercado's writings in this manner, Davis positions him as an ancestor of the abolitionists, thus obscuring how Spain's sixteenth-century commercialization prompted Mercado's critique. Here Mercado's concerns with the slave trade emerge in the context of the shifting economic practices and the emergence of a new economic sensibility in which the slave trade is a metaphor and simultaneously the idiom through which to understand the newly emerged economic relations and practices. What, in short, might be read as a critique of the slave trade is actually a critique of commercialization and the privatization of power, suggesting that the slave trade played a considerable role in the newly emergent early modern economy. Aspects of this critique can be discerned in how Davis frames Mercado's analysis of the slave trade. "While emphasizing that buying and selling Negroes was not in itself illegal, he asserted that the facts of the situation made it impossible to engage the African trade without incurring deadly sin. A buyer of any commodity was guilty of sin if he had reasons to suspect that the commodity was stolen property or that the seller lacked a legal title. And since it was common knowledge that a large proportion of Negroes had been obtained unlawfully, no one could enter into the commerce with a clear conscience."[19]

In ascribing an abolitionist ethos to such sixteenth-century Spanish thinkers as Domingo de Soto, Tomás Mercado, and Bartolomé de Albornoz, Davis offers a stunningly decontextual and ahistorical reading of their respective treatises. By critiquing the slave trade, these authors mounted a systemic attack against the nascent Atlantic complex in which the trade in Africans represented its most tangible manifestation. To conflate this critique with the genealogy of abolition, however, misses the mark and simultaneously illustrates the marginality of Spanish thought at the moment that Davis conceived his study. In light of the undeveloped and peripheral status of Spanish thought, Davis could simply attribute causality to authors and clergy but also theorists of considerable distinction, concerned with critiquing a nascent commercial sensibility and the accompanying privatization of power.

The marginalization of Spanish thought plays a considerable role in explaining how and why this early modern intellectual tradition has been misconstrued. In the introduction to *Spanish Imperialism and the Political Imagination*, the historian of political thought Anthony Pagden offers a sweeping overview concerning the theories and thoughts of the Spanish empire from the sixteenth through the eighteenth century, underscoring several points: early modern European political theorists gave considerable thought to the Spanish monarchy and the Spanish empire, which they configured as the antithesis of liberty and constitutionalism.[20] As a result of the Black Legend, we have equated this critique with writers and polemicists from the Netherlands and England—the Protestants—but Pagden recovers both an earlier and concurrent critique among Italian political theorists. For these theorists, Spain and the actions of its monarchy were a matter of concern that fostered inquiries into the nature and limits of imperial power but also the rights of imperial subjects. These inquiries understandably touched on themes (legitimate authority, tyranny, and the right to resistance) animated by imperial dominion and slavery. Spain's imperial decline in the sixteenth century obscured this vibrant history of early modern political thought since the alleged historical momentum shifted to the French and English Crowns and with it the attention of theorists. The margin of the margins—a deliberately provocative yet apt way of characterizing Iberian thought but also Spain's and Portugal's relation to Africa—has fostered a general negligence about the role of Africans and the slave in Iberian thought. Consequently, at a critical moment in the evolution of power in the West, we are left with an understanding that the most extreme manifestation of dominance—African enslavement—was irrelevant to the narrative of Western power. Yet, even a cursory reading of the existing texts illustrates how Spanish thinkers, though conceiving of Africans as barbarous, naturally assumed that laws, dominion, and civil society flourished in the "land of the blacks."

But for historians of early modern political thought, neither the process of enslavement nor the history of slavery bore any relationship to the unfolding history of power—until the eighteenth century. In the case of the slave trade, both historians of thought and political theorists note how trade in general did not invite consideration in political affairs. In his magisterial study *Jealousy of Trade*, the political theorist Istvan Hont cites Hume's observation: "Trade was never esteemed an affair of state till the last century; and there scarcely is an ancient writer on politics, who has made mention of it. Even the Italians have kept a profound silence with regard to it, though it has now engaged the chief attention, as well of ministers of state, as of speculative reasoners."[21] According to Hont, "Hume was right in stating that it was the insertion of commerce into politics that was the mark of modernity."[22] In view of this claim, as trade emerged as a subject of political affairs, slavery also invited philosophical condemnation as "evil." For Hont and especially for the political theorist Susan Buck-Morss, both trade and slavery emerged in the eighteenth-century philosophical realms as matters of concern.

"By the eighteenth century," remarks Buck-Morss, "slavery had become the root metaphor of political philosophy, connoting everything that was evil about power relations."[23] In drawing on David Brion Davis, Buck-Morss focuses on his claim that "slavery stood as the central metaphor for all the forces that debased the human spirit" but dispensed with his important qualification "for eighteenth-century thinkers who contemplated the subject," suggesting that other thinkers concerned with what "was evil about power relations" may not have considered slavery at all. For Buck-Morss, the claim that "slavery had become the root metaphor of political philosophy" looms large since she is intent on proving that the era's greatest political philosopher, Georg Wilhelm Friedrich Hegel, was intentionally silent on one of the most widely followed and discussed events: the Haitian Revolution, in which the enslaved changed the course of history. My observations here are not intended as a critique of Buck-Morss's brilliant excavation illustrating (the philosopher's radical disavowal) that Hegel could not but know of events in Haiti—events that allegedly influenced his thinking on the subject of power. Instead, I am interested in what Hegel does acknowledge about the relationship between Africans and power.[24] What Hegel underscores, precisely the point overlooked by Buck-Morss, is that despotism as a relation of power represented the greatest evil since it simultaneously engendered slavery and inhibited trade. In other words, despotism, as the modality of African sovereignty, positioned slavery as the workings of power in political, not just economic, thought, pointing back to an earlier genealogy that linked both the process of enslavement and of bondage to the larger social formation. This formulation of slavery echoes Francisco de Vitoria, Tomás de Mercado, Domingo de Soto, and Francisco Suárez, which gets lost in an eighteenth-century temporality rooted in the primacy of materialism that allegedly defined the slave experience and slavery.[25]

From another perspective—the perspective taken here—it could be argued that these claims about the eighteenth century simply reflect how Iberian thought occupies the margins of early modern thought, principally framed around Italy (Niccolò Machiavelli), France (Jean Bodin), and England (Thomas Hobbes). Stated more explicitly, trade and slavery represented a concern of early modern theorists well before the eighteenth century. For reasons that are not merely about national origins, Iberian thinkers and their ideas occupy the margins of European thought, underscoring the unwillingness of scholars and contemporaries to treat slavery, even when positioned in relation to sovereignty, as an important matter of concern. Contemporary theorists of power implicitly yet repeatedly insinuate as much in referencing power but not the theologians who commented on colonial expansion, trade, enslavement, and slavery. As a result, theorists distance and divorce the reality of colonialism and colonial slavery from its earliest encounter with the Christian commonwealth and the resulting relations that allowed early modern Europeans to actualize gains from expansion. "It was the right to new territory and new productive resources, through 'first occupation' or conquest," writes Hont, "which commanded the attention of many natural jurists." But this begs the question in what ways "new territory" acquired value if not through human labor? Here I am not insisting that enslavement and slavery need to be

theorized as distinct domains or apart from the context in which they flourished, but it seems questionable to conceptualize the features of early modern
expansion ("new territories," "new productive resources," "first occupation,"
or "conquest") without acknowledging the implicit relation to labor and enslavement's entanglement with governance. For sixteenth-century travelers—
Vitoria's contemporaries—the relationship between sovereignty, enslavement,
and trade were quite clear.

Hont's and Buck-Morss's assertions aside, the long-standing—three-
century long—disjuncture between colonial enslavement and modern power
warrants scrutiny. The simultaneity of absolutism and colonialism highlights the existence of a new modality of power that triumphed over both a
tradition of rights and legitimate resistance. In narrating absolutism, theorists
point to the sovereign as the source of power who simultaneously transcended
the embodiment of his power, the law. Characterized as the "state of exception," this configuration of power offers a striking resemblance to quintessential depictions of colonialism; the external, territorial locus where the European
presence mirrored the absolute sovereign's relationship to his subjects. The
manifest indifference to examining how the rationality of colonial rule was
expressed under absolutism brings into relief the circumscribed perspective
shaping our formulations of modern power. In this narrative of Western
power, the idea of the historicity of Europe as the sovereign subject of its
own formation—an idea largely associated with the eighteenth century—is
disavowed.

*   *   *

Another way to approach the issue of a transformation is to focus on how contemporary theorists conceive of slavery. Clearly, a modern sensibility governs
representations of early modern slavery, whereby the institution largely figures
as an economic trope. The slave appears as an abject subject under dominion
of the master but now untethered from the *oikos*, which characterized
the ancient and medieval world's instantiation of slavery. In place of
dominion—which linked the slave and slavery to politics—the market and
difference govern the institution. Through this prism, slavery no longer operated under the earlier formulation of power whose genealogy was traceable
to the ancient world. For this reason, when theorists reference the slave, they
depict modern relations in which both the master and the slave struggle for
affirmation as liberal (individual) subjects. This very (modern) subjectivity

informs the sociologist and social theorist Orlando Patterson's description of
the slave. Indeed, Patterson's depiction already embodies the subjectivity of
an individual on whom violence was continually enacted. In this respect,
Patterson—despite his emphasis on enslavement as an act of natal alienation—
configured the slave as an Enlightenment subject—the individual—while
also implicating the master-slave dialect in a drama cast and staged by the Enlightenment: beings conceiving of themselves, their autonomy, and freedom
in terms that always already assumed a form rooted in the temporality associated with the Enlightenment. This obviously represents an ahistorical representation, which has accompanied our general embrace of Patterson's social
death formulation. This realization may surprise—though curiously has attracted little attention—given that Patterson is also the scholar who long ago
claimed that we needed to historicize our representations of slavery and freedom. Contrary to his insistence that we delineate the process of making chattel, Patterson's historicizing does not extend to the Enlightenment temporality
that the slave inhabits. Since a subjectivity rooted in the late eighteenth century
could not have served as the antithesis of the very categories engendered
by the Enlightenment, which includes natal alienation, I would argue that the
dynamic of making a slave in the early modern period demands a distinct history and still requires a theorization. In lieu of such a distinct historical logic
with its accompanying social forms, the dispossessed, uprooted, and alienated
individual—forged in the eighteenth century—remains the universal subject
of the slave past. At its core, the project at hand points to an unacknowledged
and unwritten history in which the subject, the individual, is seen as a process that involves uprooting persons from the only form of sociality, the *polis*—
however conceived—and thereby attending to how the making of a slave as
the progenitor of the modern individual entails an engagement with a more
nuanced story of power with which former selves were associated. To excavate this long-neglected history demands configuring slavery in relationship
to sovereign power. Until such time, we will not have a complicated history
of power in the framing of the African past and in the early modern African
diaspora: such histories are of critical importance in narrating the story of
power. For this reason, I have insisted on bringing sovereign power into our
discussion of the African-European encounter and the history of the African
diaspora, and also to suggest that this history of the state, as one instantiation
of sovereign power, represents a foundational framing for understanding how
the individual (but also the ethnic and the cultural) emerges. Here it might
be useful to recall my earlier claim: the African diaspora has moved away from

its conceptualization rooted in state destruction—an act whereby an external or imperial assault—destroys the polity of another people, thus rendering them stateless beings. The African diaspora, in turn, has become an analytical framing that varies on a continuum of shared consciousness, culture, and racial ancestry, while the state remains noticeably absent. Stated differently, slavery once figured prominently in the discourse on power, yet in its recent history, early modern political theorists conceived of slavery as an economic system and a means for coercing labor, thereby reducing its more complicated relationship to power; even Hegel who repositions the master-slave dialectic back into the realm of power does so around the modern abstraction of the individual embodied in the slave and the master. Early modern theorists and travelers, however, were not in a position to conceive of autonomous individuals and seemed not to have lost sight of the relationship between trade and sovereignty.

*   *   *

In 1508, the year that Duarte Pacheco Pereira published *Esmeraldo de situ orbis* and more than a half century after Cà da Mosto completed his second voyage to Guinea, nine Germans, four Italians, and three Portuguese composed sixteen accounts of the African continent.[26] Despite their varied nationalities, the authors manifested a discursive unity on the purported relationship between sovereignty and trade. For them, the exchange process mediated the Christian encounter with Guinea, representing a discursive prism through which they, as European Christians, located the various nations and their inhabitants in their cosmos. The materiality of trade—symbolizing social organization, cultural development, and *civitas*—constituted the discursive site through which Europe's early modern travelers produced their understanding of Guinea, its polities, and the inhabitants' customary practices. Through the exchange mechanism, they inscribed nations, peoples, and specific traits. By means of exchange, or lack thereof, local historical memory assumed meaning for Christian travelers and guided them in their interaction with Guinea's diverse *ethnos*. Exchange, in short, symbolized the sovereign ethnic nation, the very vessel that manifested history.[27]

For scholars of the early modern African diaspora, the term nation (*nación* in Spanish, *nacão* in Portuguese) poses serious, if not irreconcilable, analytical difficulties. Used as a cultural signifier, the problem resides in discerning the basis on which the collective was constituted. "In its primary form," one scholar remarked, "the nation was recognized by language."[28] In precolonial Africa, as in early modern Europe, the nation symbolized ethnolinguistic boundaries, which often transcended a sovereign's jurisdiction. In fact, juridical and national boundaries rarely overlapped in a neat manner. Cà da Mosto stated as much when observing that various lords and distinct polities existed among the Jolofs. In response to Europeanists' assertions about the association between the early modern nation and the modern nation-state, Africanists insist that such a relationship did not exist in Africa and that this conceptualization is best avoided altogether. Among Africanists, ethnicity—derived from the Greek *ethnos*—represents the preferred reference for cultural collectivities. Ethnicity has, in fact, become the trope of choice for premodern and invariably non-Western peoples whose experiences remain unfettered by a single nation-state. But as one detractor proclaimed, the term gained valence in reference to Africans "because we refuse them the term 'nation,' which we attach to the modern state."[29] Indeed, imaging a premodern collective entity or ethnicity that had, at best, a tenuous relationship with an overarching kingdom, not to speak of nationality or nation-state, remains a pervasive problem. European travelers, as opposed to Guinea's inhabitants, introduced the language and the concepts on which the African archive remains based. While insisting on Guinea's inhabitants' barbarity, travelers like Cà da Mosto rendered *ethnos* into kingdoms and nations resembling those then prevalent in Christendom and now in the West.

At its core, ethnicity constituted a Western product, an effect, in contrast to a definable entity. Still, through discursive repetition, the concept garnered valence in both Europe and Africa, though now its genesis is obscured by the mercantile process, especially the slave trade. As one commentator noted, "The two areas of activity were constantly interacting."[30] In fact, in a trade noted for its shifting specificity, an imagined cultural precision, derived from language and territorial origins, informed the slaver's lexicon. From the 1450s on, traders under the Portuguese banner brought "Guinea" into relief as they encountered and contracted trade with the region's inhabitants. The more highly valued the commodity, the more visible and the more intelligible the nation that produced or sold the item of value. Anchored adjacent from the "river of slaves," Pacheco Pereira, in fact, remarked that "there is neither trade here nor anything else worthy of mention, so that we need not waste time in speaking of it."[31] As Pacheco Pereira ventured eastward beyond the kingdom of Benin, the frequency with which he recorded such comments increased. By the time this intrepid traveler reached the Bight of Biafara, he dismissed entire cultural areas with a wave of his pen, noting that "there is no trade there I will not name them."[32] After crossing the equator, such appraisals represented the norm. Even the kingdom of Kongo could do little to restore importance to the region. Even as the only "country in the whole of Guinea where they know how to make . . . cloths," Pacheco Pereira observed, "we know of no other commerce."[33] The Kongo's importance, as measured by Pacheco Pereira's ethnographic detail, remained of negligible value. Accordingly the "country called Anzica" south of the Kongo resembled "the land of the Moors" in its aridness and lack of fertility. On reaching Guinea's southern desert, Pacheco Pereira repeated his, and others, well-rehearsed descriptions of North Africa, except he identified the dwellers of the southern desert as "negros." "The country is a treeless desert," Pacheco Pereira observed, "containing nothing but sand. There is much fishing inside the bay and at certain times of the year negroes from the interior come to fish here; these make huts of whalebones covered with seaweed and sprinkled with sand and lead a miserable existence."[34] But near the Cape of Good Hope "where Africa ends," even the phenotype of the "negroes" experienced a transformation. Pacheco Pereira thus concluded, "The negroes of this region are heathen, bestial people, and they wear skins and sandals of raw hide; they are not as black as the negroes of the Jalofo, Mindingua and other parts of Guinea. There is no trade here."[35] Pacheco Pereira, like Zurara before him, associated topographical fecundity with human vitality, cultural dynamism, and commercial potential. For him, the desert had nothing to offer.

From Pacheco Pereira's observations, it becomes evident that the Portuguese (and subsequent Christian arrivals) mapped Guinea's landscape according to commodities and their respective value in Europe's expanding mercantile economy. They christened Guinea's topography with such names as the Gold Coast, Grain Coast, Pepper Coast, and Slave Coast. Rivers and other natural formations acquired names like "river of slaves" (*rio dos escravos*) and "river of gold" (*rio d' ouro*). Knowledge about peoples and places only assumed importance in relationship to regional productivity, the desirability of the respective commodities, and the inhabitants' willingness to engage in trade. Trade, in short, materialized nations and made certain languages more audible than others.

In repeated encounters along Guinea's Atlantic littoral, Christian travelers attempted to identify local lords, discern the extent of their jurisdiction, and learn whether they represented vassals of a more powerful sovereign. Cà da Mosto, for instance, simply structured his ethnographies on this formula.

From the Canary Islands to the Gambia region, he initially described the existing forms of lordship and then defined local customs in relationship to ruling practices and rituals. By identifying the existing hierarchy, or lack thereof, Cà da Mosto alerted subsequent European travelers about which areas to avoid. For him, lordship, of course, signified the potential for trade. But he warned his readers that rulers whose authority rested on natural law could not be found. Cà da Mosto accompanied this warning with repeated references to the dearth of towns (especially walled ones), currency, and private property. For Europeans, these represented obvious references to the absence of commercial opportunities. What few opportunities existed resulted from Guinea's chronic warfare, which local sovereigns perpetuated.

With trade as opposed to colonization being their objective, fifteenth-century European travelers discerned and then accommodated themselves to the diverse forms of sovereignty manifest along the Guinea coast. Implicit in their behavior was the recognition that political accommodation facilitated trade. Accordingly, the rule of law, embodied in local rulers, represented the most judicious means to sustain commercial intercourse with Guinea and its inhabitants. By means of Christian Europe's terminology of social stratification, fifteenth-century travelers configured Guinea in accordance with feudal concepts of political dominion. As Europeans secured trade by identifying local rulers, they simultaneously established a discursive domain whereby sovereignty's Janus face rendered persons into slaves.

Identifying local rulers and discerning the rules governing a particular African society subjected European travelers to the vexing task of cultural translation. As they encountered Guinea's inhabitants for the first time, European travelers had to inform themselves of the political practices prevailing along the Atlantic littoral, including the rituals of rule, gift exchanges, and customs that would foster a local sovereign's goodwill. In an encounter in which Guinea's inhabitants insisted on being understood in terms favoring them, European travelers confronted numerous difficulties as they sought to familiarize themselves with dominion in a specific locale and tried imposing their grammar on alien societies. In this encounter, designed to elicit sovereignty so as to facilitate trade, Europeans relied on a plethora of local guides and translators.[36] But in a political terrain characterized by succession disputes, the ascendancy of new dynasties, and periodic wars, these intermediaries still left the political philology of Europeans saddled with a temporary, if not fleeting, quality. As fifteenth- and sixteenth-century European travelers scoured Guinea in search of local rulers who would sanction and protect commercial ties, their understandings of dominion residing in a *polis* often shrouded the discrete meanings through which Guinea's inhabitants represented their polities and political practices. Despite the complexity on the African side, the accounts of this encounter, written for Europeans and generally devoid of relativity, rendered local practices familiar through the concept of sovereignty. By means of this representational practice, fifteenth-century travel accounts initiated the "invention of tradition" long before the nineteenth century.

Epilogue

Performances—largely those referenced in texts (codices, chronicles, and travel narratives)—figure prominently in this study. For this reason, it is fitting that a description of a performance, gleaned while traveling throughout West Africa, introduces the closure.

On January 1, 2011, I witnessed the staging of a durbar in Ouidah, one of Benin's spiritual capitals and the country's "city of historical tourism." Once a notorious port of embarkation on the Slave Coast, Ouidah now carries the title of UNESCO World Heritage Site. But this begs the question: what is the relationship between the slave trade and a durbar? Associated with the theatrics of power and nineteenth-century imperial rule, durbars allegedly did not govern the eighteenth- or nineteenth-century slave trade when Ouidah was a slaving capital. Ceremonies and rituals, though they are not labeled durbars, did, however, structure the African-European encounter and subsequent exchanges through time. Performances always accompanied contact, conquest, trade, or governance, thereby staging human interaction. Associated with the performance of imperial rule, scholars generally relegate durbars to the recent colonial past. But the ceremonial and symbolic staging of power that constituted a durbar was, as we have seen, present in the earliest encounters between Africans and Europeans, representing the ritualized nature of power that fueled the traffic in humans. As symbolic manifestations of power durbars, along with "palavars" (the ritualized dialogue that preceded the transaction in and exchange of goods), are features of the slaving and colonial past and, as the anthropologist Andrew Apter has brilliantly demonstrated, constitutive of the national order of things while figuring prominently in the postcolonial political imaginary.[1] For this reason, I reiterate having witnessed the staging of a durbar in Ouidah, a former capital of the Slave Coast.

January 1, 2011, was a national holiday in Benin—Vodon Day. Banks and administrative offices remained closed. Though the Beninese in the metropolitan center of Cotonou acknowledged the national holiday, the "gran fete" took place in Ouidah. Ouidah was buzzing with visitors, hawkers, and a steady trickle of official dignitaries. The organizers had positioned the ceremonial epicenter of the "gran fete" near the beach along "the route of no return" just meters from the "door of no return." As the dignitaries assembled on the elevated dais before which flew an assortment of national flags (Beninese, French, German, Brazilian, Cuban, and American), they were carefully positioned to the right, the left, or behind the president of the Republic of Benin, including the U.S. ambassador, his cultural attaché, and other members of his staff. Protocol was studiously observed: the Western dignitaries wore formal Western attire, shirts, ties, and jackets: only the American cultural attaché wore African attire. The drama of power was even evident in the seats reserved for Benin's president, who had the most luxurious and comfortable chair in contrast to those of the Western dignitaries to his left and right. But the area reserved for the officials of the republic and the diplomatic core was but one section—the "secular" site—where dignitaries assembled. Directly across from the "secular" authorities' grandstand separated by a stage was the area reserved for the recognized authorities of Vodon. They too sat under a canopy, though not elevated. Instead, they and their splendidly dressed adherents sat in cheap plastic chairs positioned on the ground. Aside from the lavishness of their dress, the spiritual leaders could be identified by the adherents kneeling if not prostrated before them while they remained seated under colorfully decorated umbrellas.

But there was something else quite discernible about the spiritual figures and individuals who could be identified as their seconds: they were almost to the person phenotypically lighter than the crowd that composed the audience and for that matter than most folks in Benin.[2] While their complexion invited attention, so did their composure, especially when compared to a third grouping. This other grouping drew attention for being phenotypically darker than the spiritual leaders under the canopy and therefore more representative of the Beninese that I had been accustomed to seeing. There were, moreover, no women identified in their gathering. The absence of men clad in effeminate attire performing and gesticulating in a highly feminized manner was also quite noticeable. This group, taking up a position on the right of the "secular" officials and to the left of the spiritual officials, was animated, vocal, and resistant to the laments of *merci* from the master of ceremony pleading for silence. Not accorded space under the canopy, they sat directly in the sun around three prominent statues. As spectators and participants awaited the president's imminent arrival, this group grew louder in their defiance, embodied in praise for their leaders and accompanying statues. What meaning are we to derive from the cacophonous assembly? Understandably, among the assembled were distinct crowds with competing claims and symbolic valence who registered their similarities and differenced in embodied form, by means of attire, spatially, and through performance. In the midst of rehearsed difference, not only were sociological distinctions evident; so were the poetics of power.

Throughout this study, I have insisted that representation of power pertaining to the entanglement of early modern Atlantic history and the African diaspora lacks historicity, scope, and nuance. Four centuries of slaving, as a result, have been rendered as a singular phenomenon mediated through liberalism's nineteenth-century prism. Market relations, despite having a history, appear as a transcendent feature of the human experience. The naturalization of commodification and trade nurtures the impression that all societies and their inhabitants' lives revolve around these universals. In the idealized liberal scenario, an unfettered economy fostered the circulation of commerce, thereby ensuring social equilibrium and liberty. Exceptions existed, but where they did, despots prevailed and a curtailed liberty characterized the social order. From the liberal vantage point, African rulers appeared as despots who fueled a morally repugnant and subsequently illicit trade in humans. They embodied the illileral experience defined by tyranny, despotism, and the absence of freedom. Viewing the state of exception as intrinsic to Africa's political culture, the German philosopher William Georg Hegel alongside other post-Enlightenment writers propagated the view that African despotism was the expression of African sovereignty. Fifteenth-century texts underscore how early modern Europeans manifested a different perspective on African sovereignty in the century that followed initial contact. But this earlier and far more nuanced history involving Africans and Europeans constitutes a casualty of liberal historicism. Stated differently, the problem of the "chiefs" arose in the late eighteenth century, becoming a trope for describing African rule throughout the nineteenth century as Europeans and New World blacks ascribed responsibility for the slave trade and slavery to African despots.[3] From this vantage point, colonial rule constituted a civilizing project that undermined chiefly authority so as to curtail the slave trade and African slavery.

The writings of anti- and pro-slavery advocates, active participants in the production of travel writing, engendered the now hegemonic image of the slave trade and slavery. Here African sovereignty and in particular African agency play a critical role in the continuing drama associated with the slave trade. Consequently, African sovereignty found expression in the spectacles, annual fetes, and coronation ceremonies that were central to the prevailing political culture.[4] The drama of kingship was fully on display at the durbars to which Europeans were invited or compelled to attend in hope of having a say in trade relations and the shaping of imperial policy. Many of the travel writers also focused on the link between empire—African empires—and the slave trade so that this alleged connection became a trope of colonial discourse and to this day still shapes narratives of the slave trade.[5] As a result, the slave trade acquired its status as the black man's burden.

Several weeks later—back in Ouidah again—standing in the Museum of Ouidah, I came to the realization that postcolonial, though one might stylize them as neoliberal, durbars conflated the slave trade and colonial rule, thereby condensing the histories of power into a cultural effect in the service of the nation. Durbars, previously associated with colonial rule, now represented a prominent feature of the postcolonial landscape, contributing significantly to the neoliberal "nationalist" project. The museum, housed in the former Portuguese fort, enabled this impression by narrating Ouidah's history in a manner analogous to how nineteenth-century abolitionists characterized the port city, its African hinterland, and the slave trade—the result of savage African despotism. For this reason, despotic Dahomey figured prominently in the history of Ouidah and the slave trade. Dahomey's power manifest in its military might and the tyranny of its ruler shaped the narrative of the slave trade.

*   *   *

Why should such nuances matter to historians of the African diaspora? If we imagine that the history of the early modern African diaspora signifies more than cultural identification, then discerning the earliest genealogies of power assumes considerable importance in the dialectics of subject and subjection that both accompanied and preceded the reigning narrative of economic and racial ascendance that governs the African-European encounter. Narrating colonial enslavement requires an engagement with an earlier idiom of dominance than that associated with the plantation temporality of the eighteenth century. An earlier history of power, in fact, reroutes the narrative of the African diaspora beyond cultural identification and the formation of the individual.

Students of the African-European encounter—whether historians of Africa, European expansion, Atlantic history, or the slave trade—display little nuance with regard to this historical process. In our hands, a secular conception of European expansion overshadows a more complex history featuring competing interests among theologians, merchants, and courtiers. Such histories project the idea of a monolithic Europe in which the making of the West, state formation, and the history of capital transpired well beyond the confines of the Atlantic and the African presence. Simply put, the Europe associated with the transatlantic slave trade represents a secular, singular, and omnipotent entity with a uniform political rationale. In view of this perspective, an earlier genealogy of Europe is lost; one in which natural law, dominion, and civil society extended to barbarians. In tracking this genealogy, we glean the pervasiveness of late modern (eighteenth- and nineteenth-century) representation of the enslavement process and slavery—a depiction that naturalizes the slave both as an economic and abject object subject to his or her master's whim.

It should be noted that contemporary framings of slavery and race as the enduring dilemma of Western culture bring into relief the ur-source of the problem—a liberal triumphal narrative of slavery and its decline. In view of the shifting dialectic between temporality and meaning, it seems reasonable to ponder how one might historicize the slave trade but also the relations of power that shaped it. In begging the question, my intent has resided in discerning how one might engender a more nuanced history of the early modern Atlantic slave trade, a history that transcends the liberal triumphalism of the nineteenth century that to this day frames the African-European encounter as a singular event—the slave trade.

A half-century after Philip Curtin's *The Atlantic Slave Trade: A Census* transformed how scholars write about the history of the slave trade, a voluminous yet vibrant historiography on the trade in all of its facets has come into existence. As a body of work, the slave trade historiography has engendered a revolution in how we think about the African past, both as an autonomous social phenomenon and as a constituent element in the narrative of the West, including Atlantic studies. Specialization and the steady proliferation of subfields, including the Trans-Atlantic Slave Trade Database and the Nigerian Hinterland Project, underscore the depth and sophistication defining the study of the slave trade. Indicative of the trade's historical and philosophical importance, writings on the slave trade memorialize the human tragedy. But as is often the case with romances and tragedies, they assume a transcendent quality when, in fact, the experience, event, or phenomenon embodied the contrary. Curtin confronted this phenomenon in trying to discern the slave trade's demographic realities. In *The Atlantic Slave Trade* he recounts trying to determine the actual number of Africans transported to the Americas only to find himself mired in a labyrinth of citations founded on circumstantial evidence, supposition, and inference but very little by way of facts. Even after the West defined the slave trade and slavery as its moral burden, conjecture rivaled facts in the realm of representation. As in other human tragedies, guilt, anger, and shame kept the scholarly burden of proof—facts—at bay. Since the publication of Philip Curtin's monumental study *The Atlantic Slave Trade: A Census*, numbers, but not the logic of numeracy, animate the dominant historiographical trend in the study of the slave trade. Curtin, building on the mytho-numerical claims of earlier writers, focused ostensibly on trading demographics. In doing so, he chartered the trade's shifting nature through time and space. Subsequent scholars have extended and refined Curtin's considerable findings, but few have ventured beyond the parameters established by his monumental study, which itself operates in the wake of the abolitionists' logic. Scholars exceeding Curtin's conceptual scope, usually other Africanists and historians of Atlantic Africa, tended to analyze the structure of the trade, thereby expanding our knowledge of the African past, but such studies rarely have linked the slave trade and the new modality of power.

NOTES

PROLOGUE

1. "Ceremonial performances," writes the historian Lawrence M. Bryant, "were the heart of political life, and much of late medieval and early sixteenth-century public history consists of chronicles and lists of ranks, meeting places, forms of address, and procedures in a vast number of ceremonial assemblies. Bryant, "Making History: Ceremonial Text, Royal Space, and Political Theory in the Sixteenth Century," in *Changing Identities in Early Modern France*, edited by Michael Wolfe (Durham, NC: Duke University Press, 1997), 65.

2. "In the past decades," writes the historian of political thought Anthony Pagden, "historians have become increasingly concerned with the role played by language in our understanding of social and political life . . . They have all, in different ways and with different ends in view, insisted upon the interdependence of the propositional content of an argument and the language, the discourse, in which it is made. At the most fundamental level such languages will be composed of precise vocabularies, metaphors and topoi, even recognized authorities, all readily identifiable and easily transmitted from one author to another. Such languages are, as J. G. A Pocock says here, 'distinguishable language-games of which each may have its own vocabulary, rules, preconditions and implications, tone and style' which the historian has to learn to 'read.' They are, to borrow a term from Hobbes, 'registers' in which specific kinds of propositions may intelligibly be cast." Pagden, "Introduction," in *The Languages of Political Theory in Early-Modern Europe*, edited by Anthony Pagden (New York: Cambridge University Press, 1987), 1.

3. Fredric Jameson, *The Political Unconscious: Narrative as a Socially Symbolic Act* (Ithaca, NY: Cornell University Press, 1981).

4. The historian Lawrence M. Bryant has written perceptively that "all historians, to some degree, find moments and events, such as assemblies-with-the-king, that they elevate from anecdotal to representational history, fashioning them into symbols that frame their particular narrative of an age. A central historiographical problem concerns the process through which any event first becomes publicized and then is incorporated as a privileged moment in history." Bryant, "Making History," 65.

5. Gomes Eanes de Zurara, *The Chronicle of the Discovery and Conquest of Guinea*, edited and translated by Charles Raymond Beazley and Edgar Prestage, 2 vols. (London: Hakluyt Society, 1896–1899), 51.

6. John K. Thornton, *The Kingdom of Kongo: Civil War and Transition, 1641–1718* (Madison: University of Wisconsin Press, 1983); Thornton, *The Kongolese Saint Anthony: Dona Beatriz Kimpa Vita and the Antonian Movement, 1684–1706* (New York: Cambridge University Press, 1998); Cécile Fromont, *The Art of Conversion: Christian Visual Culture in the Kingdom of Kongo* (Chapel Hill: University of North Carolina, 2014); Alisa Lagamma, *Kongo: Power and Majesty* (New York: Metropolitan Museum of Art, 2015); J. D. Y. Peel, *Religious Encounter and the Making of the Yoruba* (Bloomington: Indiana University Press, 2000); Rudolph T. Ware III, *The Walking Qur'an: Islamic Education, Embodied Knowledge, and History in West Africa* (Chapel Hill: University of North Carolina Press, 2014).

7. Robert Bartlett, *The Making of Europe: Conquest, Colonization and Culture Change* (Princeton, NJ: Princeton University Press, 1993).

8. Toby Green, *The Rise of the Trans-Atlantic Slave Trade in Western Africa, 1300–1589* (New York: Cambridge University Press, 2012).

9. Bartlett, *Making of Europe*; *The Idea of Europe: From Antiquity to the European Union*, edited by Anthony Pagden (New York: Cambridge University Press, 2002).

10. Alexander G. Weheliye, *Habeas Viscus: Racializing Assemblages, Biopolitics, and Black Feminist Theories of the Human* (Durham, NC: Duke University Press, 2014), 2–4.

11. Ibid., 3–4.

12. Paul Gilroy, *The Black Atlantic: Modernity and Double Consciousness* (Cambridge, MA: Belknap Harvard University Press, 1992), ix. The anthropologist Andrew Apter simultaneously offered a similar critique in *Black Critics and Kings: The Hermeneutics of Power in Yoruba Society* (Chicago: University of Chicago Press, 1992).

13. David Eltis, *The Rise of African Slavery in the Americas* (New York: Cambridge University Press, 2000), 1.

14. Eugene D. Genovese, "Materialism and Idealism in the History of Negro Slavery in the Americas," in *In Red and Black: Marxian Explorations in Southern and Afro-American History* (Knoxville: University of Tennessee Press, 1984), 23–52.

15. R. W. Connell, "Why Is Classical Theory Classical?" *American Journal of Sociology* 102, no. 6 (May 1997): 1511–57; Dorothy Ross, *The Origins of American Social Science* (New York: Cambridge University Press, 1991).

16. Eugene D. Genovese, *The World the Slaveholders Made: Two Essays in Interpretation* (New York: Vintage, 1971), 4.

17. Ira Berlin, *Generations of Captivity: A History of African-American Slaves* (Cambridge, MA: Belknap Harvard University Press, 2003), 3.

18. Genovese, *World the Slaveholders Made*, 3.

19. Karl Polanyi, *The Great Transformation: Political and Economic Origins of Our Times*, foreword by Joseph E. Stiglitz and new introduction by Fred Block (Boston: Beacon, 2001 [1944]).

20. Raymond Williams, *Marxism and Literature* (New York: Oxford University Press, 1977), 121–127.

21. Kathleen Davis, *Periodization and Sovereignty: How Ideas of Feudalism and Secularization Govern the Politics of Time* (Philadelphia: University of Pennsylvania Press, 2008), 24–25.

22. Cedric Robinson, *Black Marxism: The Making of the Black Radical Tradition* (Chapel Hill: University of North Carolina Press, 1983), 9.

23. Paul Gilroy captured this "structure of feeling" when professing that "striving to be both European and black requires some specific forms of double consciousness." Gilroy, *The Black Atlantic: Modernity and Double Consciousness* (Cambridge, MA: Harvard University Press, 1993), 1. While writers have for some time explored the dynamic of "double consciousness" invariably framed around black and white, far fewer have taken up the existentialist concern animating the conceptual pairing of European and black. To reduce this to an epistemological concern that simply belongs in the interstice of the postcolonial and the diasporic has obscured, among other things, meaningful distinctions between Europe's "black" immigrant and native-born black Europeans. Gilroy, *"There Ain't No Black in the Union Jack": The Cultural Politics of Race and Nation* (Chicago: University of Chicago Press, 1991 [1987]); Stuart Hall with Bill Schwarz, *Familiar Stranger: A Life Between Two Islands* (Durham, NC: Duke University Press, 2017). Interestingly enough, scholars of medieval and early modern Europe use the term *minority* in reference to "heretics, Moriscos, Jews, lepers, witches," populations native to Christian polities in Europe. David Nirenberg, *Communities of Violence: Persecution of Minorities in the Middle Ages* (Princeton, NJ: Princeton University Press, 1996), 3. *Minority* seems not, however, to include descendants of Africans who, though born in Europe, were defined both as "aliens" and commodities referred to as *negros, negros esclavos (escravos), negros libres,* and *negros forros,* underscoring how long-standing experiences with freedom get subordinated to slave status when representing blackness. Michelle Wright, *The Physics of Blackness: Beyond the Middle Passage Epistemology* (Minneapolis: Minnesota University Press, 2015).

24. Here we might note how the classic materialist narrative, which preceded the discursive framing of modernity, offers the same geography scope and temporal perspective espoused by theorists of modernity. The pioneering Latin American social historian of Peru, Karen Spalding, noted how "the role of the areas outside of Europe in the process of primitive capital accumulation that preceded and laid the basis for the rise of capitalism has been overemphasized, but the wealth garnered from other parts of the world from the sixteenth to the eighteenth centuries in the form of both open plunder and mercantile profits was considerable." Karen Spalding, *Huarochirí: An Andean Society Under Inca and Spanish Rule* (Stanford, CA: Stanford University Press, 1984), 108.

25. Polanyi, *Great Transformation*.

26. Sanjay Subrahmanyam, *Courtly Encounters: Translating Courtliness and Violence in Early Modern Eurasia* (Cambridge, MA: Harvard University Press, 2012).

27. *We People Here: Nahuatl Accounts of the Conquest of Mexico*, edited, translated, and introduced by James Lockhart (Los Angeles: UCLA Center for Medieval and Renaissance Studies, 1993).

28. Marcus Wood, *Blind Memory: Visual Representations of Slavery in England and America* (New York: Routledge, 2000).

29. Davis, *Periodization and Sovereignty.*

CHAPTER 1

1. Richard Hakluyt, *The Principal Navigations, Voiages, Traffiques Discouries of the English Nation Made by Sea or Over Land to the Most Remote and Farthest Distant Quarters of the Earth at Any Time Within the Compasse of These 1500 Years . . .* (London: Imprinted by George Bishop and Ralph Newberie, deputies to Christopher Barker, printer to the Queen's Most Excellent Majestie, 1589).

2. Arthur Helps, *The Conquerors of the New World and Their Bondsmen: Being a Narrative of the Principal Events Which Led to Negro Slavery in the West Indies and America,* 2 vols. (London: William Pickering, 1852), 5.

3. Ranjit Guha, *A Rule of Property for Bengal: An Essay on Permanent Settlement* (Durham, NC: Duke University Press, 1996 [1963]).

4. Arthur Helps, *The Spanish Conquest in America and Its Relation to the History of Slavery and the Government of Colonies* (London: John W. Parker & Son West Strand, 1855), 4.

5. Ibid., 5.

6. Uday Mehta, *Liberalism and Empire: A Study of Nineteenth-Century British Liberal Thought* (Chicago: University of Chicago Press, 1999); Lisa Lowe, *The Intimacies of Four Continents* (Durham, NC: Duke University Press, 2015); Antoinette Burton, *The Trouble with Empire: Challenges to Modern British Imperialism* (New York: Oxford University Press, 2015).

7. A number of scholars of the African diaspora have asserted as much, but James Sweet represents one of the few historians pressing us to actualize this conceptual perspective with regard to the African past. James H. Sweet, *Recreating Africa: Culture, Kinship, and Religion in the African-Portuguese World, 1441–1770* (Chapel Hill: University of North Carolina Press, 2003); Sweet, *Domingos Álvares, African Healing, and the Intellectual History of the Atlantic World* (Chapel Hill: University of North Carolina Press, 2011).

8. "Yet the understanding that 'we' all do 'European' history with our different and often non-European archive," observes the historian Dipesh Chakrabarty "opens up the possibility of a politics and project of alliance between the dominant metropolitan histories and the subaltern peripheral pasts." Dipesh Chakrabarty, *Provincializing Europe: Postcolonial Thought and Historical Difference* (Princeton, NJ: Princeton University Press, 2000), 42.

9. Jorge Klor de Alva, "Colonialism and Postcolonialism as (Latin) American Mirages," *Colonial Latin American Review* 1 (1992): 1–23; Walter D. Mignolo, *The Darker Side of the Renaissance: Literacy, Territoriality, and Colonization* (Ann Arbor: University of Michigan Press, 1995); Fernando Coronil, "Beyond Occidentalism: Towards Non-Imperial Geohistorical Categories," *Cultural Anthropology* 11, no. 1 (1996): 51–87; José Rabasa, *Writ-*

ing Violence on the Northern Frontier: The Historiography of Sixteenth-Century New Mexico and Florida and the Legacy of the Conquest (Durham, NC: Duke University Press, 2000): 16–19; María Elena Martínez, *Genealogical Fictions—Limpieza de Sangre: Religion and Gender in Colonial Mexico* (Stanford, CA: Stanford University Press, 2008).

10. The postcolonial literary critic Gaurav Desai building on the work of the Africanist V. Y. Mudimbe identifies the "colonial library" as "the set of representations and texts that have collectively 'invented' Africa as a locus of difference and alterity." In an effort "to reimagine the colonial library as a space of contestation," Desai posits that "my aim has been to understand the construction of the library and of the colonial process itself as *a complex series of interactions* between colonizers and the colonized rather than as a unidirectional practice." To this end, colonial encounters, performances, dialogues, but also histories and history writing make up the holdings of the colonial library. Gaurav Desai, *Subject to Colonial: African Self-Fashioning and the Colonial Library* (Durham, NC: Duke University Press, 2001), 4.

11. In *Conscripts of Modernity: The Tragedy of Colonial Enlightenment* (Durham, NC: Duke University Press, 2004), the anthropologist David Scott has written brilliantly on the overlapping intellectual-political critique informing C. L. R James's *The Black Jacobins: Toussaint L'Ouverture and the San Domingo Revolution* (New York: Vintage, 1963 [1938]). Scott foreshadows some of the specific concerns animating *Conscripts of Modernity* in *Refashioning Futures: Criticism After Postcoloniality* (Princeton, NJ: Princeton University Press, 1999).

12. The political scientist Cedric Robinson observed how

the construction of periods of time is only a sort of catchment for events. Their limited utility, though, is often abused when we turn from the ordering of things, that is chronological sequencing, to the order of things, that is the arrangements of their significances, meanings, and relations. Increment of time contoured to abstract measure rarely matched the rhythms of human action. . . . It is important to bear this in mind as we seek to come to terms with the Black theorists whose writings and thoughts have appeared primarily in the twentieth century. Their era began with the endings of slavery. They were, it might be said, the children of slaves. The phenomenology of slavery formed and informed them. And in the vortex of its ending, more particularly in the wake of the social forces that compelled new and different situatings of Blacks and others . . . these theorists discovered their shared social and intellectual location or the post-slavery world order. (Robinson, *Black Marxism*, 177)

13. Arguing that feudal differentiation engendered "racial capitalism," the political scientist Cedric Robinson questioned the classical materialist formulation that positioned race as a consequence of capitalist relations. Despite his prescient insight, Robinson seemed wedded to the materialist teleology that equated English capital accumulation as the exemplary form of capitalist development. "We will follow this British trade for the

moment," wrote Robinson "because it seems best documented, because it is so firmly seats slavery in the movement from mercantile to industrial capitalism, and because many of the clearest tracings of a Black radical tradition lead back to it." Robinson, *Black Marxism*, 116.

14. The continuing historiographical salience of Walter Rodney, *A History of the Upper Guinea Coast* is clearly manifest in the following works that extend and nuance his initial contributions. George E. Brooks, *Landlords and Strangers: Ecology, Society and Trade in Western Africa, 1000–1630* (Boulder: Westview, 1993); Rosalind Shaw, *Memories of the Slave Trade: Ritual and the Historical Imagination in Sierra Leone* (Chicago: University of Chicago Press, 2002); Walter Hawthorne, *Planting Rice and Harvesting Slaves: Transformations Along the Guinea-Bissau Coast, 1400–1900* (Portsmouth, NH: Heinemann, 2003); Donald R. Wright, *The World and a Very Small Place in Africa: A History of Globalization in Niumi, The Gambia* (Armonk, NY: M. E. Sharpe, 2004); Green, *Rise of Trans-Atlantic Slave Trade in Western Africa*.

15. Walter Rodney, *A History of the Upper Guinea Coast: 1545–1800* (Oxford: Clarendon, 1970), 117–18.

16. Ibid., 114.

17. Ibid., 118.

18. In a questionable move, Thornton links Walter Rodney with the Eurocentricism of the French historian Pierre Chaunu, who emphatically subscribed to the idea "European domination was founded on European superiority, and whether this was good or bad for people being dominated was not necessarily a relevant point. The history of the Atlantic still ought to be the history of Europeans, and the rest was still only background." On the basis of this characterization of Chaunu, Thornton writes,

> On the whole, Chaunu's analysis does not contradict much of the work of the nationalist historians and their more recent manifestations—dependency theory and world systems analysis, as characterized by the work of such scholars as André Gunder Frank, Walter Rodney, Immanuel Wallerstein, and Eric Wolf. These writers infused the work of the Annalistes with a neo-Marxist focus and reinforced and reiterated the essence of Chaunu's conclusions. However much they were committed to the study of the non-Western world, or however sympathetic they were to its people, they still agreed that the non-Western world, including Africa, had played a passive role in the development of the Atlantic. Although their radical perspective and their advocacy of Third World causes tended to make them sympathetic to Africa, the effect was simply to reinforce the tentative conclusions of the French pioneers that Africa was a victim, and a passive victim at that, for it lacked the economic strength to put up an effective resistance. (John K. Thornton, *Africa and Africans in the Making of the Modern World: 1400–1680* [New York: Cambridge University Press, 1992], 3–4)

19. Thornton, *Africa and Africans*, 4–5.

20. Scott, *Conscripts of Modernity*, 110–11.

21. Ibid., 111.

22. Thornton, *African and Africans*, 6; Paul E. Lovejoy, "Identifying Enslaved Africans in the African Diaspora," in *Identity in the Shadow of Slavery*, edited by Paul E. Lovejoy (New York: Continuum, 2000), 1–29.

23. From its inception, Thornton's argument was already dated since anthropology was experiencing a profound epistemological critique. Indeed, anthropologists continue to ask explicitly under what conditions can their discipline represent the human experiment in the past and the present. This foundational question informs some of the most engaging historical writing on the African past—a past that is explicitly involved with historical representations of Africa that had implications for how the experiences of millions of Africans ensnared in the Middle Passage should be characterized. Anthropologists have also been exploring, perhaps more so than historians, the cultural and social framings of the African past in the Americas. In doing so, they address another concern that Thornton seems only to ascribe as the historian vocation—the careful reading of contemporary sources and primary sources. Historians, it should be noted, are not the only scholars who read sources. Indeed, anthropologists have been far more attentive than historians of the early black experience to engage in source criticism, questioning of the social logic of the text, asking under what circumstances a writer or an archive was produced, and wondering what the intent of the recorder was. As a result, historical anthropologists and ethnohistorians have been at the forefront of the production of knowledge and the relationship between the archive as an epistemological site. Consequently, they have generated some of the most nuanced and complex renderings of social and cultural formations involving Africans in the Americas. For this reason, these scholars are framing questions of creolization, ethnicity, and cultural change in fundamentally transformative ways, pressing us ever deeper into the very production of African history, which, in turn, would shape the formation of social and cultural action in the Americas.

24. Unlike the anthropologists who critiqued their founders and repudiated their colonial foundations, this has not been the case among historians. Historians may not explicitly embrace the most extreme variations of, say, the Dunning School, but the profession implicitly still values the agenda set by scholars of Southern vindication who along with their Northern allies insist on the triumphalist narrative of American history, which always already frames the black experience as an aside in the history of politics, economics, and American democracy. David W. Blight, *Race and Reunion: The Civil War in American Memory* (Cambridge, MA: Belknap Press of Harvard University Press, 2001); Ross, *Origins of American Social Science*; Peter Novick, *The Noble Dream: The "Objectivity Question" and the American Historical Profession* (New York: Cambridge University Press, 1988).

25. The historian Walter C. Rucker illustrates an awareness of this dilemma when he writes, "Missing from most historical analysis regarding the circulation of people, cultures and ideas throughout the Black Atlantic is the notion that enslaved Atlantic Africans originated from particular sociocultural circumstances that shaped their sense of New World identity and consciousness as much as—if not more than—their cultural and

linguistic backgrounds." Rucker, *Gold Coast Diasporas: Identity, Culture, and Power* (Bloomington: Indiana University Press, 2015), 8. João José Reis, *Slave Rebellion in Brazil: The Muslim Uprising of Bahia in 1835,* translated by Arthur Brakel (Baltimore: Johns Hopkins University Press, 1993).

26. Charles Piot, *Remotely Global: Village Modernity in West Africa* (Chicago: University of Chicago Press, 1999).

27. Sweet, *Domingos Álvares.*

CHAPTER 2

1. References from *The Asia of João de Barros* come from the version included in *The Voyages of Cadamosto* (hereafter cited as Barros, *Asia,* and then according to decade, book, and chapter). Barros, *Asia,* 1st decade, book 2, chapter 2, 107. *The Voyages of Cadamosto and Other Documents on Western Africa in the Second Half of the Fifteenth Century,* translated and edited by Gerald Doe Crone (London: The Hakluyt Society, 1937).

2. "The Foundation of the Castle and City of São Jorge da Mina: 1482," in *Europeans in West Africa, 1450–1560: Documents to Illustrate the Nature and Scope of Portuguese Enterprise in West Africa, the Abortive Attempt of Castilians to Create an Empire There, and the Early English Voyages to Barbary and Guinea,* translated and edited by John William Blake (London: Hakluyt Society, 1942), I, 73.

3. Barros, *Asia,* 1st decade, book 3, chapter 1, 117–18.

4. Ibid., 116–17.

5. Greg Dening, *Performances* (Chicago: University of Chicago Press, 1996); Clifford Geertz, *Negara: The Theatre State in Nineteenth-Century Bali* (Princeton, NJ: Princeton University Press, 1980). In offering a genealogy of the "secular," the anthropologist Talal Asad conveys how thinkers from the ancient to the early modern period configured their landscape as being simultaneously inhabited by deities and royalty. Talal Asad, *Formations of the Secular: Christianity, Islam and Modernity* (Palo Alto, CA: Stanford University Press, 2003), 26–36;

6. The Italian political philosopher Giorgio Agamben introduced his most recent work by noting that

> the inquiry into the genealogy—or, as one used to say, the *nature*—of power
> in the West, which I began more than ten years ago with *Homo Sacer,* reaches
> a point that is in every sense decisive. The double structure of the governmental
> machine, which in *State of Exception* (2003) appeared in the correlation
> between *auctoritas* and *potestas,* here takes the form of the articulation
> between Kingdom and Government and, ultimately, interrogates the very
> relation—which initially was not considered—between *oikonomia* and Glory,
> between power as government and effective management, and power as
> ceremonial and liturgical regality, two aspects that have been curiously

neglected by both political philosophers and political scientists. Even historical studies of the insignia and liturgies of power from Peterson to Kantorowicz, Alföldi to Schramm, have failed to question this relation, precisely leaving aside a number of rather obvious questions: Why does power need glory? If it is essentially force and capacity for action and government, why does it assume the rigid, cumbersome, and "glorious" form of ceremonies, acclamations, and protocols? What is the relation between economy and Glory? (Agamben, *The Kingdom and the Glory: For a Theological Genealogy of Economy and Government*, translated by Lorenzo Chiesa, with Matteo Mandarini [Palo Alto, CA: Stanford University Press, 2011], xi–xii)

In the acknowledged shift from an examination into "the nature" to "the inquiry into the genealogy . . . of power in the West," Agamben signifies a conceptual shift toward a more robust engagement with context.

7. Why is the "simulacural regime" (to quote a term employed by the political scientist Achille Mbembe in *On the Postcolony* [Berkeley: University of California Press, 2001]) seen as lacking in substance when postcolonial authoritarians "remained in power throughout . . . through a mix of cunning, ruthlessness and election fraud"? "It was," writes the anthropologist Charles Piot (citing Mbembe), "a state that has been little more than a simulacural regime," subsisting on performance . . . and the staging of dramatic events—false coup attempts, hyperbolic celebrations of national holidays—as much as anything substantial." In viewing performance as a stand-in for something real, it suggests that the state requires substance and structure privileges a rather narrow definition of the state and reduces it to Max Weber's "monopoly over violence." Charles Piot, *Nostalgia for the Future: West Africa After the Cold War* (Chicago: University of Chicago Press, 2010), 3.

8. In the acclaimed *Ceremonies of Possession in Europe's Conquest of the New World: 1492–1640* (New York: Cambridge University Press, 1995), the historian Patricia Seed implicitly disavowed the relationship between the symbolic, Africa, and sovereignty. In so doing, she builds on a more explicitly framed genealogy associated with such modern classics as Arthur S. Keller, Oliver J. Lissitzyn, and Frederick J. Mann's *Creation of Rights of Sovereignty Through Symbolic Acts 1400–1800* (New York: Columbia University Press, 1938). As the political scientist Siba N'Zatioula Grovogui observed in *Sovereigns, Quasi Sovereigns, and Africans* (Minneapolis: University of Minnesota Press, 1996), political science alongside international law and international relations initially configured Africans as the antithesis of sovereigns.

9. Jan Vansina, *Paths in the Rainforests: Toward a History of Political Tradition in Equatorial Africa* (Madison: University of Wisconsin, 1990), 69, 73–77; Shaw, *Memories of the Slave Trade.*

10. Alejandro Cañeque, *The King's Living Image: The Culture and Politics of Viceregal Power in Colonial Mexico* (New York: Routledge, 2004); Barbara Fuchs, *Exotic Nation: Maurophila and the Construction of Early Modern Spain* (Philadelphia: University of Pennsylvania Press, 2009); Carina L. Johnson, *Cultural Hierarchy in Sixteenth-Century*

Europe: The Ottomans and Mexicans (New York: Cambridge University Press, 2011); Teofilo F. Ruiz, *A King Travels: Festive Traditions in Late Medieval and Early Modern Spain* (Princeton, NJ: Princeton University Press, 2012).

11. As religion emerged as a category of social abstraction leading to the decline of magic, the power once associated with rites and rituals became encased in the concept of tradition. Keith Thomas, *Religion and the Decline of Magic* (New York: Charles Scribner's Sons, 1971); and Talal Asad, *Genealogies of Religion: Discipline and Reasons of Power in Christianity and Islam* (Baltimore: Johns Hopkins University Press, 1993). Despite this metamorphosis, one might legitimately ask if and when magic ceased to inform the "political"? Postcolonial states in Africa, for instance, have thrived on the magical. While scholars equate state magic with the simulacrum, as in "simulacural regime" (Mbembe, *On the Postcolony*), the question of its efficacy, if not potency, at least for its citizens cannot be in doubt. Rather than ascribe this to the primitiveness of Africans, we should recall that well into the twentieth century, Europeans perpetuated the belief surrounding the mystery of the African ruler or the "magical state" since they imprisoned and then exiled erstwhile sovereigns like Prempeh I (Asante's ruler) and Agaja (Dahomey's ruler) but also their relatives, including among others Dahomey's sovereign King Guezo's mother. By sending Pempeh I to Elmina and Agaja to Martinique, Europeans were not simply disciplining and punishing recalcitrant rulers but actually removing a competing source of authority by taking hostage, containing, or removing the magic of the ruling dynasty. In doing so, Europeans were not just punishing defeated armies and native subjects; they were securing their own right to rule at a moment when their own polities were still engaged in the politics of magic, even though nation-states, republics, and constitutional monarchies were on the horizon. In other words, Europeans—though disavowing the belief in state magic were enraptured enough to remove the existing authorities and potential challengers to the new (colonial) order. They were not simply acting on the basis of a secularized political rationality. See Burton, *Mission to Gelele*; Vansina, *Paths in the Rainforest* (Madison: University of Wisconsin Press, 1990), 239; Annie E. Coombes, *Reinventing Africa: Museums, Material Culture and Popular Imagination* (New Haven, CT: Yale University Press, 1994); Suzanne Preston Blier, *The Royal Arts of Africa: The Majesty of Form* (Upper Saddle River, NJ: Prentice Hall, 1998).

12. Sidney W. Mintz and Richard Price, *An Anthropological Approach to the Afro-American Past: A Caribbean Perspective* (Philadelphia: Institute for the Study of Human Issues, 1976), and also published as Sidney W. Mintz and Richard Price, *The Birth of African-American Culture: An Anthropological Perspective* (Boston: Beacon, 1992); Ira Berlin, *Many Thousands Gone: The First Two Centuries of Slavery in North America* (Cambridge, MA: Harvard University Press, 2000), 4; Linda M. Heywood and John K. Thornton, *Central Africans, Atlantic Creoles, and the Foundations of the Americas, 1585–1660* (New York: Cambridge University Press, 2007); Niagni Batulukisi, "The Introduction of European Icons in the Lower Congo and Northern Angola," in *Through African Eyes: The European in African Art, 1500 to Present*, edited by Nii O. Quarcoopome (Detroit: Detroit Institute of Art, 2010), 38–47. A distinctive perspective emerges from anthropologists:

see Shaw, *Memories of the Slave Trade*; Andrew Apter, *The Pan-African Nation: Oil and the Spectacle of Culture in Nigeria* (Chicago: University of Chicago Press, 2005).

13. Marshall Sahlins, *Historical Metaphors and Mythical Realities: Structure in the Early History of the Sandwich Islands Kingdoms* (Ann Arbor: University of Michigan Press, 1981); Sahlins, *Islands of History* (Chicago: University of Chicago Press, 1985).

14. In framing the earliest moment of contact between Africans and Europeans, the anthropologist Rosalind Shaw observes how "when Europeans arrived on this coast, then, they did not suddenly propel untouched and isolated African localities into the wide, cosmopolitan world: a translocal sphere of commercial relations was already in place, and it intersected with a trans-Saharan trade that linked three different continents. Instead, the growth of European trade brought about the integration of the upper Guinea coast's existing commercial system with new kinds of transregional circulations. This new integration was, however, to transform the region in unprecedented ways." Shaw, *Memories of the Slave Trade*, 27. While I concur with Shaw's framing, I would suggest that the exclusive focus on the commercial circuit and networks at the expense of the political process, while germane to her project, warrants reconsideration given the vibrant and residual nature of the political process in the process of memorizing. In other words, memory of the political seems much more commonplace than memory of commodification and other economic processes. Rituals often derive from a political process or phenomenon that results in dislocation disruption, including conquest, slavery, and colonialism. While the objectives and the result have economic implications, they are often experienced and represented as political (cultural) phenomena. Barbara W. Blackmun, "Iwebo and the White Men in Benin," in Quarcoopome, *Through African Eyes*, 29–37; Thornton, *Kongolese Saint Anthony*. On the new locus of authority see Rodney, *History of the Upper Guinea Coast*; Robin Law, *Ouidah: The Social History of a West African Slaving Port* (London: James Currey, 2004); Kristin Mann, *Slavery and the Birth of an African City: Lagos, 1760–1900* (Bloomington: Indiana University Press, 2007).

15. Rodney, *History of the Upper Guinea Coast*; Joseph C. Miller, *Way of Death: Merchant Capitalism and the Angolan Slave Trade, 1730–1830* (Madison: University of Wisconsin Press, 1988), 22, 23, 26, 35. For a distinct perspective, see Vansina, *Paths in the Rainforest*.

16. Garrett Mattingly, *Renaissance Diplomacy* (New York: Dover, 1955).

17. A useful foundation for engaging but also theorizing Western forms of knowledge and power as a problematic begins with Megan Vaughan, *Curing Their Ills: Colonial Power and African Illness* (Palo Alto, CA: Stanford University Press, 1991); Chakrabarty, *Provincializing Europe*, 4–5; Scott, *Conscripts of Modernity*, 87–89.

18. Most recently, the anthropologist Irene Silverblatt drew on Weber's configuration of the state in making the case that the sixteenth-century Spanish experience in the Americas inaugurated the modern era. "From the sixteenth century through the mid-seventeenth century," observed Silverblatt, "Spain was in the vanguard of the modern world." Building on Weber's idea that the state was instrumental in ushering forth the modern experience, Silverblatt writes that "we trace our modern beginnings to the effort

of European monarchs to extend their power and consolidate their victories—the initial moments of state-making." Irene Silverblatt, *Modern Inquisitions: Peru and the Colonial Origins of the Civilized World* (Durham, NC: Duke University Press, 2004), 4.

19. In a recent work on postcolonial social formations, the anthropologists Jean and John Comaroff have pointed to the limits of Western theorizations of power but inadvertently also make a case for its universality. In postcolonies, one struggles to locate a theory, concept, or phenomenon that invites comparison with Weber's alleged universalism, although the Comaroffs note "the modernist states put in place with 'decolonization'" represented "the Weberian ideal type always more idealized than typical, always more the object of aspiration than accomplished fact." *Law and Disorder in the Postcolony*, edited by Jean Comaroff and John L. Comaroff (Chicago: University of Chicago Press, 2006), vii.

20. The continuing ease with which scholars of early modern Spain and Latin America conceive and write histories that overlook Africa and Africans beyond the modality of property represents far more than an oversight. See, for instance, Tamar Herzog, *Frontiers of Possession: Spain and Portugal in Europe and the Americas* (Princeton, NJ: Princeton University Press, 2015).

21. In describing the intellectual rationale of his recent study of Nigerian oral traditions, the writer and folklorist Isidore Okpewho directs attention to the marginalization that indigenous narratives of subordination experience in relation to the Nigerian pantheon of "national" narration and inadvertently delineates the chasm that distances the African diaspora and its cultural memories from Nigeria's past—arguably a manifestation of political thought. "I think," writes Okpewho, "it is about time we broke the monotony of our glorification of great 'emperors' and 'warrior kings' of the romantic past and looked at the other side of the equation. What about the peoples they destroyed in pursuit of their greatness: have they no stories of their own to tell? . . . If we continue to sing the praises of successful warmongers and usurpers of other people's lands and wealth, what right do we have to chastise European colonizers who did exactly the same? And do we not see a disturbing resemblance between some of these figures from the 'heroic' past and the ignoble villains who continue to lead their nations to ruin in the Africa of our own day?" Okpewho, *Once upon a Kingdom: Myth, Hegemony, and Identity* (Bloomington: Indiana University Press, 1998), xi. As a theorization of culture rooted in natal alienation, the scholarship on the African diaspora rarely directs its critique at contemporary African narration of the past. Though natal alienation frames her critique, Saidiya Hartman brings scrutiny to elite state formation and its narrative form. See Hartman, *Lose Your Mother* (New York: Farrar & Strauss, 2007).

22. The absence of "concern" represents a constituent feature of the "American dilemma." As the Swedish sociologist Gunnar Myrdal observed in relation to the modern American dilemma, "The result is an astonishing ignorance about the Negro on the part of the white public in the North. While Southerners, too, are ignorant of many phases of the Negro's life, but their ignorance has not such a simple and unemotional character as that in the North." Cited in Gene Robert and Hank Klibanoff, *The Race Beat: The Press, the Civil Rights Struggle, and the Awakening of a Nation* (New York: Alfred A. Knopf, 2006), 3–23.

23. Istvan Hont, *Jealousy of Trade: International Competition and the Nation-Sate in Historical Perspective* (Cambridge, MA: Harvard University Press, 2005).

24. By 1550 enslaved Africans totaled more than 10 percent of the population in Spain. Mark Meyerson, *The Muslims of Valencia in the Age of Fernando and Isabel: Between Coexistence and Crusade* (Berkeley: University of California Press, 1991); David Nirenberg, *Communities of Violence: Persecution of Minorities in the Middle Ages* (Princeton, NJ: Princeton University Press, 1996); Debra Blumenthal, *Enemies and Familiars: Slavery and Mastery in Fifteenth-Century Valencia* (Ithaca, NY: Cornell University Press, 2009); William D. Phillips Jr., *Slavery in Medieval and Early Modern Iberia* (Philadelphia: University of Pennsylvania Press, 2014).

25. Nancy E. van Deusen, *Global Indios: The Indigenous Struggle for Justice in Sixteenth-Century Spain* (Durham, NC: Duke University Press, 2015), 2 and passim.

26. Steven A. Epstein, *Speaking of Slavery: Color, Ethnicity, and Human Bondage in Italy* (Ithaca, NY: Cornell University Press, 2001), xiv.

27. James Muldoon, *The Americas in the Spanish World Order: The Justification for Conquest in the Seventeenth Century* (Philadelphia: University of Pennsylvania Press, 1994), 1.

28. *Slavery and Serfdom in the Middle Ages: Selected Essays by Marc Bloch*, translated by William R. Beer (Berkeley: University of California Press, 1975).

29. Classical distinctions between Greeks and Asiatic barbarians represent a manifestation of difference that inhabits early modern and modern discourses of race. Mary Nyquist, *Arbitrary Rule: Slavery, Tyranny, and the Power of Life and Death* (Chicago: University of Chicago Press, 2013), 26–37.

30. David Scott, "The Paradox of Freedom: An Interview with Orlando Patterson," *Small Axe* (March 2013), 96–242.

31. Marcus Rediker, *The Slave Ship: A Human History* (New York: Penguin, 2008).

32. Christopher Leslie Brown, *Moral Capital: Foundations of British Abolitionism* (Chapel Hill: University of North Carolina Press, 2006), 3. In view of "the abolitionist and post-abolitionist view that chattel slavery is fundamentally unjust," Mary Nyquist writes that "tempted as some may be to understand political slavery as expressive of identification on the part of those who happened to be 'free' with those who were not, the genealogical analysis undertaken here will critique this assumption as an anachronistic projection from later liberalism(s)." Nyquist, *Arbitrary Rule*, 1–3, 20.

33. In relation to the Indies (the New World), the genealogy of this act of displacement can be tacked in Jorge Cañizares-Esguerra, *How to Write the History of the New World: Histories, Epistemologies, and Identities in the Eighteenth-Century Atlantic World* (Palo Alto, CA: Stanford University Press, 2001).

34. Tamar Herzog, *Frontiers of Possession: Spain and Portugal in Europe and the Americas* (Cambridge, MA: Harvard University Press, 2015).

35. Anthony Pagden, *The Fall of Natural Man: The American Indian and the Origins of Comparative Ethnology* (New York: Cambridge University Press, 1982), 32–33. Interestingly enough, the foundational discussions framed around the right to possession and

property rights conveniently overlook an iconic manifestation of property: the enslaved African. Herzog, *Frontiers of Possession*, 17–133.

36. Christopher Schmidt-Nowara writes perceptively that "one must reassess the power and complexity of the Spanish colonial project in the nineteenth century as a backdrop for understanding the dynamics of the growth and destruction of Antillean slavery. . . . Representing nineteenth-century Spain as a feeble relic of its former greatness fails to capture the renewal of the colonial project after the 1820s and the complexity of the bonds linking Spain and its colonies." Schmidt-Nowara, *Empire and Anti-Slavery: Spain, Cuba, and Puerto Rico, 1833–1874* (Pittsburgh: University of Pittsburgh Press, 1999), 2–3. Schmidt-Nowara challenges the optic of scholars whose spatial perspective resides in the mainland where the Spanish presence was increasingly "feeble" and subsequently terminated. Such a perspective offers a narrow configuration of Spain's empire and overlooks the dynamism of the Spanish Caribbean, where modernizing forces had gained a stronghold in the economy, including the plantation sector. The framing of empire as a shifting colonial project ("the power and complexity of the Spanish colonial project") offers an analytic for reconfiguring empire in the course of the eighteenth century, which has been framed as the second conquest. Rather than narrowly configure Bourbon ascendancy in terms of the fiscalization of the state and economy, we might begin to think of the eighteenth-century reforms as a process of state-making born in response to the new demographic and therefore a racial reality (thereby also constituting a new colonial reality signified by the imperial shift that no longer accorded the Indies equivalence with Spain, symbolized in the act of designating former kingdoms [the kingdom of New Spain and the kingdom of Peru] as "colonies." The Bourbon state, consequently, undergoes what the French political philosopher Michel Foucault identified as a shift in political rationale from sovereignty to governmentality where governance grafted itself around the regulation of population rather than the control over territory. Jeremy Adelman, *Sovereignty and Revolution in the Iberian Atlantic* (Princeton, NJ: Princeton University Press, 2009).

37. Robin Blackburn, *The Making of New World Slavery: From the Baroque to the Modern, 1492–1800* (New York: Verso, 1997).

38. Daviken Studnicki-Gizbert, *A Nation upon the Ocean Sea: Portugal's Atlantic Diaspora and the Crisis of the Spanish Empire, 1492–1640* (New York: Oxford University Press, 2007).

39. Sherwin K. Bryant, *Rivers of Gold, Lives of Bondage: Governing Through Slavery in Colonial Quito* (Chapel Hill: University of North Carolina, 2014).

40. Herman L. Bennett, *Africans in Colonial Mexico: Absolutism, Christianity, and Afro-Creole Consciousness, 1570–1640* (Bloomington: Indiana University Press, 2003).

41. In offering a critique of Mexican nationalism and the ways in which historians of Mexico reproduce the violence of exclusion, I have long privileged the colonial as social field for framing the past, the period before the emergence of the Mexican Republic that Mexican nationalists framed as the proto-nation, thereby rendering what I now understand to be a much narrower configuring of the Spanish imperial that in all of its expansiveness always already incorporated forms of difference. To acknowledge this—the

distinction between the colonial and imperial state—is not simply a matter of semantics but entails acknowledging the larger heuristic and epistemological terrain in which the African and black figured well beyond an abstracted demographic presence. Obviously, the state of African history related to nineteenth-century Brazil and Cuba represents an anomaly in contrast to a colonial Latin configured around the viceroyalties of New Spain and Peru. Representative works would include Paul Christopher Johnson, *Secrets, Gossip and Gods: The Transformations of Brazilian Candomblé* (New York: Oxford University Press, 2002); Sweet, *Recreating Africa*; J. Lorand Matory, *Black Atlantic Religion: Tradition, Transnationalism, and Matriarchy in the Afro-Brazilian Candomblé* (Princeton, NJ: Princeton University Press, 2005).

42. Historical representations of the African past cannot simply mimic the demands and conceptual requirements of colonial British America or for that matter those of the United States. Since different cultural logics shaped the engagement with Africa and Africans, the pioneering work on African cultural formation that currently frames eighteenth-century (British) Atlantic studies cannot stand in for the African history of sixteenth- and seventeenth-century Latin America. In making this claim, I am mindful of the peculiar historical moment in British American history and the ideological formation through which the authors framed their questions and answers. The context that, for example, animated the historian Michael Gomez's study of slavery and ethnicity in *Exchanging Their Country Marks: The Transformation of African Identities in the Colonial and Antebellum South* (Chapel Hill: University of North Carolina Press, 1998) is peculiar to a historical moment in American history and the specificity of U.S. black cultural formation in the late twentieth century. For this reason, the political and economic context in which the European-African encounters took place, shaped the slave trade, defined the basis for slavery and the formation of ethnicity and racialized communities has to acknowledge the centrality of capitalism and its social logic. A distinct social logic characterized the early modern period and the various categories we treat as universals: the African, the slave, the slave trade, ethnicity, culture, and so on. African history in the United States, for instance, reflects the specificity of its historical-political formation that simply cannot be imposed universally or seen as relevant in different national-cultural contexts (one might note that even terms such as *Middle Passage* or *African diaspora* reference a specific intellectual formation that is constitutive of American studies). Yet in acknowledging as much, we need also to contend with a nationalist denial: the elite configuration of Latin American history in which the black and therefore the African is not validated or valorized. How then does one engage in conceiving of an African history in and for such a context? Asked differently, what then are the configurations or dominant representations of the African past required for the polities of Latin America?

43. Martínez, *Genealogical Fictions*, 13.

44. "I agree with all of those insisting that colonialism is not homogenous, that we should pay more attention to the diversity of colonial discourses," writes the literary historian Walter Mignolo, insisting that "postcoloniality cannot be generalized, and so forth. It is precisely because I agree with the need to diversify colonial experiences that I am

interested in diversifying the loci of enunciation from where colonial legacies are studied and re-inscribed in the present. It would be misleading to assume . . . that postcolonial theories could only emerge from the legacies of the British Empire, or be postulated as monological and theoretical models to describe the particularities and diversity of colonial experiences." Mignolo, *Darker Side of the Renaissance*, ix. The literary historian José Rabasa writes, "I welcome J. Jorge Klor de Alva's reminder of the different meanings the term colonialism has had in Western history and the fact that we should avoid projecting nineteenth-century British understandings of colonialism and its specific economic structures onto the sixteenth- and seventeenth-century Spanish possession in the New World." Earlier in the same text, Rabasa observes,

> We must keep in mind that the theoretical work in these fields (i.e., postcolonial theory and subaltern studies) has been conceived for the most part with other areas of the world and historical moments in mind. . . . Hence, postcolonialism, understood as a new condition of thought, cannot be equated with the end of a colonial period, nor should the questions postcolonial scholars raise be limited to the specific experiences of nineteenth- and twentieth-century colonialisms. For now, let me point out that this genealogy has had two detrimental consequences for the study of earlier periods in the Americas. At best, Enlightenment forms of producing otherness—for example, the opposition between peoples with and without history, or between peoples in a state of nature and those living under a state—assumes a transhistorical applicability that erases historical specificity. At worst, postcolonial theorists reduce the colonial enterprises before the Enlightenment to crude modes of raping the land—with no coherent civilizing mission worth mentioning. This book argues the exception of the Spanish imperial project, but a similar argument could be made for Portuguese modes of colonization in the early modern period. (Rabasa, *Writing Violence on the Northern Frontier*, 16–17, 18–19)

45. Since the publication of Philip Curtin's monumental study *The Atlantic Slave Trade*, numbers, but not the logic of numeracy, animate the dominant historiographical trend in the study of the slave trade. Curtin, building on the mytho-numerical claims of earlier writers, focused ostensibly on trading demographics. In doing so, he charted the trade's shifting nature through time and space. Subsequent scholars have extended and refined Curtin's considerable findings, but few have ventured beyond the parameters established by his study. Scholars that did exceed Curtin's conceptual scope, usually other Africanists, tended to analysis the structure of the trade thereby expanding our knowledge of the African past. Curtin, *The Atlantic Slave: A Census* (Madison: University of Wisconsin Press, 1969).

46. Tzvetan Todorov, *The Conquest of America: The Question of the Other*, translated by Richard Howard (New York: Harper Perennial, 1982), 5.

47. Writers have long and largely confined this intellectual genealogy to the eighteenth century and the intellectual tradition associated with political economy. See Cañizares-Esguerra, *How to Write the History of the New World*. By no means, however, do most writers attribute Europe's modernity to imperial expansion. In Michael McKeon's magisterial examination of how the private and public domains gradually emerged in the wake of absolutism "devolution" in early modern England, the reader is hard pressed to discern an opening or insights as to how the imperial configured in the cultural formation of the modern. McKeon, *The Secret History of Domesticity: Public, Private, and the Division of Knowledge* (Baltimore: Johns Hopkins University Press, 2005). In offering his critique of the culturally exclusive framing of European modernity in general and its English variety in particular, Paul Gilroy rightly questioned such restrictive hermeneutics. Gilroy, *Black Atlantic*, 14.

48. We may need to be reminded that invocation of 1492 served as a corrective to the framings of commentators of various intellectual traditions (the Enlightenment, Liberalism, and so on) that collectively exorcised an earlier history of imperial expansion associated with Portugal and Spain from the narrative of modernity.

49. Reinhart Koselleck, *Futures Past: On the Semantics of Historical Time*, translated and with an introduction by Keith Tribe (New York: Columbia University Press, 2004); Johannes Fabian, *Time and the Other: How Anthropology Makes Its Object* (New York: Columbia University Press, 1983); J. G. A. Pocock, "Time, Institutions and Action: An Essay on Traditions and Their Understanding," in J. G. A Pocock, *Politics, Language and Time: Essays on Political Thought and History* (Chicago: University of Chicago Press, 1960), 233–72.

50. The political theorist Richard Tuck has written perceptively on the matter of the hegemonic status of the eighteenth-century historical sensibility. "This deeper understanding of the humanist roots of the modern moral science," writes Tuck, "is merely one example of the kind of insight which is available to us once the post-Kantian history is replaced with a pre-Kantian one. The moral theories of the late seventeenth- and eighteenth-century natural lawyers constituted in many ways the most important language of politics and ethics in Europe, influential over a huge area and in a wide variety of disciplines. Their essential unity has been fractured and their character has been misunderstood for the last two centuries; but if we allow ourselves to be guided by 'the history of morality' which they themselves inspired, we can recover a truer sense of what they represented. Not the least important consequence of this is then that we can put into proper perspective the invention at the end of the eighteenth century of the political and ethical theories by which in one way or another we all still live." Tuck, "The 'Modern' Theory of Natural Law," in Pagden, *Languages of Political Theory in Early-Modern Europe*, 118–19.

51. Bennett, *Africans in Colonial Mexico*, 51–61.

52. "Deposition of John Hawkins, of the City of London, Gentleman," in *Documents Illustrative of the History of the Slave Trade to America: Volume I, 1441–700*, edited by Elizabeth Donnan (Washington, DC: Carnegie Institution, 1930), 70.

53. Ibid., 71.

54. Ibid.

55. "Deposition of William Clarke," in Donnan, *Documents Illustrative of the History of the Slave Trade to America,* 69.

56. For conceiving imperial expansion as "privateering," see Heywood and Thornton, *Central Africans, Atlantic Creoles,* 5–48.

57. Karl Marx, *Capital: A Critique of Political Economy,* vol. 1, translated by Ben Fowkes and introduction by Ernest Mandel (New York: Vintage, 1977), 874–75.

58. Ibid., 875.

59. Even in the wake of "discovering" Cedric Robinson's *Black Marxism,* statecraft as opposed to racial capitalism remains woefully underexamined in relation to the earliest African-European encounter and histories whereby the African assumes the status of a commodity.

60. In acknowledging how primitive capital accumulation entails both an economic and a political practice, Marx underscores the symbiosis between the two. Moreover, he points to the social process resulting from this structural transition, thereby reducing the peasant but giving rise to other social entities that occupy specific niches in the transitory economy that existed before the ascendance of capitalism. I am keen on stressing two matters: the acknowledgment of the political process (in the form of an alliance between the absolutist sovereign and the landed gentry, legislation, and so forth) and how in thinking through the genealogy of capitalism, we often lose sight of the existence of previous states of economic and political practice that existed for substantial periods and represented far more than transitory moments, instances, and expressions in the triumphant narrative of capitalism.

CHAPTER 3

1. Gomes Eanes de Zurara, *The Chronicle of the Discovery and Conquest of Guinea,* edited and translated by Charles Raymond Beazley and Edgar Prestage, 2 vols., (London: Hakluyt Society, 1896–1899), 40.

2. Thornton, *Africa and Africans;* Eric R. Wolf, *Europe and the People Without History* (Berkeley: University of California Press, 1982); Immanuel Wallerstein, *The Modern World-System I: Capitalist Agriculture and the Origins of the European World-Economy in the Sixteenth Century* (New York: Academic, 1974), 43–44, 86–89.

3. Robin Blackburn introduced his recent survey of slavery, noting how "this book furnishes an account of the making of the European systems of colonial slavery in the Americas, and seeks to illuminate their role in the advent of modernity." For Blackburn, commercialized nature of the slave systems delineates their relationship to modernity. "They [the European systems of colonial slavery in the Americas] became intensely commercial, making Atlantic trade the pacemaker of global exchanges from the sixteenth century to the nineteenth." In working out his understanding of modernity, Blackburn rarely strayed from commercialization and commodification. Blackburn,

Making of New World Slavery, 1, 4–5. Orlando Patterson's suggestion that "it is not the condition of slavery that must be defined in terms of absolute notions of property, as is so often attempted; rather it is the notion of absolute property that must be explained in terms of ancient Roman slavery" can easily be extended to track and historicize modernity's genealogy. Patterson, *Slavery and Social Death: A Comparative Study* (Cambridge, MA: Harvard University Press, 1982), 32. David Harvey's discussion of modernity, though it varies from the ways that scholars of slavery and colonialism employ it, has significantly influenced my thinking. Harvey, *The Condition of Postmodernity: An Enquiry into the Origins of Cultural Change* (Cambridge, MA: Blackwell, 1990), 11–16. For a rethinking of modernity's scope and nature see Gilroy, *Black Atlantic*.

4. Alan Watson, *Slave Law in the Americas* (Athens: University of Georgia Press, 1989), xi, 2–3, 22–62, 83–86, 91–101, 115–24.

5. For scholars of Latin American slavery, Frank Tannenbaum's *Slave and Citizen* (New York: Alfred Knopf, 1947) represents the classic formulation examining Roman law's influence on the *Siete Partidas* and by implication on the slave experience. Rome's colonization of Iberia and the subsequent Romanization of the Visgothic invaders who ruled over much of the peninsula from the fifth century until the Islamic invasion in 711 CE help explain Roman law's cultural and intellectual legacy, especially after its reemergence in the eleventh century. As Iberia's Christians imposed invented traditions during the Reconquista's long history (732–1492), they consciously embraced practices and customs that purportedly predated both the Emirate and the Caliphate of Córdoba. Because of Constantine's Christian conversion and the imperial support that Christian leaders received from successive emperors, Roman law and Christianity converged ideologically in the minds of many medieval Christians. Joseph F. O'Callaghan, *A History of Medieval Spain* (Ithaca, NY: Cornell University Press, 1975), 46–49, 63–68; *The Cambridge History of Medieval Political Thought c. 350–c. 1450*, edited by J. H. Burns (New York: Cambridge University Press, 1988), 11–20, 37–47, 123–53; Richard L. Kagan, *Lawsuits and Litigants in Castile: 1500–1700* (Chapel Hill: University of North Carolina, 1981), 21–51.

6. James Muldoon, *Popes, Lawyers and Infidels: The Church and the Non-Christian World, 1250–1550* (Philadelphia: University of Pennsylvania Press, 1979), 8.

7. Kenneth Pennington, *The Prince and the Law, 1200–1600: Sovereignty and Right in the Western Legal Tradition* (Berkeley: University of California Press, 1993), 6. My understanding of medieval historiography, canon law, and Innocent IV draws heavily on the works of James Muldoon, Kenneth Pennington, and James Brundage. See Brundage, *Law, Sex, and Christian Society*; Muldoon, *Popes, Lawyers and Infidels*; James Muldoon, *The Americas in the Spanish World Order: The Justification for Conquest in the Seventeenth Century* (Philadelphia: University of Pennsylvania, 1994); Pennington, *The Prince and the Law*.

8. Muldoon's observation about shifting domains seems quite pertinent. Muldoon concluded that: "there was yet another reason for the failure of the popes and lawyers of the late Middle Ages to develop further the work of their thirteenth-century predecessors regarding infidels. The initiative in dealings with non-European societies was passing to secular rulers." Muldoon, *Popes, Lawyers and Infidels*, 156.

9. Nirenberg, *Communities of Violence*; R. I. Moore, *The Formation of a Persecuting Society: Power and Deviance in Western Europe, 950–1250* (Cambridge, MA: Blackwell, 1987); John Boswell, *Christianity, Social Tolerance and Homosexuality: Gay People in Western Europe from the Beginning of the Christian Era to the Fourteenth-Century* (Chicago: University of Chicago Press, 1980); O'Callaghan, *History of Medieval Spain*, 185.

10. Woodrow Wilson Borah, *Justice by Insurance, the General Indian Court of Colonial Mexico and the Legal-Aides of the Half-Real* (Berkeley: University of California Press, 1983) 10.

11. Richard Kagan, *Lawsuits and Litigants in Castile, 1500–1700* (Chapel Hill: University of North Carolina Press, 1981), 22–32.

12. Larry Siedentop, *Inventing the Individual: The Origins of Western Liberalism* (Cambridge, MA: Belknap Press of Harvard University Press, 2014).

13. After the court's destruction, the corporate identities of Jews and Moors continued to be forged around customs and traditions that now lacked legal enforcement and sanctioned violence. Consequently, the role of shame and community disapprobation gained a more prominent role.

14. Deborah Root, "Speaking Christian: Orthodoxy and Difference in Sixteenth-Century Spain," *Representations* (Summer 1988): 118–34.

15. Zurara, *Chronicle*, I, 1. According to Ivana Elbl, the Hakluyt edition of *The Chronicle* still represents the most authoritative version available. "Cross-Cultural Trade and Diplomacy: Portuguese Relations with West Africa, 1441–1521," *Journal of World History* (Fall 1992): 165–204. For a favorable literary assessment of the Hakluyt edition, see Kenneth Baxter Wolf's article "The 'Moors' of West Africa and the Beginnings of the Portuguese Slave Trade," *Journal of Medieval and Renaissance Studies* (Fall 1994): 449–69. Joining the royal court in the 1440s as a historian under the command of João I's royal archivist and chronicler, Fernão Lopes, Zurara initially was commissioned to complete a chronicle of the Portuguese kings. He subsequently crafted the *Crónica de tomada de Ceuta* (The Conquest of Ceuta). In 1449, Zurara started the *Crónica dos feitos de Guinea* (The Chronicle of the Discovery and Conquest of Guinea), which he completed in 1453.

16. Zurara, *Chronicle*, I, 4. The text, consequently, [the "consequently" does not obviously follow on a point] embodied the very same tension rendered in the process of recording and silencing specific histories. Wolf attends to this tension in *The Chronicle*. Wolf, "'Moors' of West Africa," 451–54. Similar concerns permeate the work of various literary critics, historians, and historically minded anthropologists. Mary Poovey, *Uneven Developments: The Ideological Work of Gender in Mid-Victorian England* (Chicago: University of Chicago Press, 1988), 1–23; H. Avram Vesser, "Introduction," in *The New Historicism*, edited by H. Avaram Vesser (New York: Routledge, 1989), ix–xvi; Gabrielle M. Spiegel, *Romancing the Past: The Rise of Vernacular Prose Historiography in Thirteenth-Century France* (Berkeley: University of California Press, 1993); Spiegel, *The Past as Text: The Theory and Practice of Medieval Historiography* (Baltimore: Johns Hopkins University Press, 1997); David William Cohen, *The Combing of History* (Chicago: University of Chicago Press, 1994), 1–23; Michel-Rolph Trouillot, *Silencing the Past: Power and the Production of History* (Boston: Beacon, 1995).

17. Iberian preoccupation, then and now, with an unbroken Christian tradition underscores a deep-seated romance that in its nostalgia stands in as an ideology. Northrop Frye has observed that "in every age the ruling social and intellectual class tends to project its ideals in some form of romance where the virtuous heroes and the beautiful heroines represent the ideals and the villains the threats to their ascendancy. This is the general character of chivalric romance in the Middle Ages. . . . The perennially child-like quality of romance is marked by its extraordinary persistent nostalgia, its search for some kind of imaginative golden age in time and space." Frye, *Anatomy of Criticism: Four Essays* (Princeton, NJ: Princeton University Press, 1957), 186. Peter Hulme, to whom I am indebted for this formulation, has brilliantly examined the discursive implication of the "colonial romance." Hulme, *Colonial Encounters: Europe and the Native Caribbean, 1492–1797* (New York: Routledge, 1986).

18. Wolf, "'Moors' of West Africa," 449–69. In an insightful reading of Richard Hakluyt's *Principal Navigations*, the literary theorists Emily C. Bartels has shown that this conflating process continued throughout the sixteenth century and transcended national boundaries. Bartels, "Imperialist Beginnings: Richard Hakluyt and the Construction of Africa," *Criticism* (Fall 1992): 517–38.

19. On the relationship between wonderment and otherness: see Stephen Greenblatt, *Marvelous Possessions: The Wonder of the New World* (Chicago: University of Chicago Press, 1992); *New World Encounters*, edited by Stephen Greenblatt (Berkeley: University of California Press, 1993); Enrique Dussel, *The Invention of the Americas: Eclipse of "the Other" and the Myth of Modernity*, translated by Michael D. Barber (New York: Continuum, 1995); Hulme, *Colonial Encounters*; Anthony Pagden, *Fall of Natural Man*; Pagden, *European Encounters with the New World: From Renaissance to Romanticism* (New Haven, CT: Yale University Press, 1993); Stuart B. Schwartz, ed., *Implicit Understandings: Observing, Reporting, and Reflecting on the Encounters Between Europeans and Other Peoples in the Early Modern Era* (Cambridge: Cambridge University Press, 1994); Todorov, *Conquest of America*. A curious silence on the African presence permeates many of the works cited above. The subjectivity of the New World, the Indies, and their original inhabitants seems always posited around a binary that features Indians and Spaniards as givens as opposed to contested representations. Though most scholarship on New World encounters acknowledge in passing the enslaved and colonized African presence, very little of that scholarship questions the salience of the Spanish-Indian binary as the principal analytical category. Yet a half century ago, Tannenbaum noted that colonization and settlement of the Americas represented "a joint Afro-European enterprise." Tannenbaum, *Slave and Citizen*, 40. Today, this silence remains complicit in the historiography that examines the intersection of race and nation formation throughout Latin America. By exorcising blackness from the "collective memory" nationalist discourses, which includes the historical discipline, have naturalized a Christian, hispanicized whiteness and in the process have regimented the racial discourse largely around the indigenous presence. Peter Wade, *Blackness and Race Mixture: The Dynamics of Racial Identity in Colombia* (Baltimore: Johns Hopkins University Press, 1993), 3–47; Richard Graham, ed., *The Idea of Race in Latin America, 1870–1940* (Austin: University of Texas

Press, 1990); Winthrop R. Wright, *Café con Leche: Race, Class, and National Image in Venezuela* (Austin: University of Texas Press, 1990); Thomas E. Skidmore, *Black into White: Race and Nationality in Brazilian Thought* (Durham, NC: Duke University Press, 1993); Enrique Florescano, *Memory, Myth and Time in Mexico: From the Aztecs to Independence*, translated by Albert G. Bork (Austin: University of Texas Press, 1994).

20. Lyle McAlister noted that "conquest" (*conquista*) "meant the establishment of *señorio* over land and people by force of arms but, within a context established by Reconquest experience and the subjugation of the Canaries, for particular ends: the extension of Christendom and the dominions of Christians kings at the expense of infidels and pagans; and the extraction of tribute and booty from the conquered. It is interesting that the Spaniards avoided the word *conquista* in describing their territorial aggrandizements in Christian Italy." Lyle McAlister, *Spain and Portugal in the New World: 1492–1700* (Minneapolis: University of Minnesota Press, 194), 89–90; for the medieval trajectory, see Bartlett, *Making of Europe.*

21. Accord to Patricia Seed, this behavior should surprise since the Portuguese grounded their acts of possession in the nautical science and navigational technology of which they were early modern pioneers. Seed, *Ceremonies of Possession in Europe's Conquest of the New World, 1492–1640* (Cambridge: Cambridge University Press, 1995), 100–48.

22. Zurara was careful not to conflate the activities of the merchants, including "trade," "trafficking," or "bargaining," with the idea of conquest. In 1448, Zurara signals the end of the "Guinea's" conquest since "the matters that follow were not accomplished with such toil and bravery as in the past." Zurara, *Chronicle*, II, 289.

23. Bennett, *Africans in Colonial Mexico.*

24. Zurara, *Chronicle*, I, 16.

25. Ibid., I, 28.

26. Ibid., I, 29.

27. Ibid., I, 31.

28. Ibid., I, 99.

29. Valorizing Zurara's pronouncement simultaneously clarifies and obscures geographical and purportedly related cultural differences between Islamic Moors and Guinea's pagan inhabitants. As a discursive entity, there never has been one "Africa" but many "Africas." In this pantheon of representations, "Africa" often stood in for the whole continent but before the Renaissance usually symbolized the northern regions of the continent with which the ancient Greeks and Romans were quite familiar. "Libya" and "Libia" often represented the area bordering the Mediterranean and its hinterland over which Rome ruled. "Ethiopia" often competed with "Libya" and "Africa" as the toponym for the northern region of the continent but occasionally found itself in competition with the term "Guinea" as the signifier for "the land of blacks." Over the centuries, Europeans also included the "Sudan" and the "Niger" to reference pagan Africans, and "black Moors," "Negroes," or simply "blacks." Christopher Miller, *Blank Darkness: Africanist Discourse in French* (Chicago: University of Chicago Press, 1986), 6–14, 16–65;

V. Y. Mudimbe, *The Idea of Africa* (Bloomington: Indiana University Press, 1994), 1–104; Bartels, "Imperialist Beginnings," 520–25; Kim Hall, *Things of Darkness: Economies of Race and Gender in Early Modern England* (Ithaca: Cornell University Press, 1995), 25–61; Margo Hendricks and Patricia Parker, eds. *Women, "Race" and Writing in the Early Modern Period* (New York: Routledge, 1994), 1–14, 35–54, 84–100, 118–37.

30. Zurara, *The Chronicle*, I, 42–43.

31. Ibid., I, 45–49.

32. Ibid., I, 51.

33. Ibid., I, 55.

34. Ibid., I, 56.

35. Ibid., I, 52–53.

36. Ibid., I, 53.

37. Ibid., I, 54.

38. For imperial competition among European Christians in the late Middle Ages and the nascent early modern period, see McAlister, *Spain and Portugal*, 46–51, 55–69; Bartlett, *Making of Europe*, 306–14.

39. The numerous fifteenth-century papal bulls underscore this point. *European Treaties Bearing on the History of the United States and Its Dependencies to 1648*, edited by Frances Gardiner Davenport (Washington, DC: Carnegie Institution, 1917); Pagden, *Fall of Natural Man*, 57–108; Pennington, *The Prince and the Law*; Muldoon, *Popes, Lawyers and Infidels*; Muldoon, *The Americas in the Spanish World Order*.

40. Conciliar canons preceded the twelfth century; however, the systematic deployment of canon law started with the jurist Gratian. Brundage, *Law, Sex, and Christian Society*, 229–416, specifically 235–39.

41. Pennington, *The Prince and the Law*; 8–37; Brundage, *Law, Sex, and Christian Society*, 325–486.

42. Since the Church received a share of the spoils, Zurara, like subsequent commentators, focused on the *diezmos* (tenth of share) taken from Guinea, which the ecclesiastical authorities appropriated at the various ports of entry. Over time, contemporary and subsequent historians have naturalized this perspective but at the expense of reducing the Church's ambivalence. The Church sought both to benefit materially from colonization and to increase the number of Christian souls. The focus on the former process has obscured canon laws' importance and ability to be both the protector of the colonized and colonialism's beneficiary. Zurara, *Chronicle*, I, 54.

43. Zurara, *Chronicle*, I, 58–80.

44. Ibid., I, 81.

45. James H. Sweet, "The Iberian Roots of American Racist Thought," *William and Mary Quarterly* (January 1997): 143–66.

46. Zurara, *Chronicle*, I, 96, 136.

47. Ibid., II, 177.

48. Ibid., I, 99.

49. Ibid., II, 192.

50. Ibid., II, 194.

51. Ibid., II, 268.

52. Ibid., II, 281–82.

53. Ibid., II, 289.

54. In a recent work examining possession ceremonies, Patricia Seed states that Portuguese discovery "signified the established of legitimate dominion," which rested on navigational technology, nautical innovations, and scientific knowledge. Though laudable for the specificity it accords English, French, Portuguese, Spanish, and Dutch understandings of possession, some of the conclusions seem distinctly applicable to the Indies. In the various texts related to the Portuguese and Spanish encounter with Guinea, the ceremonies identified in the New World do not play an important role. Seed, *Ceremonies of Possession*, 9–10, 101–48, esp. 128–40. In light of this observation, I rely on the more textually based definition of discovery employed by Anthony Pagden to situate the Europe's early modern encounters. Pagden, *European Encounters*, 5–12.

55. Pagden, *European Encounters*, 10; also see Pagden, *Fall of Natural Man*, 4–6.

56. Romans, the rulers of the Iberian Peninsula after they defeated the Carthaginians, referred to the region as Hispania. O'Callaghan, *History of Medieval Spain*, 26–29; Seed, *Ceremonies of Possession*, 179–84; Anthony Pagden, *Lords of All the World: Ideologies of Empire in Spain, Britain and France c. 1500–c. 1800* (New Haven: Yale University Press, 1995), 11–28.

57. Wolf, "'Moors' of West Africa," 452. Barbara Fuchs's brilliant work redefines how we approach sixteenth-century Spanish historiography and representations of Spanish-Muslim relations. Commenting on the literary scholar Ramón Menéndez Pidal's discussion of *maurophilia*, Fuchs notes that this representation "by no means depends on the defeat of the Moors. The earliest medieval *cantares de gesta* and romances evince a sympathetic view of an enemy with whom Christians frequently allied, and with whom they lived." Fuchs, *Exotic Nation: Maurophilia and the Construction of Early Modern Spain* (Philadelphia: University of Pennsylvania Press, 2009), 73. It should be noted that the interest and admiration shown by the Portuguese and Spaniards toward Muslims and Africans not only flourished after the enemies had been "conquered" but surfaced in the context of encounters when the Iberians sought to establish "contact" or trade. As we shall see, curiosity takes a political form in that it brings into relief despotism. Here then is not a simple romance, a distance that allows sympathy but a respect that emerges in a real context in which Spanish and Portuguese desires or objectives have yet to be realized. Obviously, the savage, the cruel, the tyrannical, and the despotic resulted in and framed the Black Legend, but its relationship to Africa and Africans precedes the English-French narrative directed against the cruel Spaniards.

58. Zurara, *Chronicle*, I, 81.

59. Ibid., I, 54. For a critical assessment of the deployment of the curse of Ham and its shifting plot structure, see Benjamin Braude, "The Sons of Noah and the Construction of Ethnic and Geographical Identities in the Medieval and Early Modern Periods," *William and Mary Quarterly* (January 1997): 103–42; William McKee Evans, "From the

Land of Canaan to the Land of Guinea: The Strange Odyssey of the 'Sons of Ham,'"
American Historical Review 85 (February 1980): 15–43.

60. D. A. Brading, *The First America: The Spanish Monarchy, Creole Patriots and the Liberal State* (New York: Cambridge University Press, 1991), 15–18, 23–24, 44–50.

61. Zurara, *Chronicle*, I, 101.

62. Ibid., I, 109–10.

63. Ibid.; Aristotle, *The Politics*, translated and with an introduction by Carnes Lord (Chicago: University of Chicago Press, 1984).

64. J. H. Elliott, *The Old World and the New, 1492–1650* (Cambridge: Cambridge University Press, 1970); Pagden, *Fall of Natural Man*; Pagden, *European Encounters*; Anthony Grafton, *New Worlds, Ancient Texts: The Power of Tradition and the Shock of Discovery* (Cambridge, MA: Harvard University Press, 1992); Peter Burke, "America and the Rewriting of World History," in *America in European Consciousness, 1493–1750*, edited by Karen Ordahl Kupperman (Chapel Hill: University of North Carolina Press, 1995), 33–51; Sabine MacCormack, "Limits of Understanding: Perceptions of Greco-Roman and Amerindian Paganism in Early Modern Europe," in *America in European Consciousness:1493–1750*, edited by Karen Ordahl Kupperman (Chapel Hill: University of North Carolina Press, 1995), 79–129.

65. Zurara, *Chronicle*, I, 85.

CHAPTER 4

1. *The Portuguese in West Africa, 1415–1670: A Documentary History*, edited by Malyn Newitt (New York: Cambridge University Press, 2010); Rodney, *History of the Upper Guinea Coast*; Brooks, *Landlords and Strangers*; Thornton, *Africa and Africans*; John Iliffe, *Honour in African History* (New York: Cambridge University Press, 2005); Green, *Rise of the Trans-Atlantic Slave Trade in Western Africa*.

2. V. Y. Mudimbe, *The Idea of Africa* (Bloomington: Indiana University Press, 1994), 37; Siba N'Zatioula Grovogui, *Sovereign, Quasi Sovereigns, and Africans: Race and Self-Determination in International Law* (Minneapolis: University of Minnesota Press, 1996).

3. Jean Bodin observed that "sovereignty is the absolute and perpetual power of a commonwealth, which the Latins call *maiestas*; the Greeks *akra exousia*, *kurion arche*, and *kurion politeuma*; and the Italians *segnioria*, a word they use for private persons as well as for those who have full control of the state, while the Hebrews call it *tomech shévet*—that is, the highest power of command." Bodin, *The Six Bookes of a Commonweale*, edited and introduced by Kenneth Douglas McRae (Cambridge, MA: Harvard University Press, 1962), book 1, chapter 8, 84.

4. K. Davis, *Periodization and Sovereignty*.

5. Natalie Zemon Davis, *Trickster Travels: A Sixteenth-Century Muslim Between Worlds* (New York: Hill and Wang, 2006), 2–4; *Merchants and Marvel: Commerce, Science and Art in Early Modern Europe*, edited by Pamela H. Smith and Paula Findlen (New York:

Routledge, 2002), 1–4; *Black Africans in Renaissance Europe*, edited by T. F. Earle and K. J. P. Lowe (New York: Cambridge University Press, 2005).

6. My intention here is merely to signify that in a space that came to be synonymous with slaving and the slave trade, the process of encounter and early modern expansion operated within and yet beyond the domain of force. At the same time that the Europeans manifested force, they were also cognized or were made to be cognizant of the force Africans exerted, including the rules of engagement that shaped the European presence, encounter, and subsequent desire to impose order on their presence and relations in a specific area. Subrahmanyam, *Courtly Encounters.*

7. Andrew C. Hess, *The Forgotten Frontier: A History of the Sixteenth-Century Ibero-African Frontier* (Chicago: University of Chicago Press, 1978); Mark D. Meyerson, *The Muslims of Valencia in the Age of Fernando and Isabel: Between Coexistence and Crusade* (Berkeley: University of California Press, 1991); Nirenberg, *Communities of Violence*; Blumenthal, *Enemies and Familiars.*

8. "For, in the end," writes Anthony Pagden, "Vitoria and his successors were far less concerned with the particulars of the American case than they were with the opportunities it provided for a refutation of Lutheran and, later, Calvinist theories of sovereignty." Pagden, "Dispossessing the Barbarian," in *Languages of Political Theory in Early-Modern Europe*, 83.

9. Fernand Braudel, *The Mediterranean and the Mediterranean World in the Age of Philip II*, translated by Sîan Reynolds (Berkeley: University of California Press, 1995 [1966 translated; 1949]; Carl Schmitt, *The Nomos of the Earth in the International Law of the* Jus Publicum Europeum, translated by G. L. Ulmen (New York: Telos, 2006 [1950]); Wallerstein, *Modern World-System I: Capitalist Agriculture*; Eric Wolf, *Europe and the People Without History* (Berkeley: University of California Press, 1982); Mbembe, *On the Postcolony.*

10. The cultural theorist Walter Mignolo has written perceptively about how the Castilian court sought to introduce Castilian as the lingua franca among indigenous peoples in the early sixteenth-century New World, an act that conflicted with the desires and objectives of the mendicant friars who insisted on local vernaculars. The court and missionary policies represented much more than distinct perspectives on language. As discrete philosophies of language and conflict over their implementation, these positions touched on distinct (political) rationalities shaping the nature of the Christian order. Mignolo, *Darker Side of the Renaissance*, 52–55.

11. According to Andrew Hess,

How to govern the newly conquered populations, absorbed the attention of the royal bureaucracy. For the Crown, the end of the Reconquista complicated the task of ruling the peninsula's Muslim minority. An irregular passage of Islamic territories into the hands of Christian rulers since the eleventh century had given birth not to one large Mudéjar society but to a mosaic of separate groups. This spasmodic progress of the reconquest had also formed a varying set of relationships between the subjected populations and the aristocracy the crown had established as the local rulers of its new Muslim subjects. (Hess, *The Forgotten Frontier: A History of the Sixteenth-Century Ibero-African Frontier* [Chicago: University of Chicago Press, 1978], 128)

12. Here we might want to ask why we should accept the Castilian historical formulation (its chronology, its narrative, and its momentous events) as the framing device for Spain and for that matter Iberia? In conflating Castile's narrative with the history of Spain, the conquest of the Moors is conflated with the fall of Granada, which in turn is linked with the expulsion of the Jews and the Columbus voyage. But this conflates too much, including asymmetrical subject formation that resulted from the complex configuration of Islamic subjects on the Iberian Peninsula and throughout the Hispanic-Islamic frontier.

13. Blumenthal, *Enemies and Familiars.*

14. Hess, *Forgotten Frontier*, 132.

15. Nyquist, *Arbitrary Rule*; Patterson, *Slavery and Social Death*; Meyerson, *Muslims of Valencia in the Age of Fernando and Isabel.* On the basis of their wealth, meager in most instances, alongside their symbolic marginalization, Muslims in tandem with Jews became lenders of money but also royal tax farmers. By such means, Muslims and Jews came to be identified as the "royal treasure."

16. African studies originated in the idea that a distinct cultural logic, specific experiences, and particular institutional formation characterized the continent and its peoples, thus serving as the baseline for the production of knowledge on Africa and Africans. But in view of a European presence forged around the slave trade and colonialism, African studies specialists asserted that the narrative of European power wielded a disproportionate influence over the continent and its inhabitants. For this reason, deconstructing Europe's epistemological hegemony still represents a precondition for inscribing the story of Africa and Africans. In framing matters as such, I explore an earlier instantiation of the "colonial library" about which the literary theorist Gaurav Desai has written with considerable perception: "My project is to investigate the conditions of possibility and the actual manifestations of precisely such an epistemological colonization as it emerges throughout the study of the colonial library. Inspired by the Asantehene's rebuke, however, my aim has been to understand the construction of the library and of the colonial process itself as a complex series of interactions between colonizers and the colonized rather than as a unidirectional practice." Desai, *Subject to Colonialism*, 4.

17. Kenneth Pennington, *The Prince and the Law: 1200–1600, Sovereignty and Rights in the Western Legal Tradition* (Berkeley: University of California Press, 1993), 2.

18. Pennington, *The Prince and the Law*, 9.

19. Thomas N. Bisson, *The Crisis of the Twelfth Century: Power, Lordship, and the Origins of European Government* (Princeton, NJ: Princeton University Press, 2009).

20. Pagden, "Introduction," in *Languages of Political Theory in Early-Modern Europe*, 1–17.

21. Margaret T. Hogden, *Early Anthropology in the Sixteenth and Seventeenth Centuries* (Philadelphia: University of Pennsylvania Press, 1964).

22. David Northrup, *Africa's Discovery of Europe: 1450–1850* (New York: Oxford University Press, 2009), ix–x.

23. Christopher Fyfe, "Race, Empire, and the Historians," *Race and Class* 33, no. 4 (1992): 15. Cited in Gaurav Desai, who goes on to write that "Fyfe's project in the essay is to challenge historians, both African and non-African, to rethink the role of race in the project of African colonialism. That white historians may feel ashamed and embarrassed to raise the issue may be understandable, suggests Fyfe, but the fact that African historians in the majority also sweep the issue under the carpet seems astounding to him." Desai, *Subject to Colonialism*, 19.

24. Mudimbe, *Idea of Africa*, 45; Grovogui, *Sovereign, Quasi Sovereigns, and Africans*, 8.

25. Seed, *Ceremonies of Possession*, 70–72.

26. Spiegel, *Romancing the Past*, passim.

27. Mbembe, *On the Postcolony*, 2.

28. V. Y. Mudimbe, *The Invention of Africa: Gnosis, Philosophy, and the Order of Knowledge* (Bloomington: University of Indiana Press, 1988), 6.

29. Mudimbe, *Invention of Africa*, 16.

30. Ibid., 46.

31. Ibid., 47.

32. Ibid., 45.

33. Ibid., 45.

34. Ibid., 37.

35. Mudimbe, *Idea of Africa*, 33.

36. A similar slippage characterizes the study of the International Relations specialists and Africanist Siba Grovogui who in *Sovereigns, Quasi Sovereigns, and Africans* makes claims that align with those of Mudimbe.

37. "The Bull *Romanus pontifex*, January 8, 1455," in *European Treaties Bearing on the History of the United States and its Dependencies to 1648*, edited by Frances Gardiner Davenport (Washington, D.C. Carnegie Institution of Washington, 1917), 21.

38. Ibid., 22.

39. In a subsequent work, Mudimbe wrote that *terra nullius* enabled Christians "to dispossess all Saracens and other non-Christians of all their goods, the right to invade and conquer these peoples' lands, to expel them from it, and when necessary, to fight them and subjugate them in a perpetual servitude, and to expropriate all their possessions." Mudimbe, *Idea of Africa*, 33. In transporting nineteenth-century colonialism across time and space, readings such as Mudimbe's lose sight of earlier colonial historicity that engendered distinct possibilities. Here the postcolonial critique raised by scholars of Latin America is of critical importance:

> To dialogue with postcolonial scholars, we must elicit the categories and
> concepts from sixteenth- and seventeenth-century Spanish texts that articulate
> tutelage, civilizing mission, native collaboration, and colonial law and that are
> still influential today. Hence, postcolonialism, understood as a new condition

of thought, cannot be equated with the end of a colonial period, nor should the questions postcolonial scholars raise be limited to the specific experiences of nineteenth- and twentieth-century colonialisms. For now, let me point out that this genealogy has had two detrimental consequences for the study of earlier periods in the Americas. At best, Enlightenment forms of producing otherness—for example, the opposition between peoples with and without history, or between peoples in a state of nature and those living under a state—assumes a transhistorical applicability that erases historical specificity. At worst, postcolonial theorists reduce the colonial enterprises before the Enlightenment to crude modes of raping the land—with no coherent civilizing mission worth mentioning. This book argues the exception of the Spanish imperial project, but a similar argument could be made for Portuguese modes of colonization in the early modern period. (Rabasa, *Writing Violence on the Northern Frontier*, 16–17)

40. Bryant, "Making History," 46.

41. Ibid.

42. Mudimbe, *Idea of Africa*, 33.

43. Lamin Sanneh, *Abolitionists Abroad: American Blacks and the Making of Modern West Africa* (Cambridge, MA: Harvard University Press, 1999); Brown, *Moral Capital*; Wood, *Blind Memory*; Coombes, *Reinventing Africa*.

44. Tannenbaum, *Slave and Citizen*, 62.

45. Ibid.

46. Mudimbe, *Invention of Africa*, 32.

47. Tannenbaum, *Slave and Citizen*, 62.

48. Scott, *Conscripts of Modernity*, 118; Frederick Cooper, *Colonialism in Question: Theory, Knowledge, History* (Berkeley: University of California Press, 2005), 3–55.

49. Note that Scott's understanding of modern power, though focused on its deployment in the eighteenth-century New World, resembles Mudimbe's characterization of the earliest encounter between Europeans and Africans. Earlier, I argued that Mudimbe's perspective privileged a mature form of colonialism. Scott's formulation of power warrants a similar critique. Even as he historicizes power, Scott obscures earlier incarnations of its modern form that embodied distinct rationalities in relation to sovereign subjects in Africa and those deemed devoid of sovereignty who were enslaved. Scott, *Conscripts of Modernity*, 117.

50. Marcus Rediker, *The Slave Ship: A Human History* (New York: Penguin, 2007); Trevor Burnard, *Masters, Tyranny, and Desire: Thomas Thistlewood and His Slaves in the Anglo-Jamaican World* (Chapel Hill: University of North Carolina Press, 2004); Alexander Byrd, *Captives and Voyagers: Black Migrants Across the Eighteenth-Century British Atlantic World* (Baton Rouge: Louisiana State University Press, 2009).

51. Ironically, early modern commentators on absolutism rooted the origins of this novel political tradition in Roman law, which as we saw in the previous chapter was simultaneously the basis of empire and slavery. J. H. Franklin noted how

the opinions of these commentators reflect the ambiguity of the system they expound, and maintain a delicate balance between monarchist and constitutionalist ideas. If the former element (monarchist) sometimes seems overwhelming to the modern reader, it is because the lawyers are so heavily dependent on the terminology of Roman law. The status of Roman law in medieval France is a highly complicated question which need not be considered here. We need only observe that Roman legal concepts, as elaborated by the medieval commentators, had long been accepted by French jurists as the ordinary form of learned discourse. In this process the basic equation of the position of the king of France with that of the Roman princeps became the tacit starting point for all reflections. (J. H. Franklin, *Jean Bodin and the Rise of Absolutist Theory* [New York: Cambridge University Press, 1973], 6)

52. Writing perceptively on the sixteenth-century culture of power, the scholar of Spanish empire Alejandro Cañeque criticizes representations of modern colonialism that influence how early modernists narrate power. To illustrate his point, Cañeque cites the brilliant Irving Leonard who wrote that "inherent in the colonial order was an arbitrary, monolithic state headed by a vice-sovereign with nearly absolute authority who functioned essentially as an overseer of the enormous estate of its absentee owner. . . . His Majesty's representations often were little less than unrestrained despots." It is interesting to see Leonard appropriating the very language that the Protestants employed in their critique of Catholic tyranny [recall the genealogy of (Catholic) despotism, resides in idolatry. For Cañeque, however, this represents the language and the discourse of modern power which obscures the nature of power in the sixteenth century. In this sense, Cañeque overlooks the genealogy of power invoked by Leonard that privileges the Protestant critique (the Protestant who since Weber has embodied the modern)—in this case the modern critique of despotic power.] Cañeque then goes on to ask,

But, was this the real nature of viceregal power? Were the viceroys who ruled over New Spain in the sixteenth and seventeenth centuries "tyrants" who governed in a despotic way? No doubt, one can understand how tempting it is to see the figure of the viceroy through the prism of a modern governor or president of the republic (it is interesting to observe that Cañeque doesn't really attend to the fact that Leonard's representation draws on the modern form of power associated with the planter and the plantation: "who function essentially as an overseer of the enormous estate of its absentee owner;" a modern form of power yet distinct from the other forms of modern power vested in the governor or president), but we should be very careful when making broad comparisons that ignore the great gulf of historical experience and cultural transformation that separates twentieth-century Mexican rulers from their supposed colonial predecessors. (cited in Alejandro Cañeque, *The King's Living Image: The Culture and Politics of Viceregal Power in Colonial Mexico* [New York: Routledge Press, 2004], 3)

Keep in mind that Leonard, a North American, makes his assertion in 1959 in a context in which a prominent form of modern domination—white supremacy—tacks its genealogy back to the slavery and the institution of the plantation, which for North Americans was one of the prominent references for describing power even in the age of modernization or developmentalism that followed in the wake of the Holocaust.

53. Hont writes that "for the case of Locke, see James Tully, 'Rediscovering America . . .', Tully, *An Approach to Political Philosophy* . . . (Cambridge, 1993); Tuck, *The Rights of War and Peace*, 166–181; and Barbara Arneil, *John Locke and America* . . . (Oxford). . . . For contrast with earlier debates, Anthony Pagden, *The Fall of Natural Man* . . . (Cambridge 1982)." "Modern histories of political thought," observes Hont "are routinely organized around a contrast between Renaissance humanism, the politics of civic virtue, and seventeenth-century natural jurisprudence, the precursor of the modern meta-legal discourse of human rights. The paradigm shift between the two is regarded by most as the beginning of modern liberalism. A very similar contrast between humanism and natural jurisprudence is also deployed to explain the birth of political economy." Hont, *Jealousy of Trade*, 10, 17.

54. Wallerstein, *Modern World-System I: Capitalist Agriculture*, book 1, 67.

55. Andrew Apter, *The Pan-African Nation: Oil and the Spectacle of Culture in Nigeria* (Chicago: University of Chicago Press, 2005).

56. The point I want to be grasped here for the kind of *strategic* reading I am commending in this book is that there were at least two conditions that made possible the posing of this question of the politics of colonialist representation as a question in the first place: one was precisely the existence of the space enabled by the prior moment of anticoloniality in which the problem of the horizon of politics (i.e., nation-state sovereignty) had appeared resolved; the other was the emergence in the humanities and social sciences of practices of criticism (call them poststructuralist) concerned with the interrogation of representation as such. These latter made visible the persistence of the colonial in the heart of sovereignty (in the vocabulary of anticoloniality, these were theorized as neocolonialism and cultural imperialism) and enabled postcoloniality to problematize colonialism as a discursive formation enduring into the present.

Scott continues noting how

at the same time, however, this practice of criticism—like its affiliated practices in cultural criticism—operated through a certain suspension or deferral of the question of the political, a deferral of the question of the renewal of a theory of politics. Or, rather, postcoloniality operated by implicitly occupying the horizon of nationalist politics already defined by the anticolonial project. It is, in a sense, precisely this deferral of the question of the political that made possible a sustained interrogation of the internal structures of the cultural reason of colonialist knowledges. However, there is reason to doubt the contemporary efficacy of this strategy of criticism. This doubt is not about its internal cognitive coherence, but about, on the one hand, whether there is much more . . . that can be accomplished with it; and, on the other hand, whether the new global conditions . . . do not urge us to rethink the target that this criticism was constructed to meet. (Scott, *Refashioning Futures*, 12–14)

57. Rucker, *Gold Coast Diaspora*.

58. See David Scott interview with Orlando Patterson in "Paradox of Freedom"; Orlando Patterson, *The Sociology of Slavery: An Analysis of the Origins, Development, and Structure of Negro Slave Society in Jamaica* (New Jersey: Associated University Press, 1969); Edward Brathwaite, *The Development of Creole Society in Jamaica: 1770–1820* (Oxford: Oxford University Press, 1971). Scott writes that "the problem-space of the anticolonial project had, of course, been defined by the demand for political decolonization, the demand for the overthrow of colonial power. Its goal was the achievement of political sovereignty." Scott, *Refashioning Futures*, 11. "The new question for postcoloniality turned not so much on the old idea of colonialism as a structure of material exploitation and profit (the question for anticoloniality) as on the idea of colonialism as a structure of organized authoritative knowledge (a formation, an archive)" Scott, *Refashioning Futures*,12.

59. For compelling departures from the conventional framing, see Stephanie Smallwood, *Saltwater Slavery: A Middle Passage from Africa to the American Diaspora* (Cambridge, MA: Harvard University Press, 2008); Vincent Brown, *The Reaper's Garden: Death and Power in the World of Atlantic Slavery* (Cambridge, MA: Harvard University Press, 2008); Byrd, *Captives and Voyagers*.

60. Paul Lovejoy, "Identifying Enslaved Africans in the Diaspora," in *Identity in the Shadow of Slavery*, edited by Paul E. Lovejoy (New York, Continuum, 2000), 9.

61. Patterson writes that "of the 1.6 million Africans brought to the New World before the end of the seventeenth century, as many as 60 percent may have been captives of genuine warfare, while slightly less than a third were kidnapped." Patterson, *Slavery and Social Death*, 119. But Patterson is keen on historicizing the process of enslavement. While warfare prevailed as the principal means of slave acquisition in the period before the seventeenth century, that practice declined with time. "In all, then," writes Patterson, "the overwhelming majority of slaves brought to all regions of the New World were kidnapped persons, with no more than 30 percent being genuine prisoners of war." Patterson, *Slavery and Social Death*, 120.

62. Brown, *Reaper's Garden*, 7–8.

63. What I am really after is the lingering effects of politics and their impact on the formation of African ethnicity both in African history and the history of the New World.

64. Byrd, *Captives and Voyagers*, 18. See Chambers, "'My own nation,' Igbo Exiles in the Diaspora" *Slavery & Abolition* 18, 1 (1997): 84–91; Michael Gomez, *Exchanging Our Country Marks: The Transformation of African Identities in the Colonial and Antebellum*

South (Chapel Hill: University of North Carolina, 1998), 114–34. David Northrup's critique of Chambers's work flows mostly from just this kind of oversight. See Northrup, "Igbo and Myth Igbo: Culture and Ethnicity in the Atlantic World, 1600–1850" *Slavery & Abolition* 21, 3 (2000): 1–20.

65. Byrd, *Captives and Voyagers*, 18.

66. See note 49.

67. Michel Foucault, *Security, Territory, Population: Lectures at the College de France, 1977–1978*, edited by Michel Senellart and translated by Graham Burchell (New York: Palgrave, 2007).

68. Scott, *Conscripts of Modernity*, 112.

69. Scott, *Conscripts of Modernity*, 116.

> My own view is that as we stare into the bleak face of the various dead-ended modernities constructed by the postcolonial state we ought perhaps to be less enthusiastic about the heroic story embodied in the alternative modernities thesis and more concerned to inquire into the modern concepts and institutions upon which these resisting projects themselves depended. This, I want to urge, is where the stakes for us are as we undertake to think and work our way out of the present. I am urging, therefore, that we need a way of describing the regime of slave plantation power in which what is brought into view is less what it restricts and what resists this restriction, less what it represses and what escapes or overcomes this repression, and more the modern conditions it created that positively shaped the way in which language, religion, kinship, and so were reconstituted. (Scott, *Conscripts of Modernity*, 115)

70. Scott's understanding of modern power, though focused on its deployment in the eighteenth-century New World, resembles Mudimbe's characterization of the earliest encounter between Europeans and Africans. Earlier, I argued that Mudimbe's perspective privileged a mature form of colonialism.

71. While an industrial temporality characterized slave ships—factories on the sea—plantations—factories in the fields and cities—factories of the urban landscape—positioning New World blacks at the forefront of modernity, this dynamic represents an obscuring anachronism when describing fifteenth- and sixteenth-century experiences.

72. Wolf, *Europe and the People Without History*.

73. Fuchs, *Exotic Nation*, 1.

CHAPTER 5

1. "The Bull *Romanus pontifex* (Nicholas V), January 8, 1455," in Gardiner, *European Treaties*, 22; Duarte Pacheco Pereira, *Esmeraldo de situ orbis*, edited by George H. T. Kimble (London: Hakluyt Society, 2010); Zurara, *Chronicle*, I, 27–29, 58. Useful summaries

include Charles R. Boxer, *The Portuguese Seaborne Empire 1415–1825* (New York: Alfred A. Knopf, 1969); McAlister, *Spain and Portugal in the New World*; A. H. de Oliveira Marques, *History of Portugal, Volume I: From Lusitania to Empire* (New York: Columbia University Press, 1972); A. J. R. Russell-Wood, *A World on the Move: The Portuguese in Africa, Asia, and America 1415–1808* (New York: St. Martin's, 1992).

2. Zurara, *Chronicle*, I and II, passim; Alvise da Cà da Mosto, *The Voyages of Cadamosto and Other Documents on Western Africa in the Second Half of the Fifteenth Century*, translated and edited by Gerald R. Crone (London: Hakluyt Society, 1937); McAlister, *Spain and Portugal*, 48; Brooks, *Landlords and Strangers*, 125–35; Thornton, *Africa and Africans*, 29–32.

3. "The Bull *Romanus pontifex* (Nicholas V), January 8, 1455," in Gardiner, *European Treaties*, 22; Zurara, *Chronicle*, I, 53–54, 61.

4. In the closing decades of the fifteenth century, crown officials modified the duties on the Guinea trade. The *vintena* (a 5 percent duty) and the *quarto* (a 25 percent duty) replaced the *quinto*. During Dom Sebastião's reign, crown officials introduced the *dízima* (a 10 percent tax) and the *sisa* (a 10 percent sales tax). As the Guinea trade grew in complexity, a series of new regulatory institutions emerged. In 1486, João II united the various officials overseeing the Guinea trade in the Casa da Mina e Tratos de Guiné, often referred to as the Casa da Mina and the Casa da Guiné. The Casa dos Escravos within the Casa da Mina e Tratos de Guiné controlled the slave trade. A. C. de C. M. Saunders, *A Social History of Black Slaves and Freedom in Portugal: 1441–1555* (New York: Cambridge University Press, 1982), 7–11.

5. Terms like *peça de escravo*, *pieza de india*, *boçal*, *bozal*, *ladinhos*, and *ladino*, which early modern Portuguese and Castilians employed to represent Guinea's diverse inhabitants, reflected the Crown's regulatory impulse. This terminology had a lasting impact since subsequent European arrivals employed Portuguese terms in their encounter with Guinea's inhabitants. See, among numerous examples, "Deposition of William Fowler of Ratcliffe, Merchant, 30 April 1569," *Documents Illustrative of the History of the Slave Trade to America*, edited by Elizabeth Donnan (Washington, DC: Carnegie Institution, 1930), I, 72.

6. Zurara, *Chronicle*, I, 46.

7. David Brion Davis, *The Problem of Slavery in Western Culture* (Ithaca, NY: Cornell University Press, 1996); Meyerson, *Muslims of Valencia in the Age of Fernando and Isabel*; Blumenthal, *Enemies and Familiars*.

8. "The Voyage of 1453–4, King John II of Castile to King Afonso of Portugal, Valladolid, 10 April 1454," in *Europeans in West Africa, 1450–1560: Documents to Illustrate the Nature and Scope of Portuguese Enterprise in West Africa, the Abortive Attempt of Castilians to Create an Empire There, and the Early English Voyages to Barbary and Guinea*, translated and edited by John William Blake (London: Hakluyt Society, 1942), 200; "The Bull *Romanus pontifex* (Nicholas V), January 8, 1455," in Gardiner, *European Treaties*, 22.

9. "Negotiations about Castilian Claim to Guinea. 1454," in Blake, *Europeans in West Africa*, I, 201.

10. As we shall see, in Guinea, Portugal's "possession" rites and rituals differed markedly from those that Seed describes in the New World. Seed, *Ceremonies of Possession*, 100–78.

11. "A Castilian Interloper in Guinea. c. 1460," in Blake, *Europeans in West Africa*, I, 203; Diogo Gomes de Sintra, *El descubrimiento de Guinea y de las Islas Occidentales*, introduction, translation, and notes by Daniel Lopez-Canete Quiles (Seville: Secretario de Publicaciones de la Universidad de Sevilla, 1991), 63, 65. For an abridged English version, see "The Voyages of Diogo Gomes," in Cà da Mosto, *Voyages of Cadamosto*, 100–102. During the Third Lateran Council (1179), ecclesiastical officials stipulated that the sale of arms to "Saracens, infidels and pagans" represented a sin. Well into the sixteenth century, Church officials repeated this prohibition, underscoring the extent to which the phenomenon occurred. In *Romanus pontifex*, Nicholas V consistently cautioned his flock against selling arms and "other things prohibited by law from being in any way carried to the Saracens" under the threat of excommunication. "The Bull *Romanus pontifex* (Nicholas V), January 8, 1455," in Gardiner, *European Treaties*, 22, 24, 25.

12. From Afonso's perspective in the case cited, the incarcerated Castilians represented interlopers who were subject to his justice. But unlike the Genoese merchant, who in strict violation of Christian law sold arms to Guinea's inhabitants for which Portuguese officials severed his hands before burning him at the stake, Castilians would receive lighter sentences. As legitimate heir and Portugal's sovereign, Dom Afonso thought that he possessed Guinea, allowing him to decide who could trade with its inhabitants. Nicholas V decreed as much when ruling that in Guinea, King Afonso, his successors, and the Infante "might and may, now and henceforth, freely and lawfully . . . make any prohibitions, statutues, and decrees whatsoever, even penal ones." "The Voyage of 1453–4, King John II of Castile to King Afonso of Portugal, Valladolid, 10 April 1454," in Blake, *Europeans in West Africa*, I, 201.

13. "Another Account of These Negotiations," in Blake, *Europeans in West Africa*, I, 202.

14. In developing a legal basis for Christian interaction with the *extra ecclesiam*, the canonist Sinibaldo Fieschi who became Pope Innocent IV concerned himself explicitly with the question of lawful authority. Even as Innocent asserted that the law of nations superseded natural law in mediating the interaction among competing parties and "princes," he noted that lawful authorities represented individuals "who possess the power to do justice and impose discipline on those who do not abide by the laws governing the relationship of men with their neighbors." Muldoon, *Popes, Lawyers and Infidels*, 8.

15. McAlister, *Spain and Portugal*, 42–52, 55–69.

16. "The Bull *Romanus pontifex* (Nicholas V), January 8, 1455," in Gardiner, *European Treaties*, 9–26; "The Bull Aeterni Regis (Sixtus IV), June 21, 1481," in Blake, *European Treaties*, 49–55.

17. In stating that Guinea represented *terra nullius*, Mudimbe initially cites "Inter Coetera" (sic), which was issued on May 3, 1493, and then briefly moves forward to "*Inter Coetera II*" (sic), *Eximiae devotionis*, *Dudum siquidem*, *Aeterni Regis*, and finally *Eximiae devotionis II* before working back to "*Romanus Pontifex*" (sic). Unduly influenced by a literal

reading of the bulls and *terra nullius* at the expense of the all-important canon law tradition, Mudimbe concludes that "non-Christians have no right to possess or negotiate any
dominion in the then-existing international context, and thus their land is objectively a
terra nullius that may be occupied and seized by Christians in order to exploit the rich-
ness meant by God to be shared by all humankind." Furthermore, Mudimbe's decontextualized reading of the papal texts and fifteenth-century accords allows for the erroneous
assertion that in "the great number of agreements and contracts that were made in this
connection, no European power considered the natives to have any sovereignty or any
accepted rights over their lands." Mudimbe, *Idea of Africa*, 30–37. The pervasiveness of
this perspective contributes to the slippage that immediately renders all Africans into
European victims as slaves or the colonized. Even now, with resistance theories ascendant, this perspective confines Africans to structuralist objects (slaves and colonized) as
opposed to agents and juridical subjects. See, for instance, Siba N'Zatioula Grovogui, in
Sovereigns, Quasi Sovereigns, and Africans, who examines this problem and its implication
for political theory and the field of international relations but whose lack of historicity
ensures that he too reproduces this phenomenon.

18. "The Bull *Romanus pontifex* (Nicholas V), January 8, 1455," in Gardiner, *European Treaties*, 24.

19. Mudimbe, *Idea of Africa*, 33.

20. Ibid. Though his work on Castilian and Portuguese expansion in the early modern period is noted for its subtlety, Lyle McAlister makes a questionable claim that "the
Portuguese crown took the position that it acquired lordship in these territories by the
simple act of discovery and occupation, because they were terra nullius; that is, they
were not under any true lordship, they were empty, or their people were savages who lived
without polity." McAlister, *Spain and Portugal*, 52.

21. Pacheco Pereira, *Esmeraldo de situ orbis*, 104–5; "The Bull *Romanus pontifex* (Nicholas V), January 8, 1455," in Gardiner, *European Treaties*, 14 n. 26.

22. "The Bull *Romanus pontifex* (Nicholas V), January 8, 1455," in Gardiner, *European Treaties*, 22; "The Bull *Inter caetera* (Calixtus III), March 13, 1456," in *European
Treaties*, 27, 30–32.

23. "The Bull *Romanus pontifex*, January 8, 1455," in Gardiner, *European Treaties*, 25.

24. The bulls consistently focused on "islands," "ocean seas," and "harbors" belying
the claims that the pope authorized Portuguese *senhorio* over Guinea proper. In *Romanus
pontifex*, Nicolas noted that the Portuguese sovereign "has peopled with orthodox Christians certain solitary islands in the ocean sea." He similarly remarked that the Portuguese
had "very many inhabitants or dwellers in divers islands situated in the said sea." Of
these two quotes, the first referenced the Canary Islands while the latter pertained to
the contested Atlantic Islands, which, among others, included Madeira and the Azores.
Even in the most explicit reference to Guinea, claims about Portuguese dominion cannot
be easily established. "And so it has come to pass that when a number of ships . . . had
explored and taken possession of very many harbors, islands, and seas, they at length
came to the province of Guinea, and having taken possession of some islands and harbors

and the sea adjacent to that province . . . war was waged . . . in the name of the said King
Affonso and of the infante and in it very many islands in that neighborhood were sub-
dued and peacefully possessed as they are still possessed together with the adjacent sea."
But in the one reference to "land," Nicolas does not refer specifically to Guinea, though
he stated that Afonso "justly and lawfully has acquired and possessed and doth possess,
those islands, *lands*, harbors, and seas" [my emphasis]. Perhaps the land that Nicolas
mentioned belonged to Afonso's conquests in North Africa. "The Bull *Romanus pontifex*
(Nicholas V), January 8, 1455," in Gardiner, *European Treaties*, 21–23.

25. C. H. Haring noted that "and like the Romans they [Castilians] were pre-
eminently creators of laws and builders of institutions. Of all the colonizing peoples of
modern times, the Spaniards were the most legal-minded." This observation can easily be
extended to the Portuguese. Haring, *The Spanish Empire in America* (New York: Harcourt,
Brace & World, 1947), 25. In his magisterial study of Iberian expansion, McAlister suggests as much in *Spain and Portugal*, 47–52, 55–75. For an understanding of the law and
its pervasiveness over the colonial arena, see Roberto González Echevarría, *Myth and
Archive: A Theory of Latin American Narrative* (Durham, NC: Duke University Press,
1998 [1990]), 43–92. González Echevarria essentially affirms the conclusions of colonial
Latin American historians for whom the law represented the starting point for an understanding of Iberian colonialism and resistance to it.

26. In this of line inquiry, Walter Rodney's *History of the Upper Guinea Coast* represented an important breakthrough. Ironically, his detractors have largely focused on the final chapter in his study on the Upper Guinea Coast, which constituted a drastic departure
from the earlier parts of the book. See, for instance, Thornton, *Africa and Africans*, 43–125.

27. The works of medievalists sustain this assertion. W. Eugene Shiels, *King and
Church: The Rise and Fall of the Patronato Real* (Chicago: Loyala University Press, 1961), 33–54;
Pennington, *Popes, Canonists and Texts*, 3–15; Muldoon, *Popes, Lawyers, and Infidels*, passim.

28. Hulme, *Colonial Encounters*, 2.

29. By the first decade of the sixteenth century, Europeans had produced a total of
sixteen accounts on Guinea. José da Silva Horta, "A Representação do Africano na Literatura de Viagens, do Senegal À Serra Leoa (1453–1508)," *Mare Liberum: Revista de História
dos Mares* (1991), no. 2 (Lisbon: Comissão Nacional para as Comemorações dos Descobri-
mentos Portugueses).

30. Muldoon, *Popes, Lawyers and Infidels*, 156.

31. Ibid., 133.

32. Franciscus de Vitoria, "Reflection of the Very Reverend Father Friar Francisco
de Vitoria, Master of Theology and Most Worthy Prime Professor at the University of Salamanca, Delivered in the Said University, A. D. 1539," in *Vitoria: Political Writings*, edited
by Anthony Pagden and Jeremy Lawrence (Cambridge: Cambridge University Press, 1991),
115–62.

33. Muldoon, *Popes, Lawyers and Infidels*, 156. W. Eugene Shiels noted, however, that
"in confronting the fact that these bulls put large quasi-religious powers into the hands of
laymen, it is recognized that medieval times made no sharp distinction between the church

and state. What is found there is two parallel laws, civil and canon, and two parallel courts. Both often dealt with the same matter, though on different grounds, and no static unanimity affected thought on the subject. It was understood that sacerdotium and regnum were not rival but coworks, that neither could interfere with the other in his rightful sphere." Shiels, *King and Church*, 48.

34. "The Bull *Romanus pontifex*, January 8, 1455," in Gardiner, *European Treaties*, 23.

35. Wyatt MacGaffey, "Dialogues of the Deaf: Europeans on the Atlantic coast of Africa," in Schwartz, *Implicit Understandings*, 261.

36. William Pietz, "The Problem of the Fetish IIIa: Bosman's Guinea and the Enlightenment Theory of Fetishism," *Res* (Autumn 1988): 116–17; In a series of provocative essays, Pietz argued that the "fetish" as a term and concept "originated in the cross-cultural spaces of the coast of West Africa." "The Problem of the Fetish, I" *Res* (Spring 1985): 5. See also Pietz, "The Problem of the Fetish, II: The Origin of the Fetish," *Res* (Spring 1997): 23–45; Pietz, "Fetishism and Materialism: The Limits of Theory in Marx," in *Fetishism as Cultural Discourse*, edited by Emily Apter and William Pietz (Ithaca: Cornell University Press, 1993); MacGaffey, "Dialogues of the Deaf," 251. More recently, the anthropologist Michael Ralph has taken up and built on Pietz's original formulations around the question of the fetish. Ralph, *The Forensics of Capital* (Chicago: University of Chicago Press, 2015).

37. John and Jean Comaroff, *Ethnography and the Historical Imagination* (Boulder, CO: Westview, 1992), 6, 3–48 passim. Margaret T. Hodgen noted that "one of the major differences between the thought of the Middle Ages and that of the Renaissance was the value attached to the trait of curiosity." *Early Anthropology in the Sixteenth and Seventeenth Centuries* (Philadelphia: University of Pennsylvania Press, 1964), 207.

38. Cà da Mosto, *Voyages of Cadamosto*, 5.

39. Hodgen, *Early Anthropology*, 222.

40. For a recent treatment of this theme, see Schwartz's exemplary edited collection *Implicit Understandings*.

41. By the first decade of the sixteenth century, Europeans had produced a total of sixteen accounts on Guinea. da Silva Horta, "A Representação do Africano na Literatura de Viagens." A pervasive if not *the* omnipresent theme informing these texts centers on the question "under what law or lordship . . . do (Guinea's inhabitants) live?" Zurara, *Chronicle*, I, 46.

42. In the European imaginary from the early modern era to imperialism's heyday, despotism constituted the representative form of African polities. In his engaging study, Mahmood Mamdani notes that "like all colonial powers, the British worked with a single model of customary authority in pre-colonial Africa. That model was monarchical, patriarchal, and authoritarian. It presumed a king at the center of every polity, a chief on every piece of administrative ground, and a patriarch in every homestead or kraal. Whether in the homestead, the village, or the kingdom, authority was considered an attribute of a personal despotism." Mahmood Mandani, *Citizen and Subjects: Contemporary Africa and the Legacy of Late Colonialism* (Princeton: Princeton University Press, 1996). Similarly, the German philosopher Georg Wilhelm Friedrich Hegel concluded that sovereignty in

Africa was entirely unrestrained. He asserted that "there is absolutely no bond, no restraint upon that arbitrary volition. . . . A ruler stands at the head, for sensuous barbarism can only be restrained by despotic power." Hegel, *The Philosophy of History*, translated by J. Sibree with prefaces by Charles Hegel and J. Sibree and an introduction by C. J. Friedrich (New York: Dover, 1956), 96. By reading Hegel's appraisal of Africans, one gleans the subject position Guinea's inhabitants held in the modern Western intellectual tradition which, in turn, shaped—through a discourse on despotism—the early development of African Studies, especially the historiography of African state formation. But as Mamdani insightfully observed, "notions of a pre-colonial tradition are far more constraining than illuminating." Mamdani, *Citizen and Subject: Contemporary Africa and the Legacy of Late Colonialism* (Princeton: Princeton University Press, 1996), 39. For an introduction to critical developments in the study of the state in Africa, see, among others, M. Fortes and E. E. Evans-Pritchard, *African Political Systems* (London: Kegan Paul International, 1940); Joseph C. Miller, *Kings and Kinsmen: Early Mbundu States in Angola* (Oxford: Clarendon, 1976); Vansina, *Paths in the Rainforests*; Iliffe, *Honour in African History*; Jean-François Bayart, *The State in Africa: The Politics of the Belly* (New York: Polity, 2009).

43. Cà da Mosto, *Voyages of Cadamosto*, 13.

44. Ibid.

45. Ibid., 14.

46. Ibid., 17, 16.

47. Ibid., 18.

48. Ibid., 19.

49. Ibid., 18.

50. Ibid., 29.

51. Ibid., 28.

52. Ibid., 26.

53. Ibid., 29–30.

54. Ibid., 30.

55. Ibid., 33. The idea of Africans being responsible for the enslavement process entered the European imagination in the early modern period and reigned ascendant well into the modern era. Hegel attributed this process to undeveloped "moral sentiments" allowing kin to sell one another "as either has the opportunity." Undeveloped morality enabled Africans to manifest "that perfect contempt for humanity, which in its bearing on Justice and Morality is the fundamental characteristic of the race. . . . The undervaluing of humanity among them reaches an incredible degree of intensity. Tyranny is regarded as no wrong, and cannibalism is looked upon as quite customary and proper." Hegel, *Philosophy of History*, 95.

56. Cà da Mosto, *Voyages of Cadamosto*, 35.

57. Ibid., 37.

58. Ibid., 37.

59. When early modern travelers sought out lords and sovereigns, they not only made recently naturalized assumptions, but they may have been looking for a form of sovereignty

that only had recently existed in Europe. Sovereignty in Europe had been and was subject to diverse modifications. Therefore, what European travelers projected onto Guinea were specific manifestations of sovereignty—a secular polity grounded in specific territory with a commercial base. Well into the twentieth century, Europeans naturalized this phenomenon. The anthropologists M. Fortes and E. Evans-Pritchard, for instance, introduced their study on African political systems by proclaiming that "every human society has some sort of territorial structure which . . . provides the framework, not only for the political organization . . . but for other forms of social organization also, such as the economic, for example." Fortes and Evans-Pritchard, *African Political Systems*, xiv. Ernst H. Kantorowicz's *The Kings Two Bodies: A Study in Medieval Political Theology* (Princeton, NJ: Princeton University Press, 1957) reveals the transition that European kingship experiences. The important point is that Europeans invented new traditions as discrete manifestations of kingship arose in the early modern period. Travelers, in turn, might have been looking for a particular tradition that was increasingly alien.

60. Cà da Mosto, *Voyages of Cadamosto*, 39.

61. Ibid., 39–40.

62. Ibid., 40.

63. Ibid. Innocent IV defined government's origin and authority in the phenomenon that Cà da Mosto found wanting in Guinea rulers. According to Muldoon, Innocent IV saw "lawful authorities as those men who possess the power to do justice and impose discipline on those who do not abide by the laws governing the relationship of men with their neighbors." Muldoon, *Popes, Lawyers, and Infidels*, 8.

64. Cà da Mosto, *Voyages of Cadamosto*, 54.

65. Ibid., 69.

66. Ibid., 33.

67. Ibid., 57.

68. Cà da Mosto simply rendered this defensive posture as a form of incivility and as marker of savagery. He intoned that the Gambia's inhabitants "were so rude and savage that we were unable to have speech with them on land." Later on, however, we learn that Gambia's inhabitants thought the same and worse of the Christians. "They firmly believed that we Christians ate human flesh," Cà da Mosto remarked, and "that we only bought negroes to eath them." The Gambians, therefore, resisted the Christian advances, wishing only "to slaughter us all, and to make a gift of our possessions to their lord." Such tantalizing detail, derived from a European travel writer thus projecting a dialogue on the "natives," warrants more conceptual consideration than it has been accorded in the historiography. For the most part, our analysis of such dynamics has been restricted to the framework of resistance. It speaks directly to a localized (Gambian) and historically specific anthropology and a concomitant philosophy of culture. Cà da Mosto, *Voyages of Cadamosto*, 58, 60, 62–63.

69. Cà da Mosto, *Voyages of Cadamosto*, 60.

70. Even before his arrival in the "Land of the Blacks," Cà da Mosto learned, if not assumed, that Guinea's sovereigns controlled the slave trade. After arriving on Arguin

Island, Cà da Mosto noted that "these Arabs also have many Berber horses, which they trade, and take to the Land of the Blacks, exchanging them with the rulers for slaves." *Voyages of Cadamosto*, 17.

71. Cà da Mosto, *Voyages of Cadamosto*, 67.

72. Ibid., 68.

73. In light of Iberian expansion, Woodrow Borah concluded, "Europeans followed an ad hoc rule of power. Heathens organized in powerful agglomerations, easily able to retaliate, were treated with consideration, although captives taken in war could be enslaved. Heathens without significant capability to withstand the Christians, or encountered in small numbers, might be seized as slaves for transportation to Europe or elsewhere, or might be conquered." Borah, *Justice by Insurance*, 16.

74. Cà da Mosto, *Voyages of Cadamosto*, 17.

75. Ibid., 18–19.

76. "Grants of Rights of Trade in Guinea to the Santiagians, 12 June 1466," in Blake, *Europeans in West Africa*, I, 65–67; "Grant of Fernão Gomes, 1469," in *Europeans in West Africa*, I, 67–68; "Renewal of Grant to Fernão Gomes, 1 June 1473," in *Europeans in West Africa*, I, 68–69; "The Foundation of the Castle and City of São Jorge Da Mina, 1482," in *Europeans in West Africa*, I, 70.

77. Boxer, *Portuguese Seaborne Empire*; Rodney, *History of the Upper Guinea Coast*, Hawthorne, *Planting Rice and Harvesting Slaves*; Green, *Rise of the Trans-Atlantic Slave Trade in Western Africa*; David Wheat, *Atlantic Africa and the Spanish Caribbean, 1570–1640* (Chapel Hill: University of North Carolina Press, for the Omohundro Institute Early American History and Culture, 2016).

78. Stuart B. Schwartz observed how "in the islands of São Tome, Cabo Verde and those off Guine proprietors were given jurisdiction of a final nature except in cases involving a punishment by death or loss of limb." Schwartz, *Sovereignty and Society in Colonial Brazil: The High Court of Bahia and Its Judges, 1609–1751* (Berkeley: University of California Press, 1973), 19. For similar observations, see Charles Verlinden, *The Beginnings of Modern Colonization: Eleven Essays with an Introduction*, translated by Yvonne Freccero (Ithaca, NY: Cornell University Press, 1970), 204–5.

79. Verlinden, *Beginnings of Modern Colonization*, 240; Again, Stuart Schwartz noted that "what most people failed to see . . . was the way in which juridical organization had become the structural organization of empire." Schwartz, *Sovereignty and Society in Colonial Brazil*, 21.

80. "Grant of Rights to Trade in Guinea to the Santiagians, 12 June 1466," in Blake, *Europeans in West Africa*, I, 64.

81. According to the medievalist Kenneth Pennington, a few decades later, Bartholomew de las Casas would "read what the canonist had to say about papal rescripts, and he concluded that the pope could not have meant what he said. The pope could not, after all, grant letters which prejudiced a third party, and the privilege of one party could not usurp the right of another. Concessions and privileges are to be made without injury to another party." Las Casas "observed that it would be absurd if the pope had actually taken

the Indians' dominium away; all he gave the Spanish was the right to preach the faith." Pennington, *Popes, Canonists and Texts*, 14–15.

82. "Appointment of Receivers of the Customs of Guinea at Sevilla, Valladolid, 19 August 1475," in Blake, *Europeans in West Africa*, I, 209–11.

83. "Appointment of Receivers of the Customs of Guinea at Seville, Valladolid, 19 August 1475," in Blake, *Europeans in West Africa*, I, 210.

84. McAlister, *Spain and Portugal*, 56–65.

85. "Zúniga's Account of the Appointment of Customs Receivers, 1475," in Blake, *Europeans in West Africa*, I, 212.

86. A Castilian chronicler wrote that the Catholic sovereigns "seeing the profit which was to be had in that business . . . took a hand therein; and they commanded that no one was to go those parts without their license, so that they might receive the fifth part of that obtained there, which pertained to them, as to the lords of the land." "A Castilian Account of the Discovery of Mina, c. 1474," in Blake, *Europeans in West Africa*, I, 206.

87. "Raiders from Palos seize a Negro Prince in Guinea, Queen Isabella to Mosén Diego de Valera. Tordesillas, 15 May 1476," in Blake, *Europeans in West Africa*, I, 212–13; "Description of the Same Raid and of the Events Leading up to It," in Blake, *Europeans in West Africa*, I, 213–17.

88. Nyquist, *Arbitrary Rule*; Siedentop, *Inventing the Individual*.

89. The Castilians eventually returned Niumi's sovereign and the subjects who could be recovered. Brooks, *Landlords and Strangers*, 133; Wright, *The World and a Very Small Place*.

90. "Royal Authority to the Men of Palos &c. to Sail to Mina, Seville, 4 March 1478," in Blake, *Europeans in West Africa*, I, 232. Even as Castile's sovereigns demanded that their subjects obtain license to travel and trade in designated parts of Guinea, the traders of the voyages here cited also secured letters of "safe-conduct" from Portugal's sovereign through Isabel and Ferdinand's efforts. These documents speak to Castile's insistence on diplomacy and a well-regulated commerce between Christians and pagans, Castilians and Guinea's inhabitants, mediated through charters and licenses. It is vitally important to see the Portuguese-Castilian rivalry as a symbolic right to Guinea but one that does not entail territorial rights in or over "the land of blacks." The issue is who among the Europeans can legitimately trade with Guinea's inhabitants. Portugal's Afonso stated as much when he instructed his officials on April 6, 1480, to plunge interlopers who ventured beyond the Canaries into the sea "in order to defend, guard and preserve the trades of Gujnee, the barters and mines of gold, and the commerce which rightly belongs to these kingdoms." In his order, Afonso asserts no claim to possessing Guinea or the territory of its inhabitants. "Order of King Affonso V of Portugal to His Captains to Cast into the Sea the Crews of Ships Found Beyond the Canaries, Vianna, 6 April 1480," in *Europeans in West Africa*, I, 245; "The Voyage of Two Caravels, La Bolandra and La Toca, from Andalusia to Mina During the Winter of 1479–80, Decree of the Catholic Kings, Toledo, 3 February 1480," in *Europeans in West Africa*, I, 241–43; "The Voyage of Two Other Caravels, La Galiota and Sant Telmo, from Andalusia to Mina During the Winter of 1479–80," in *Europeans in West Africa*, I, 244–45.

91. Commenting on Isabel's behavior, Shiels remarked that "her civil authority did not empower her to cut the chain of ecclesiastical right." Therefore, he observed that the incursions into Guinea "carried overtones of imperial character," thus representing "a new departure in politics." Shiels, *King and Church*, 42, 47. Despite Shiels's assertion corroborated by numerous other scholars, canon law, and, by implication, Innocent IV, opinion held sway well into the second half of the sixteenth century. Pennington, *Popes, Canonists and Texts*, 6, 9, 14–15; Muldoon, *Popes, Lawyers, and Infidels*, 27, 120, 153, 156.

92. "Pulgar's Account of Cobide's Voyage, 1478," in Blake, *Europeans in West Africa*, I, 235–36; "Portuguese Version of the Voyage of Cobides, 1478," in *Europeans in West Africa*, I, 236–37; "Another Portuguese Version of the Voyage of Cobides, 1478," in *Europeans in West Africa*, I, 237; "Castilian Request for Papal Support for the Voyage, 1478 (?)," in *Europeans in West Africa*, I, 234–35.

93. "Treaty between Spain and Portugal, concluded at Alcàçovas, September 4, 1479, Ratification by Spain, March 6, 1480 [Ratification by Portugal, September 8, 1479]," in Gardiner, *European Treaties*, 33–48.

94. "The Bull Aeterni Regis (Sixtus IV), June 21, 1481," in Gardiner, *European Treaties*, 49–55.

95. "Treaty Between Spain and Portugal Concluded at Tordesillas, June 7, 1494, Ratification by Spain, July 2, 1494 [Ratification by Portugal, September 5, 1494]," in Gardiner, *European Treaties*, 84–100; "Compact Between Spain and Portugal, Signed by the Catholic Sovereigns at Madrid, May 7, 1495," in *European Treaties*, 101–6.

96. Even throughout the sixteenth century, numerous European travelers noted as much. See, for instance, "Martin Frobisher's Report About Guinea, Based upon His Experience While a Prisoner at Mina in 1555, 27 May 1562," in Blake, *Europeans in West Africa*, II, 358–59.

97. Barros, *Asia*, 1st decade, book 3, chapter 1, 117.

98. Interestingly enough, Patricia Seed associated such practices with Spanish and French possession in the Americas, whereas she noted that the Portuguese relied on nautical and astronomical practices. From the beginning of their explorations in the Atlantic, the Portuguese marked their presence with insignia, wooden crosses, and spectacles. Seed, *Ceremonies of Possession*, 41–99. João de Barros, a sixteenth-century chronicler, historian, and Portuguese official, stated that "it was not unusual that they should found this memorial cut on the trees, because at that time our men frequently did so, and some of them, in praise of Prince Henry, cut the motto of his emblem . . . because they thought that this inscription cut in the bark of the dragon-trees, in addition to wooden crosses would, be sufficient to establish possession of their discoveries. Later on King João the Second ordered Padroes to be erected with inscriptions setting forth when and by who the land had been discovered." Barros, *Asia*, 1st decade, book 2, chapter 2, 112.

99. "The Foundation of the Castle and City of São Jorge da Mina, 1482," in Blake, *Europeans in West Africa*, I, 72–73; Barros, *Asia*, 1st decade, book 3, chapter 1, 116–17.

100. "The Foundation of the Castle and City of São Jorge da Mina, 1482," in Blake, *Europeans in West Africa*, I, 74; Barros, *Asia*, 1st decade, book 3, chapter 1, 118.

101. "The Foundation of the Castle and City of São Jorge da Mina, 1482," in Blake, *Europeans in West Africa*, I, 74.

102. Ibid.

103. Barros, *Asia*, 1st decade, book 3, chapter 2, 123; "The Foundation of the Castle and City of São Jorge da Mina, 1482," in Blake, *Europeans in West Africa*, I, 77; Pacheco Pereira, *Esmeraldo de situ orbis*, 119.

104. "Diogo D' Alvarenga to King Manuel, São Jorge da Mina, 18 August 1503," in Blake, *Europeans in West Africa*, I, 94–96; "Duarte Pacheco Pereira, Governor of São Jorge da Mina, to the Factor, Joao de Figueiredo, 8 August 1520," in Blake, *Europeans in West Africa*, I, 130–31; "The Same to the Same, São Jorge da Mina, 18 August 1520," in Blake, *Europeans in West Africa*, I, 131–32. The Portuguese occasionally paid their tribute to Mina's rulers in slaves. Alberto Iria, "Da fundoção e governo do Castelo ou Fortaleza de São Jorge da Mina pelo Portugueses e da sua acçao missionária após o descrobimento desta costa," *Studia* 1 (1958), 45.

105. "King John III to Affonso de Albuquerque, Governor of Sâo Jorge Da Mina, 13 October 1523," in Blake, *Europeans in West Africa*.

106. "Appointment of Affonso de Albuquerque as Captain of São Jorge da Mina, 4 July 1522," in Blake, *Europeans in West Africa*, I, 132; "King John III to Affonso de Albuquerque, Governor of São Jorge da Mina, 13 October 1523," in Blake, *Europeans in West Africa*, I, 133–34.

107. Barros, *Asia*, 1st decade, book 3, chapter 6, 128.

108. Ibid., 128–29.

109. Pacheco Pereira, *Esmeraldo de situ orbis*, 153–54.

110. Ibid., 142.

111. Ibid., 141.

112. The point here is that the history based on the nation and nation-state is earlier configured around providence and subsequently providential figures (great men) as the makers of history. In the modern period, their ideology, nationalism, results in their assuming the helm of the nation-state. Here think of the Kwame Nkrumah adage, "Seek ye first the political kingdom."

113. Beatrix Heintze, "Der Portugiesisch-Afrikanische Vasallenvertrag in Angola im 17 Jahrhundert," *Paideuma* 25 (1979): 195–223.

114. Pacheco Pereira cites numerous examples of cannibalism, which ecclesiastical authorities defined as a violation of natural law. Pacheco Pereira, *Esmeraldo de situ orbis*, passim.

CHAPTER 6

1. "Letter 2: To Fray Bernardino de Vique, OP, Salamanca, 18 March [1546?]," in *Vitoria: Political Writings*, edited by Anthony Pagden and Jeremy Lawrance (New York: Cambridge University Press, 1991), 334–335.

2. Pagden, *Fall of Natural Man*, 60. Anthony Pagden writes that "the first . . . to achieve recognition *as* a political language was political Aristotelianism. This was the creation of St. Thomas Aquinas and his immediate followers. . . . It was, as Rubinstein says, William of Moerbeke's translation of the *Politics*, which effectively 'introduced *politicus* and its Latin equivalent *civilis* into Western political language,' and with the term came the Greek concept of the 'politic.'" Pagden, *Languages of Political Theory in Early-Modern Europe*, 3.

3. To understand these answers on the enslavement of blacks, writes Friar
   Arcos, one must know the questions, which are as follows: First, they take
   trinkets to Guinea to lure the blacks, who are seized when they come to look
   at them . . . second about those who have been enslaved in war . . . third, the
   blacks have a custom that when they are leading one their own to execution,
   if anyone can be found to buy the criminal they commute the sentence to
   slavery: the question is whether this slavery must be perpetual or temporary;
   and fourth can we rest easy in conscience on the assurance that the king of
   Portugal and the members of his Council will not permit unjust trading?
   ("Letter 2," in Pagden and Lawrance, *Vitoria*, 334)

4. William D. Phillips Jr., *Slavery in Medieval and Early Modern Iberia* (Philadelphia: University of Pennsylvania Press, 2014); Nyquist, *Arbitrary Rule*. Patterson writes, "The means of enslavement of the Africans brought to the New World still needs to be thoroughly explored. Of the Senegambian regions Philip D. Curtin has written that 'at least 80 per cent . . . were captives.'" Curtin, *Economic Change in Precolonial Africa* (Madison: University of Wisconsin Press, 1975), 154. "It would be wrong to assume that the same held true for other areas of West Africa throughout the period of the trade. A safer claim is that under the pressure of European demand, the majority of slaves shipped from Africa until the early decades of the eighteenth century were war captives." Patterson, *Slavery and Social Death*, 397n54.

5. We can, in fact, surmise that the largely enslaved African population along with the free population of African descent constituted an even greater percentage of the total population on the Iberian Peninsula. A number of scholars have pointed to Isabel's order that curtailed the trade in Indian slaves precipitating the end of Indian slavery—in theory—in the Spanish Indies. In tandem with Bartolomé de la Casas's disavowing the enslavement of Indians and subsequent repudiation of slavery, scholars have been keen to point to Castilian ambivalence on the issue of slavery as a way of underscoring the "Spanish struggle for justice" in relation to the treatment of Africans but particularly Indians. Often framed in relation to treatment and the Black Legend, the salient issued revolved around sovereignty. Nancy E. van Deusen, *Global Indios: The Indigenous Struggle for Justice in Sixteenth-Century Spain* (Durham, NC: Duke University Press, 2015).

6. Foucault, *Security, Territory, Population*, 96.

7. Ibid., 106.

8. Saunders, *Social History of Black Slaves and Freedom in Portugal*.

9. Elvira Vilches, *New World Gold: Cultural Anxiety and Monetary Disorder in Early Modern Spain* (Chicago: University of Chicago Press, 2010); Daviken Studnicki-Gizbert, *A Nation upon the Ocean Sea: Portugal's Atlantic Diaspora and the Crisis of the Spanish Empire, 1492–1640* (New York: Oxford University Press, 2007).

10. Studnicki-Gizbert, *Nation upon the Ocean Sea*, 31–34.

11. It might be argued that not until the process of devolution of absolutism had been enacted could the authority of masters as owners of chattel be totally assured. After all, sovereigns could (and in the case of Catholic absolutists did) intervene for reasons of state in the affairs of their subjects despite their claims of dominion in the case of property. For a genealogy of this claim, see Michael McKeon, *The Secret History of Domesticity: Public, Private, and the Division of Knowledge* (Baltimore: Johns Hopkins University Press, 2005).

12. Albert O. Hirschman, *The Passions and the Interests: Political Arguments for Capitalism Before Its Triumph* (Princeton, NJ: Princeton University Press, 1977); J. G. A. Pocock, "Virtue and Property: The Question of Liberal Origins," in *Virtue, Commerce, and History: Essays on Political Thought and History, Chiefly in the Eighteenth Century*, J. G. A. Pocock (New York: Cambridge University Press, 1985), 51–71.

13. The historian Sherwin K. Bryant has brilliantly chartered the linkage between slavery and colonial Spanish governance in *Rivers of Gold, Lives of Bondage: Governing Through Slavery in Colonial Quito* (Chapel Hill: University of North Carolina Press, 2014).

14. In a recent and at times brilliant discussion on piety and Islamic revival among Egyptian women, the anthropologist Saba Mahmood writes that the "cultural critic Jeffery Minson has argued persuasively that one way in which the legacy of humanist ethics, particularly in its Kantian formulation, has continued to be important to post-Enlightenment thought is in the relative lack of attention given to the morphology of moral actions, that is, to their precise shape and form." According to Mahmood, Minson tracks this tradition back to Kant "for whom morality proper was primarily a rational matter that entailed the exercise of the faculty of reason, shorn of the specific context (of social virtues, habit, character formation, and so on) in which the act unfolded." To Minson's argument, Mahmood contributes that "the Kantian legacy . . . becomes particularly important in light of the tradition of Aristotelian ethics it displaces—a tradition in which morality was both realized through, and manifest in, outward behavioral forms." In light of the neo-Scholasticism shaping political thought in sixteenth- and seventeenth-century Spain and its dependencies, the discussion between Kantian and Aristotelian ethics seems far from misplaced. The behavioral patterns of New Spain's subjects—though not necessarily Aristotelian in its cultural logic—were nonetheless processed by Spanish officials and thinkers through that light. For this reason, we might profit from seeing and thinking about other forms of behavior, not just ethical behavior as being embedded in a tradition of practice. Stated differently, rather than attributing a consciousness to the behavior of Africans that mirrors the Kantian legacy, we might be able to see consciousness and behavior as being mutually constitutive of meaning. And in the case of seventeenth-century African marriage patterns, we might discern how an individual in that instance wished

to be defined. This shift could be interpreted as a shift from a Kantian to an Aristotelian formulation of context. Here Saba Mahmood is useful. Mahmood writes that "one consequence of this Kantian conception of ethics is the relative lack of attention paid to the manifest form ethical practices take, and a general demotion of conduct, social demeanor, and etiquettes in our analysis of moral systems." As Minson points out, even scholars like Bourdieu, whose work focuses on practices of dress, physical bearing, and styles of comportment—things that Bourdieu calls "the practical mnemonics of culture"—consider these practices interesting only insofar as a rational evaluation reveals them to be signs and symbols of a much deeper and more fundamental reality of social structures and cultural logics (Jeffrey Minson, "Men and Manners: Kantian Humanism, Rhetoric and the History of Ethics," *Economy & Society* 18, no. 1 (February 1989): 191–220). I agree with Minson: "when Bourdieu considers the variety of practices that characterize a particular social group (such as their styles of eating, socializing, and entertainment), he is primarily concerned with how these practices embody and symbolize the doxa and ethos of the group such that the ideologies the members inhabit come to be congealed in their social or class habitus. One may argue, however, that the significance of an embodied practice is not exhausted by its ability to function as an index of social and class status or a group's ideological habitus." Saba Mahmood, *Politics of Piety: The Islamic Revival and the Feminist Subject* (Princeton, NJ: Princeton University Press, 2005), 25, 26. The political theorist Richard Tuck writes succinctly on the matter of historical sensibility. "This deeper understanding of the humanist roots of the modern moral science," notes Tuck,

> is merely one example of the kind of insight which is available to us once the post-Kantian history of morality is replaced with the pre-Kantian one. The moral theories of the late seventeenth- and eighteenth-century natural lawyers constituted in many ways the most important language of politics and ethics in Europe, influential over a huge area and in a wide variety of disciplines. Their essential unity has been fractured and their character misunderstood for the last two centuries; but if we allow ourselves to be guided by "the history of morality" which they themselves inspired, we can recover a truer sense of what they represented. Not the least important consequence of this is then that we can put into a proper perspective the invention at the end of the eighteenth century of the political and ethnical theories by which in one way or another we all still live. (Tuck, "The 'Modern' Theory of Natural Law," in Pagden, *Languages of Political Theory in Early-Modern Europe*, 118–19)

15. Franklin, *Jean Bodin and the Rise of Absolutist Theory*, 6.

16. Patterson, *Slavery and Social Death*, 35. Again, the historian Sherwin Bryant is one of the few scholars working on early Latin America and slavery who seems to have taken up this observation. Bryant, *Rivers of Gold*.

17. Davis, *Problem of Slavery in Western Culture*, 187.

18. Ibid., 187, 188.

19. Finally, Davis identifies Bartolomé Frías de Albornoz as another Spanish writer offering a critique of the sixteenth-century slave trade. "An even more radical attack on Negro slavery," notes Davis,

> appeared in 1573 from the hand of Bartolomé de Albornoz, who had become a professor of law at the University of Mexico at the time of its founding, and who had later been called to study at Talavera. Like Mercado, Albornoz challenged both the methods by which Africans were captured and the legality of their subsequent sale. He went beyond the theologian, however, in his contempt for sophistry and rationalization. In the ironic tone of a philosophe, Albornoz said that the purchase of Negroes from the Portuguese must be in conformity with both statute law and the law of conscience, since it was accepted by kings and public opinion; no member of a religious order had spoken out against the trade, and indeed the clergy were as active as other people in buying and selling slaves.

For Davis such sentiments were sufficient for him to conclude that "Bartolomé de Albornoz . . . had the outlook of a genuine abolitionist. It would appear that no one else attacked Negro slavery with such uncompromising boldness until the late seventeenth century." Davis, *Problem of Slavery in Western Culture*, 188–190.

20. J. H. Franklin, "The Persistence of Medieval Constitutionalism," in Franklin, *Jean Bodin and the Rise of Absolutist Theory*, 1–22.

21. Hont, *Jealousy of Trade*, 8–9.

22. Ibid., 21. Hume's perspective—a perspective shared by other figures of the Scottish Enlightenment—underscores both the novelty and critique associated with identifying modernity with 1492 and the Iberian experience.

23. Interestingly, Buck-Morss quotes David Brion Davis: "For eighteenth-century thinkers who contemplated the subject, slavery stood as the central metaphor for all the forces that debased the human spirit." Davis, *Problem of Slavery in the Age of Revolution*, 263, cited in Susan Buck-Morss, "Hegel and Haiti," *Critical Inquiry* 26, no. 4 (Summer 2000): 821–65.

24. Hegel identifies the brutal despotism of the African sovereign as the sign that disqualifies Africa and Africans from civilization. In doing so, Hegel is far from the first to point to the symbiotic relationship between African sovereigns and African despotism. John Iliffe notes in the opening of his book on honor in Africa that the "Buganda's heroes displayed greater concern for loyalty to chief and king than those of *The Iliad*, while real heroes, of course, pursued additional routes to honor, perhaps by generosity, gifts of leadership, or arts of peace, but the repeated demonstration of martial prowess in the pursuit of individual preeminence remained indispensable." Iliffe, *Honour in African History*, 2. This comparative reference along with the constant refrain that Africans were invariably more deferential to their leaders or that the despotic rulers were intent on the debasement

of their subjects represents a persistent theme in European writings on African governance or the dominion of the African ruler but that nonetheless has a history.

25. My concern with Buck-Morss's claim is that it frames slavery but also the slave trade in a singular mode. Consequently, the writers' moral center experiences a shift— "slavery had become the root metaphor of political philosophy, connoting everything that was evil about power relations." Aside from centering the conscience of European philosophers as the principal agents who found fault with the institution, Buck-Morss loses sight of the critique that emanates from the thinking of Scottish political economists and French physiocrats attentive to the fact that "New World slavery developed a novel ferocity, scale and focus. . . . It brought about what might be termed a degradation of slavery violating on a massive scale even traditional notions of what slavery meant." Blackburn, *Making of New World Slavery*, 41–42.

26. da Silva Horta, "A Representação do Africano na Literatura de Viagens."

27. Wolf, *Europe and the People Without History*.

28. Thornton, *Africa and Africans*, 184.

29. B. Jewsiewicki, "The Production of History and Social Conscience, Or How to 'Civilize' the Other," *History in Africa* 8 (1981), 75–87.

30. Rodney, *History of the Upper Guinea Coast*, 166.

31. Pacheco Pereira, *Esmeraldo de situ orbis*, 128.

32. Ibid., 132.

33. Ibid., 130.

34. Ibid., 147.

35. Ibid., 154.

36. P. E. H. Hair, "The Use of African Languages in Afro-European Contacts in Guinea: 1440–1560," *Sierra Leone Language Review* 5 (1966): 5–26.

EPILOGUE

1. Andrew Apter, *Black Critics and Kings: The Hermeneutics of Power in Yoruba Society* (Chicago: University of Chicago Press, 1992); Charles Piot, *Remotely Global: Village Modernity in West Africa* (Chicago: University of Chicago Press, 1999); Piot, *Nostalgia for the Future: West Africa After the Cold War* (Chicago: University of Chicago Press, 2010).

2. The phenotypes, though synonymous with the colonial legacy, preceded the advent of European rule. Indeed, the da Silva family in Porto Novo, Benin, traces its genealogy back to a white Brazilian paterfamilias who after making his fortune in trade—the slave trade—among other things opted not to return to Brazil in the second half of the nineteenth century. He was not alone. A number of whites, derived from Brazilian, Spanish, Cuban, and vague European origins, established roots in Benin. As founding fathers, many of these men took both Afro-Brazilian and African mistresses and wives who, in turn, afforded them local and circum-Atlantic kinship ties that engendered protection and trade. From these conjugal unions, a process of Afro-Brazilian ethnogenesis,

familiar to us through the work of J. Michael Turner and J. Lorand Matory, took hold. Generations later these families and their descendants continue to date their origins with the arrival of the white patriarch and the kinship ties afforded by the union with an Afro-Brazilian or African wife. In the case of the da Silvas, this phenomenon was on display through hundreds of passport-sized photos that identified the individual and her or his specific relationship to the family. Rather than assuming the form of a family tree in descending order, the pictures resemble a spread in police archives. While this format might be designed to save space or reflects the creative limitations of the family curator, Karim da Silva, it underscores the deep and dense network of da Silva that took hold in Porto Novo.

Porto Novo [J. Lorand Matory, *Black Atlantic Religion: Tradition, Transnationalism, and Matriarchy in the Afro-Brazilian Candomblé* (Princeton: Princeton University Press, 2005), 81–84] no doubt, is remarkable in its architecture in contrast to say Ouidah, Cotonou, or Abomey. Indeed, some of the most distinctive buildings warrant analogy with Salvador da Bahia, Illheus, or those brilliant villages in Minas Gerais. There is no mistaking that the structure that houses the Musée da Silva reflects its Brazilian influences, with its large patio and the two-story structure resembling the *fazendas* of Brazil. There was understandably a difference between the material culture of Benin and Brazil. I did not arrive in Porto Novo or for that matter at the Musée da Silva with the highest expectations. Architectural history had never been my forte. I often appreciated the novelty or distinction in what I saw but still mostly missed the nuance that informed writers alerted me to when looking at say a cathedral, a castle, or a mosque. Brazilian architecture? I thought its significance would blow right over me. And to a certain extent it has. But in Porto Novo, and in Benin generally, one cannot but notice the relationship between migration, cultural influence, and material culture.

In the museum of the da Silva family, tangible diasporic links, among other things, underscored how Afro-Brazilian families served as harbingers of black modernity that included the rise of African nationalism. In the complex nineteenth- and early twentieth-century landscape in which slavery, freedom, colonialism, and nationalism have become iconic tropes, the da Silva family museum and archive enables us to viscerally see how former slaves and their descendants served as the architects of a modern nationalist political project that culminated in African independence. In terms of the modern political project, one need only note the constant emphasis on dignitaries: local officials and represented men (the doctors, the well-heeled merchant, the successful printer, the lawyers, the judges, and colonial officials); but this was not simply limited to the Christian or Catholic officials, the ones often linked to the French colonial state. It also included Muslim and traditional African figures (kings that would subsequently be identified as chiefs or who held a sinecure in the colonial administration). The family valued and evidently nurtured these associations, and this would eventually serve as the basis of a localized African public sphere and the localized basis of the imagined nation.

3. Sanneh, *Abolitionists Abroad*.

4. Coombes, *Reinventing Africa*.

5. Desai, *Subject to Colonialism*, 1–4.

BIBLIOGRAPHY

Abulafia, David. *The Discovery of Mankind: Atlantic Encounters in the Age of Columbus.* New Haven, CT: Yale University Press, 2008.

Adelman, Jeremy. *Sovereignty and Revolution in the Iberian Atlantic.* Princeton, NJ: Princeton University Press, 2006.

Africa's Ogun: Old World and New. Edited by Sandra T. Barnes. Bloomington: Indiana University Press, 1997.

Agamben, Giorgio. *The Kingdom and the Glory: For a Theological Genealogy of Economy and Government.* Translated by Lorenzo Chiesa. Palo Alto, CA: Stanford University Press, 2011.

———. *State of Exception.* Translated by Keven Attell. Chicago: University of Chicago Press, 2005.

Anderson, Perry. *Lineages of the Absolutist State.* New York: Verso, 1974.

Appiah, Kwame Anthony. *In My Father's House: Africa in the Philosophy of Culture.* New York: Oxford University Press, 1992.

Apter, Andrew. *Black Critics and Kings: The Hermeneutics of Power in a Yoruba Society.* Chicago: University of Chicago Press, 1992.

———. *The Pan-African Nation: Oil and the Spectacle of Culture in Nigeria.* Chicago: University of Chicago Press, 2005.

Arendt, Hannah. *The Human Condition.* Introduction by Margaret Canovan. Chicago: University of Chicago Press, 1958.

———. *On Revolution.* Introduction by Jonathan Schell. New York: Penguin, 1963.

Aristotle. *Aristotle, The Politics.* Translated and with an introduction by Carnes Lord. Chicago: University of Chicago Press, 1984.

Asad, Talal. *Formations of the Secular: Christianity, Islam, Modernity.* Palo Alto, CA: Stanford University Press, 2003.

Barry, Boubacar. *The Kingdom of Waalo: Senegal Before the Conquest.* New York: Diasporic Africa Press, 2012.

Bartlett, Robert. *The Making of Europe: Conquest, Colonization and Cultural Change, 950–1350.* Princeton, NJ: Princeton University Press, 1993.

Baucom, Ian. *Specters of the Atlantic: Finance Capital, Slavery and the Philosophy of History.* Durham, NC: Duke University Press, 2005.

Bayart, Jean-François. *The State in Africa: The Politics of the Belly.* Malden, MA: Polity, 2009.

Bennett, Herman. *Africans in Colonial Mexico: Absolutism, Christianity, and Afro-Creole Consciousness, 1570–1640*. Bloomington: Indiana University Press, 2003.

———. *Colonial Blackness: A History of Afro-Mexico*. Bloomington: Indiana University Press, 2009.

Benton, Lauren. *Law and Colonial Cultures: Legal Regimes in World History, 1400–1900*. New York: Cambridge University Press, 2002.

———. *A Search for Sovereignty: Law and Geography in European Empires,1400–1900*. New York: Cambridge University Press, 2010.

Bison, Thomas N. *The Crisis of the Twelfth Century: Power, Lordship, and the Origins of European Government*. Princeton, NJ: Princeton University Press, 2009.

Black, Jeremy. *Kings, Nobles and Commoners: States and Societies in Early Modern Europe: A Revisionist History*. New York: I. B. Tauris, 2004.

Black Africans in Renaissance Europe. Edited by T. F. Earle and K. J. P. Lowe. New York: Cambridge University Press, 2005.

Blackburn, Robin. *The American Crucible: Slavery, Emancipation and Human Rights*. New York: Verso, 2011.

———. *The Making of New World Slavery: From the Baroque to the Modern, 1492–1800*. New York: Verso, 1997.

Blier, Suzanne Preston. *The Royal Arts of Africa: The Majesty of Form*. Upper Saddle River, NJ: Prentice Hall, 1998.

Block, Marc. *Slavery and Serfdom in the Middle Ages: Selected Essays*. Translated by William R. Beer. Berkeley: University of California Press, 1975.

Blumenthal, Debra. *Enemies and Familiars: Slavery and Mastery in Fifteenth-Century Valencia*. Ithaca, NY: Cornell University Press, 2009.

Bodin, Jean. *Method for the Easy Comprehension of History*. Translated by Beatrice Reynolds. New York: Octagon, 1966.

———. *On Sovereignty: Four Chapters from the Six Books of the Commonwealth*. Edited and translated by Julian H. Franklin. New York: Cambridge University Press, 1992.

Bonilla, Yarimar. *Non-Sovereign Futures: French Caribbean Politics in the Wake of Disenchantment*. Chicago: University of Chicago Press, 2015.

Brading, D. A. *The First America: The Spanish Monarchy, Creole Patriots, and the Liberal State: 1492–1867*. New York: Cambridge University Press, 1991.

Brooks, George E. *Landlords and Strangers: Ecology, Society, and Trade in Western Africa, 1000–1630*. Boulder, CO: Westview, 1993.

Brown, Christopher Leslie. *Moral Capital: Foundations of British Abolitionism*. Chapel Hill: University of North Carolina Press, 2006.

Brown, Vincent. *The Reaper's Garden: Death and Power in the World of Atlantic Slavery*. Cambridge, MA: Harvard University Press, 2008.

Brown, Wendy. *Walled States, Waning Sovereignty*. New York: Zone, 2014.

Brundage, James A. *Law, Sex, and Christian Society in Medieval Europe*. Chicago: University of Chicago Press, 1987.

———. *Medieval Canon Law*. New York: Longman, 1995.

———. *The Medieval Origins of the Legal Profession: Canonists, Civilians, and Courts.* Chicago: University of Chicago Press, 2008.

Bryant, Sherwin K. *Rivers of Gold, Lives of Bondage: Governing Through Slavery in Colonial Quito.* Chapel Hill: University of North Carolina Press, 2014.

Burton, Antoinette. *The Trouble with Empire: Challenges to Modern British Imperialism.* New York: Oxford University Press, 2015.

Byrd, Alexander X. *Captives and Voyagers: Black Migrants Across the Eighteenth-Century British Atlantic World.* Baton Rouge: Louisiana State University Press, 2008.

The Cambridge History of Medieval Political Thought c. 350–1450. Edited by J. H. Burns. New York: Cambridge University Press, 1988.

Campbell, Mary B. *The Witness and the Other World: Exotic European Travel Writing, 400–1600.* Ithaca, NY: Cornell University Press, 1988.

Candido, Mariana P. *An African Slaving Port and the Atlantic World: Benguela and Its Hinterland.* New York: Cambridge University Press, 2013.

Cañeque, Alejandro. *The King's Living Image: The Culture and Politics of Viceregal Power in Colonial Mexico.* New York: Routledge, 2004.

Cañizares-Esguerra, Jorge. *How to the Write the History of the New World: Histories, Epistemologies, and Identities in the Eighteenth-Century Atlantic World.* Palo Alto, CA: Stanford University Press, 2001.

Central Africans and Cultural Transformations in the American Diaspora. Edited by Linda M. Heywood. New York: Cambridge University Press, 2002.

Changing Identities in Early Modern France. Edited by Michael Wolfe. Durham, NC: Duke University Press, 1997.

Comaroff, Jean. *Body of Power Spirit of Resistance: The Culture and History of a South African People.* Chicago: University of Chicago Press, 1985.

Comaroff, Jean, and John Comaroff. *Of Revelation and Revolution: Christianity, Colonialism and Consciousness in South Africa.* Volume I. Chicago: University of Chicago Press, 1991.

Cooper, Frederick. *Colonialism in Question: Theory, Knowledge, History.* Berkeley: University of California Press, 2005.

Coronil, Fernando. *The Magical State: Nature, Money, and Modernity in Venezuela.* Chicago: University of Chicago Press, 1997.

Crowley, Roger. *1453: The Holy War for Constantinople and the Clash of Islam and the West.* New York: Hyperion, 2005.

Curtin, Philip D. *The Atlantic Slave Trade: A Census.* Madison: University of Wisconsin Press, 1969.

Davis, David Brion. *The Problem of Slavery in Western Culture.* Ithaca, NY: Cornell University Press, 1996.

Davis, Kathleen. *Periodization and Sovereignty: How Ideas of Feudalism and Secularization Govern the Politics of Time.* Philadelphia: University of Pennsylvania Press, 2008.

Davis, Natalie Zemon. *Trickster Travels: A Sixteenth-Century Muslim Between Worlds.* New York: Hill and Wang, 2006.

De Oliveíra Marques, A. H. *History of Portugal, Volume I: From Lusitania to Empire*. New York: Columbia University Press, 1972.

De Wet, Chris L. *Preaching Bondage: John Chrysostom and the Discourse of Slavery in Early Christianity*. Berkeley: University of California Press, 2015.

Dening, Greg. *Performances*. Chicago: University of Chicago Press, 1996.

Desai, Gaurav. *Subject to Colonialism: African Self-Fashioning and the Colonial Library*. Durham, NC: Duke University Press, 2001.

El Hamel, Chouki. *Black Morocco: A History of Slavery, Race, and Islam*. New York: Cambridge University Press, 2013.

Elias, Norbert. *The Civilizing Process: Sociogenetic and Psychogenetic Investigations*. Translated by Edmund Jephcott. Oxford: Blackwell, 1994.

Elliot, J. H. *The Old World and the New: 1492–1650*. New York: Cambridge University Press, 1970.

Eltis, David. *The Rise of African Slavery in the Americas*. New York: Cambridge University Press, 2000.

Fabian, Johannes. *Out of Our Minds: Reason and Madness in the Exploration of Central Africa*. Berkeley: University of California Press, 2000.

Ferguson, James. *Expectations of Modernity: Myths and Meanings of Urban Life on the Zambian Copperbelt*. Berkeley: University of California Press, 1999.

———. *Global Shadows: African in the Neoliberal World Order*. Durham, NC: Duke University Press, 2006.

Fernández-Armesto, Felipe. *1492: The Year the World Began*. New York: Harper Collins, 2009.

———. *The Americas: A Hemispheric History*. New York: Random House, 2003.

Ferreira, Roquinaldo. *Cross-Cultural Exchange in the Atlantic World: Angola and Brazil During the Era of the Slave Trade*. New York: Cambridge University Press, 2012.

Foucault, Michel. *Discipline and Punish: The Birth of the Prison*. Translated by Alan Sheridan. New York: Vintage, 1979.

———. *The History of Sexuality: An Introduction*. Volume I. Translated by Robert Hurley. New York: Vintage, 1990.

———. *Security, Territory, Population: Lectures at the Collège de France: 1977–1978*. Edited by Michel Senellart and translated by Graham Burchell. New York: Picador, 2007.

The Foucault Effect: Studies in Governmentality, with Two Lectures by and an Interview with Michel Foucault. Edited by Graham Burchell, Colin Gordon, and Peter Miller. Chicago: University of Chicago Press, 1991.

Francisco de Vitoria: Political Writings. Edited by Anthony Pagden and Jeremy Lawrance. New York: Cambridge University Press, 1991.

Franklin, Julian H. *Jean Bodin and the Rise of Absolutist Theory*. New York: Cambridge University Press, 1973.

Fromont, Cécile. *The Art of Conversion: Christian Visual Culture in the Kingdom of Kongo*. Chapel Hill: University of North Carolina Press, 2014.

Fuchs, Barbara. *Exotic Nation: Maurophilia and the Construction of Early Modern Spain.* Philadelphia: University of Pennsylvania Press, 2009.

Geertz, Clifford. *Negara: The Theatre State in Nineteenth-Century Bali.* Princeton, NJ: Princeton University Press, 1980.

Gilroy, Paul. *The Black Atlantic: Modernity and Double Consciousness.* Cambridge, MA: Harvard University Press, 1993.

Given, James B. *Inquisition and Medieval Society: Power, Discipline and Resistance in Languedoc.* Ithaca, NY: Cornell University Press, 1977.

Glassman, Jonathon. *War of Words, War of Stones: Racial Thought and Violence in Colonial Zanzibar.* Bloomington: Indiana University Press, 2011.

Green, Toby. *The Rise of the Trans-Atlantic Slave Trade in Western Africa, 1300–1589.* New York: Cambridge University Press, 2012.

Greene, Molly. *A Shared World: Christians and Muslims in Early Modern Mediterranean.* Princeton, NJ: Princeton University Press, 2000.

Grovogui, Siba N'Zatioula. *Sovereigns, Quasi Sovereigns, and Africans: Race and Self-Determination in International Law.* Minneapolis: University of Minnesota Press, 1996.

Hall, Bruce S. *A History of Race in Muslim West Africa, 1600–1960.* New York: Cambridge University Press, 2011.

Hanchard, Michael George. *Orpheus and Power: The Movimento Negro of Rio de Janeiro and São Paulo, Brazil, 1945–1988.* Princeton, NJ: Princeton University Press, 1994.

Harper, Kyle. *Slavery in the Late Roman World: AD 275–425.* New York: Cambridge University Press, 2011.

Hartman, Saidiya V. *Scenes of Subjection: Terror, Slavery, and Self-Making in Nineteenth-Century America.* New York: Oxford University Press, 1997.

Harvey, L. P. *Islamic Spain: 1250–1500.* Chicago: University of Chicago Press, 1990.

Hawthorne, Walter. *Planting Rice and Harvesting Slaves: Transformations Along the Guinea-Bissau Coast, 1400–1900.* Portsmouth, NH: Heinemann, 2003.

Helms, Mary W. *Ulysses' Sail: An Ethnographic Odyssey of Power, Knowledge, and Geographical Distance.* Princeton, NJ: Princeton University Press, 1988.

Herzog, Tamar. *Frontiers of Possession: Spain and Portugal in Europe and the Americas.* Cambridge, MA: Harvard University Press, 2015.

Hess, Andrew C. *The Forgotten Frontier: A History of the Sixteenth-Century Ibero-African Frontier.* Chicago: University of Chicago Press, 1978.

Heywood, Linda M., and John K. Thornton. *Central Africans, Atlantic Creoles, and the Foundations of the Americas, 1585–1660.* New York: Cambridge University Press, 2007.

Hirschman, Albert O. *The Passions and the Interests: Political Arguments for Capitalism Before Its Triumph.* Princeton, NJ: Princeton University Press, 1977.

Hobbes, Thomas. *Leviathan.* Edited with an introduction by J. C. A. Gaskin. New York: Oxford University Press, 1996.

Hodgen, Margaret T. *Early Anthropology in the Sixteenth and Seventeenth Centuries.* Philadelphia: University of Pennsylvania Press, 1964.

Holt, Thomas C. *The Problem of Freedom: Race, Labor, and Politics in Jamaica and Britain, 1832–1938*. Baltimore: Johns Hopkins University Press, 1992.

Hopkins, A. G. *An Economic History of West Africa*. New York: Longman, 1973.

Hulme, Peter. *Colonial Encounters: Europe and the Native Caribbean, 1492–1797*. New York: Routledge, 1986.

Iliffe, John. *Honour in African History*. New York: Cambridge University Press, 2005.

Johnson, Carina L. *Cultural Hierarchy in Sixteenth-Century Europe: The Ottomans and Mexicans*. New York: Cambridge University Press, 2011.

Kagan, Richard L. *Clio and the Crown: The Politics of History in Medieval and Early Modern Spain*. Baltimore: Johns Hopkins University Press, 2009.

Kalusa, Walima T., and Megan Vaughan. *Death, Belief and Politics in Central African History*. Lusaka, Zambia: Lembani Trust, 2013.

Kantorowicz, Ernest H. *The King's Two Bodies: A Study in Medieval Political Theology*. Princeton, NJ: Princeton University Press, 1957.

Kazanjian, David. *The Brink of Freedom: Improvising Life in the Nineteenth-Century Atlantic World*. Durham: Duke University Press, 2016.

———. *The Colonizing Trick: National Culture and Imperial Citizenship in Early America*. Minneapolis: University of Minnesota, 2003.

Kelleher, Marie A. *The Measure of Woman: Law and Female Identity in the Crown of Aragon*. Philadelphia: University of Pennsylvania Press, 2010.

Kelley, Donald R. *Foundations of Modern Historical Scholarship: Language, Law, and History in the French Renaissance*. New York: Columbia University Press, 1970.

———. *The Human Measure: Social Thought in the Western Legal Tradition*. Cambridge, MA: Harvard University Press, 1990.

Kim, Keechang. *Aliens in Medieval Law: The Origins of Modern Citizenship*. New York: Cambridge University Press, 2000.

Koselleck, Reinhart. *Futures Past: On the Semantics of Historical Time*. Translated and with an introduction by Keith Tribe. New York: Columbia University Press, 2004.

Landau, Paul S. *Popular Politics in the History of South Africa, 1400–1948*. New York: Cambridge University Press, 2010.

The Languages of Political Theory in Early-Modern Europe. Edited by Anthony Pagden. New York: Cambridge University Press, 1987.

Larkin, Brian. *Signal and Noise: Media, Infrastructure, and Urban Culture in Nigeria*. Durham, NC: Duke University Press, 2008.

Law and Disorder in the Postcolony. Edited by Jean Comaroff and John L. Camaroff. Chicago: University of Chicago Press, 2006.

Lester, Toby. *The Fourth Part of the World: The Race to the Ends of the Earth and the Epic Story of the Map That Gave America Its Name*. New York: Free Press, 2009.

Lewis, David Levering. *God's Crucible: Islam and the Making of Europe, 570–1215*. New York: W. W. Norton, 2008.

Lovejoy, Paul E. *Transformations in Slavery: A History of Slavery in Africa*. 2nd ed. New York: Cambridge University Press, 1983.

MacCormack, Sabine. *On the Wings of Time: Rome, the Incas, Spain, and Peru*. Princeton, NJ: Princeton University Press, 2007.

Mackenthun, Gesa. *Metaphors of Dispossession: American Beginnings and the Translation of Empire, 1492–1637*. Norman: University of Oklahoma Press, 1997.

Major, J. Russell. *From Renaissance Monarchy to Absolute Monarchy: French Kings, Nobles and Estates*. Baltimore: Johns Hopkins University Press, 1994.

Malkki, Liisa H. *Purity and Exile: Violence, Memory, and National Cosmology Among Hutu Refugees in Tanzania*. Chicago: University of Chicago Press, 1995.

Mamdani, Mahmood. *Citizen and Subject: Contemporary Africa and the Legacy of Late Colonialism*. Princeton, NJ: Princeton University Press, 1996.

———. *Saviors and Survivors: Darfur, Politics, and the War on Terror*. New York: Pantheon, 2009.

———. *When Victims Become Killers: Colonialism, Nativism, and the Genocide in Rwanda*. Princeton, NJ: Princeton University Press, 2001.

Mann, Gregory. *From Empires to NGOs in the West African Sahel: The Road to Nongovernmentality*. New York: Cambridge University Press, 2015.

Mann, Kristin. *Slavery and the Birth of an African City: Lagos, 1760–1900*. Bloomington: Indiana University Press, 2007.

Manning, Patrick. *Slavery and African Life: Occidental, Oriental, and African Slave Trades*. New York: Cambridge University Press, 1990.

Martin-Márquez, Susan. *Disorientations: Spanish Colonialism in Africa and the Performance of Identity*. New Haven, CT: Yale University Press, 2008.

Martínez, María Elena. *Genealogical Fictions: Limpieza de Sangre, Religion, and Gender in Colonial Mexico*. Palo Alto, CA: Stanford University Press, 2008.

Materialities of Rituals in the Black Atlantic. Edited by Akinwumi Ogundiran and Paula Saunders. Bloomington: Indiana University Press, 2014.

Matory, J. Lorand. *Black Atlantic Religion: Tradition, Transnationalism, and Matriarchy in the Afro-Brazilian Candomblé*. Princeton, NJ: Princeton University Press, 2005.

Mbembe, Achille. *On the Postcolony*. Berkeley: University of California Press, 2001.

McAlister, Lyle N. *Spain and Portugal in the New World: 1492–1700*. Minneapolis: University of Minnesota Press, 1984.

McKeon, Michael. *The Secret History of Domesticity: Public, Private, and the Division of Knowledge*. Baltimore: Johns Hopkins University Press, 2005.

Meier, Christian. *A Culture of Freedom: Ancient Greece and the Origins of Europe*. Translated by Jefferson Chase. New York: Oxford University Press, 2012.

Meillassoux, Claude. *The Anthropology of Slavery: The Womb of Iron and Gold*. Translated by Alide Dasnois. Chicago: University of Chicago Press, 1991.

Merchants and Marvels: Commerce, Science, and Art in Early Modern Europe. Edited by Pamela H. Smith and Paula Findlen. New York: Routledge, 2002.

Mignolo, Walter D. *The Darker Side of the Renaissance: Literacy, Territoriality, and Colonization.* Ann Arbor: University of Michigan Press, 1995.

———. *Local Histories/Global Designs: Coloniality, Subaltern Knowledges, and Border Thinking.* Princeton, NJ: Princeton University Press, 2000.

Miller, Christopher L. *Blank Darkness: Africanist Discourse in French.* Chicago: University of Chicago Press, 1985.

———. *Theories of Africans: Francophone Literature and Anthropology in Africa.* Chicago: University of Chicago Press, 1990.

Miller, Joseph C. *The Problem of Slavery as History: A Global Approach.* New Haven, CT: Yale University Press, 2012.

———. *Way of Death: Merchant Capitalism and the Angolan Slave Trade, 1730–1830.* Madison: University of Wisconsin Press, 1988.

Milton, Gregory B. *Market Power: Lordship, Society, and Economy in Medieval Catalonia (1276–1313).* New York: Palgrave MacMillan, 2012.

Moore, R. I. *The Formation of a Persecuting Society: Power and Deviance in Western Europe, 950–1250.* Cambridge: Blackwell, 1987.

Morgan, Jennifer L. *Laboring Women: Reproduction and Gender in New World Slavery.* Philadelphia: University of Pennsylvania Press, 2004.

Mudimbe, V. Y. *The Idea of Africa.* Bloomington: Indiana University Press, 1994.

———. *The Invention of Africa: Gnosis, Philosophy, and the Order of Knowledge.* Bloomington: Indiana University Press, 1988.

Newberry, David. *Kings and Clans: Ijwi Island and the Lake Kivu Rift, 1780–1840.* Madison: University of Wisconsin Press, 1991.

Newson, Linda A., and Susie Minchin. *From Capture to Sale: The Portuguese Slave Trade to Spanish South America in the Early Seventeenth Century.* Boston: Brill, 2007.

Nirenberg, David. *Communities of Violence: Persecution of Minorities in the Middle Ages.* Princeton, NJ: Princeton University Press, 1996.

Northrup, David. *Africa's Discovery of Europe: 1450–1850.* 2nd ed. New York: Oxford University Press, 2009.

Nyquist, Mary. *Arbitrary Rule: Slavery, Tyranny, and the Power of Life and Death.* Chicago: University of Chicago Press, 2013.

Obeyesekere, Gananath. *The Apotheosis of Capitan Cook: European Mythmaking in the Pacific.* Princeton, NJ: Princeton University Press, 1992.

Okpewho, Isídore. *Once upon a Kingdom: Myth, Hegemony, and Identity.* Bloomington: Indiana University Press, 1998.

Osborn, Emily Lynn. *Our New Husbands Are Here: Households, Gender, and Politics in a West African State from the Slave Trade to Colonial Rule.* Athens: Ohio University Press, 2011.

Out of One, Many Africas: Reconstructing the Study and Meaning of Africa. Edited by William G. Martin and Michael O. West. Urbana: University of Illinois Press, 1999.

Pagden, Anthony. *European Encounters with the New World: From Renaissance to Romanticism.* New Haven, CT: Yale University Press, 1993.

————. *The Fall of Natural Man: The American Indian and the Origins of Comparative Ethnology*. New York: Cambridge University Press, 1982.

————. *Lords of All the World: Ideologies of Empire in Spain, Britain and France, c. 1500–c. 1800*. New Haven, CT: Yale University Press, 1995.

————. *Spanish Imperialism and the Political Imagination: Studies in European and Spanish-American Social and Political Theory 1513–1830*. New Haven, CT: Yale University Press, 1990.

Patterson, Orlando. *Freedom, Volume I: Freedom in the Making of Western Culture*. New York: Basic, 1991.

————. *Slavery and Social Death: A Comparative Study*. Cambridge, MA: Harvard University Press, 1982.

Peel, J. D. Y. *Religious Encounter and the Making of the Yoruba*. Bloomington: Indiana University Press, 2000.

Pennington, Kenneth. *The Prince and the Law, 1200–1600: Sovereignty and Rights in the Western Legal Tradition*. Berkeley: University of California Press, 2002.

Phillips, William D., Jr. *Slavery in Medieval and Early Modern Iberia*. Philadelphia: University of Pennsylvania, 2014.

Pierre, Jemima. *The Predicament of Blackness: Postcolonial Ghana and the Politics of Race*. Chicago: University of Chicago Press, 2013.

Piot, Charles. *Nostalgia for the Future: West Africa After the Cold War*. Chicago: University of Chicago Press, 2010.

————. *Remotely Global: Village Modernity in West Africa*. Chicago: University of Chicago Press, 1999.

Pocock, J. G. A. *Virtue, Commerce, and History: Essays on Political Thought and History Chiefly in the Eighteenth Century*. New York: Cambridge University Press, 1985.

The Portuguese in West Africa, 1415–1670: A Documentary History. Edited by Malyn Newitt. New York: Cambridge University Press, 2010.

Portuguese Oceanic Expansion: 1400–1800. Edited by Francisco Bethencourt and Diogo Ramada Curto. New York: Cambridge University Press, 2007.

Powell, Eve M. Troutt. *A Different Shade of Colonialism: Egypt, Great Britain, and the Mastery of the Sudan*. Berkeley: University of California Press, 2003.

Rabasa, José. *Writing Violence on the Northern Frontier: The Historiography of Sixteenth-Century New Mexico and Florida and the Legacy of the Conquest*. Durham, NC: Duke University Press, 2000.

Ralph, Michael. *Forensics of Capital*. Chicago: University of Chicago Press, 2015.

Ringrose, David R. *Expansion and Global Interaction, 1200–1700*. New York: Addison Wesley Longman, 2001.

Roberts, Neil. *Freedom as Marronage*. Chicago: University of Chicago Press, 2015.

Robinson, Cedric. J. *Black Marxism: The Making of the Black Radical Tradition*. Foreword by Robin D. G. Kelly. Chapel Hill: University of North Carolina Press, 1983.

Rodney, Walter. *A History of the Upper Guinea Coast: 1545 to 1800*. New York: Monthly Review Press, 1970.

Rosenwein, Barbara H. *Negotiating Space: Power, Restraint, and Privileges of Immunity in Early Medieval Europe*. Ithaca, NY: Cornell University Press, 1999.

Ruiz, Teofilo F. *A King Travels: Festive Traditions in Late Medieval and Early Modern Spain*. Princeton, NJ: Princeton University Press, 2012.

Russell-Wood, A. J. R. *A World on the Move: The Portuguese in Africa, Asia, and America, 1415–1808*. New York: St. Martin's, 1992.

Sahlins, Marshall. *Islands of History*. Chicago: University of Chicago Press, 1985.

Said, Edward W. *Orientalism*. New York: Penguin, 1978.

Sanneh, Lamin. *Abolitionists Abroad: American Black and the Making of Modern West Africa*. Cambridge, MA: Harvard University Press, 1999.

Schmidt, Carl. *The Nomos of the Earth: In the International Law of the* Jus Publicum Europaeum. Translated and annotated by G. L. Ulmen. New York: Telos, 2006.

———. *Political Theology: Four Chapters on the Concept of Sovereignty*. Translated and with an introduction by George Schwab. Chicago: University of Chicago Press, 1985.

Schwartz, Stuart B. *All Can Be Saved: Religious Tolerance and Salvation in the Iberian Atlantic World*. New Haven, CT: Yale University Press, 2008.

Scott, David. *Conscripts of Modernity: The Tragedy of Colonial Enlightenment*. Durham, NC: Duke University Press, 2004.

———. *Refashioning Futures: Criticism After Postcoloniality*. Princeton, NJ: Princeton University Press, 1999.

Seed, Patricia. *Ceremonies of Possession in Europe's Conquest of the New World, 1492–1640*. New York: Cambridge University Press, 1995.

Shaw, Rosalind. *Memories of the Slave Trade: Ritual and the Historical Imagination in Sierra Leone*. Chicago: University of Chicago Press, 2002.

Siedentop, Larry. *Inventing the Individual: The Origins of Western Liberalism*. Cambridge, MA: Belknap Press of Harvard University Press, 2014.

Silverblatt, Irene. *Modern Inquisitions: Peru and the Colonial Origins of the Civilized World*. Durham, NC: Duke University Press, 2004.

Singh, Nikhil Pal. *Black Is a Country: Race and the Unfinished Struggle for Democracy*. Cambridge, MA: Harvard University Press, 2004.

Smallwood, Stephanie E. *Saltwater Slavery: A Middle Passage from Africa to American Diaspora*. Cambridge, MA: Harvard University Press, 2007.

Sparks, Randy J. *The Two Princes of Calabar: An Eighteenth-Century Atlantic Odyssey*. Cambridge, MA: Harvard University Press, 2004.

———. *Where the Negroes Are Masters: An African Port in the Era of the Slave Trade*. Cambridge, MA: Harvard University Press, 2014.

Spiegel, Gabrielle M. *The Past as Text: The Theory and Practice of Medieval Historiography*. Baltimore: Johns Hopkins University Press, 1997.

———. *Romancing the Past: The Rise of Vernacular Prose Historiography in Thirteenth-Century France*. Berkeley: University of California Press, 1993.

Stanley, Amy Dru. *From Bondage to Contract: Wage Labor, Marriage, and the Market in the Age of Slave Emancipation*. New York: Cambridge University Press, 1998.

Stoler, Ann Laura. *Race and the Education of Desire: Foucault's History of Sexuality and the Colonial Order of Things*. Durham, NC: Duke University Press, 1995.

Studnicki-Gizbert, Daviken. *A Nation upon the Ocean Sea: Portugal's Atlantic Diaspora and the Crisis of the Spanish Empire, 1492–1640*. New York: Oxford University Press, 2007.

Subrahmanyam, Sanjay. *Courtly Encounters: Translating Courtliness and Violence in Early Modern Eurasia*. Cambridge, MA: Harvard University Press, 2012.

Sweet, James H. *Domingos Álvares, African Healing, and the Intellectual History of the Atlantic World*. Chapel Hill: University of North Carolina Press, 2011.

Thomas, Hugh. *The Slave Trade: The Story of the Atlantic Slave, 1444–1870*. New York: Simon & Schuster, 1997.

Thomas, Keith. *Religion and the Decline of Magic: Religion and the Decline of Magic*. New York: Scribner's, 1971.

Thomson, Janice E. *Mercenaries, Pirates, and Sovereigns*. Princeton, NJ: Princeton University Press, 1994.

Thornton, John. *Africa & Africans in the Making of the Atlantic World, 1400–1680*. New York: Cambridge University Press, 1992.

Thornton, John K. *A Cultural History of the Atlantic World, 1250–1820*. New York: Cambridge University Press, 2012.

Todorov, Tzvetan. *The Conquest of America: The Question of the Other*. Translated by Richard Howard. New York: Harper Perennial, 1982.

Toledano, Ehud R. *As If Silent and Absent: Bonds of Enslavement in the Islamic Middle East*. New Haven, CT: Yale University Press, 2007.

Trouillot, Michel-Rolph. *Silencing the Past: Power and the Production of History*. Boston: Beacon, 1995.

Vansina, Jan. *Paths in the Rainforests: Toward a History of Political Tradition in Equatorial Africa*. Madison: University of Wisconsin Press, 1990.

Vaughan, Megan. *Creating the Creole Island: Slavery in Eighteenth-Century Mauritius*. Durham, NC: Duke University Press, 2005.

———. *Curing Their Ills: Colonial Power and African Illness*. Palo Alto, CA: Stanford University Press, 1991.

Vilches, Elvira. *New World Gold: Cultural Anxiety and Monetary Disorder in Early Modern Spain*. Chicago: University of Chicago Press, 2010.

Wallerstein, Immanuel. *The Modern World-System I: Capitalist Agriculture and the Origins of the European World-Economy in the Sixteenth Century*. New York: Academic, 1974.

———. *The Modern World-System II: Mercantilism and the Consolidation of the European World-Economy, 1600–1750*. New York: Academic, 1980.

Ware, Rudolph T. III. *The Waking Qur'an: Islamic Education, Embodied Knowledge, and History in West Africa*. Chapel Hill: University of North Carolina Press, 2014.

Weber, Max. *The Agrarian Sociology of Ancient Civilizations*. Translated by R. I. Frank. New York: Verso, 2013.

Weheliye, Alexander G. *Habeas Viscus: Racializing Assemlages, Biopolitics, and Black Feminist Theories of the Human.* Durham, NC: Duke University Press, 2014.

Wilder, Gary. *The French Imperial Nation-State: Negritude and Colonial Humanism Between the Two World Wars.* Chicago: University of Chicago Press, 2005.

Williams, Jr., Robert A. *The American Indian in Western Legal Thought: The Discourses of Conquest.* New York: Oxford University Press, 1990.

Wright, Donald R. *The World and a Very Small Place in Africa: A History of Globalization in Niumi, the Gambia.* Armonk, NY: M. E. Sharpe, 2004.

Zachernuk, Philip S. *Colonial Subjects: An African Intelligentsia and Atlantic Ideas.* Charlottesville: University of Virginia Press, 2000.

INDEX

ACKNOWLEDGMENTS
────────────

If I thanked all the individuals whom I have burdened with the ideas manifest here, this book would be a far weightier tome. Those who have been subjected to both the ideas and various chapters, along the way offering their critiques to the numerous incarnations of this project, have been kind to indulge me. I thank you all even if you are not personally acknowledged here. Too many talks and a faulty method of recording who said what, when, and where bares considerable blame. I do recall specific conversations concerning this book with Steven Amsterdam, Linda Asher, Jeremy Adelman, Ralph Bauer, Eric Bayruns, Lauren Benton, Ira Berlin, Stephen Best, Nick Biddle, John Blanton, Christopher Brown, Sherwin Bryant, Susan Buck-Morss, Antoinette Burton, Clare Carroll, Brian Connolly, Marcela Echeverria, Brent Edwards, Duncan Faherty, Ada Ferrer, Antonio Ferros, John Eric Frankson, Miles Grier, Kim Hall, Saidiya Hartman, Kristina Huang, David Joselit, Richard Kagan, David Kazanjian, Paul Landau, Uday Mehta, Max Mishler, Joseph C. Miller, Jennifer L. Morgan, Fred Moten, Stephan Palmie, Michael Ralph, Robert Reid-Pharr, Yolanda San-Miguel Martinez, Joan Scott, Nikhil Singh, Julia Skurski, Timothy Tyson, Megan Vaughan, David Wheat, and Gary Wilder. Special debts will always be due to Antoinette Burton, Clare Carroll, Henrique Espada Lima, Kristina Huang, Jennifer Morgan, Julie Skurski, Megan Vaughan, and David Wheat for their extensive critiques. Without question, you have made this a better book. Thank you! I thank the following institutions for their support or invitations to speak about the project: the Department of English at the University of Pennsylvania, Latin American and Latino Studies at the University of Pennsylvania, the McNeil Center, NYU Atlantic History Seminar, the Department of History at The Johns Hopkins University, Dwight Eisenhower Library, the Department of History at Rutgers University, Rutgers Center for Historical Analysis, University of California at Berkeley, The Graduate Center, Mina Rees Library, the Committee on Globalization & Social Change. Bob Lockhart, Lily Palladino, and the staff at the University of Pennsylvania Press need to be acknowledged for their exacting professional standards. Bob has been a terrific editor but also a friend able to coax me into writing a better book. Thank you!

From what has been signified above and is true for all scholarship, no project is crafted in isolation. Institutions and individuals matter. Antoinette Burton and David Kazanjian have modeled what it means to be brilliant but also remarkably engaged with mentoring and keeping the political at the forefront. I am humbled by the virtues they exemplify as intellectuals. I have been fortunate to enjoy the company of so many good people—my parents, Lee and Helga; my son Carl; my in-laws Cynthia Young and Zachary Morgan; Julie Livingston; Behrooz Ghamari-Tabrizi; Nikhil Singh; Thuy Tu; and, of course, the usuals—who have sustained me in the writing of this book. Working with the CUNY Pipeline Fellows, the Pipeline Staff, the MAGNET Fellows, Eric Frankson, and the good folks whose lives have intersected with the Office of Educational Opportunity & Diversity Programs (EOD) has been a steady source of inspiration. My daughter Emma has been intrigued about this project from the beginning to its completion and so has her great-grandmother Maymette. Their interest mattered at crucial moments. What links Emma and Maymette, beyond being related, is deep curiosity and Jennifer Morgan, respectively the mom and the granddaughter. Jennifer has often taken time from her extensive intellectual and institutional involvements to make so much possible. It is with love and affection that I dedicate this book to her.

CPSIA information can be obtained
at www.ICGtesting.com
Printed in the USA
BVHW032151070719
552815BV00003B/6/P